A PROFESSIONAL'S PRIMER FOR SUCCESSFUL
FEATURE STORIES

Whether it's a general profile on big-tree logging or a feature
on a minor league relief pitcher, William E. Blundell shows
writers how to create a story that grabs the reader's attention
and doesn't let go. Used to teach *Wall Street Journal* writers
the tricks of the trade—and a system for producing top-quality
articles—this guide was created by a working newsman for
working newspeople. It deals with the nitty-gritty of coming up
with ideas, gathering the right kind of information, and
getting past the most common roadblocks that crop up during
the writing process. Chock full of ideas and expert instruction,
it is an invaluable book for both beginning writers and
experienced pros alike.

THE ART AND CRAFT
OF FEATURE WRITING

William E. Blundell, currently a news editor for features at
The Wall Street Journal, has been a reporter, page-one
writer, Los Angeles bureau chief, and national correspondent
for the paper. He is a winner of the Mike Berger Award,
granted by the trustees of Columbia University, for
distinguished metropolitan reporting in New York; the Ray
Howard Public Service Award of the Scripps-Howard
Foundation; and the Distinguished Writing Award for non-
deadline feature writing, granted by the American Society
of Newspaper Editors.

THE ART AND CRAFT OF FEATURE WRITING

Based on *The Wall Street Journal Guide*

WILLIAM E. BLUNDELL

A PLUME BOOK

PLUME
Published by the Penguin Group
Penguin Books USA Inc., 375 Hudson Street, New York, New York 10014,
U.S.A.
Penguin Books Ltd, 27 Wrights Lane, London W8 5TZ, England
Penguin Books Australia Ltd, Ringwood, Victoria, Australia
Penguin Books Canada Ltd, 10 Alcorn Avenue, Toronto, Ontario, Canada
M4V 3B2
Penguin Books (N.Z.) Ltd, 182-190 Wairau Road, Auckland 10, New Zealand
Penguin Books Ltd, Registered Offices: Harmondsworth, Middlesex, England

Published by Plume, an imprint of Dutton Signet, a division of Penguin Books
USA Inc.

First Plume Printing, November, 1988

15   14   13   12   11   10   9   8

Library of Congress Cataloging-in-Publication Data

Blundell, William E.
  The art and craft of feature writing.

  1. Feature writing—Handbooks, manuals, etc.
2. Technical writing—Handbooks, manuals, etc.
3. Authorship.   I. Wall Street journal.   II. Title.
PN4784.F37B58   1988   808′.02   88-25307
ISBN 0-452-26158-9

PRINTED IN THE UNITED STATES OF AMERICA

CONTENTS

INTRODUCTION

During arid stretches of meetings I attend—which is to say, an appalling amount of the time—the rumpled, morose figure of Mel Bookstein plods into my daydreams. He lives only in these imaginings, but his plight is real enough. Bookstein is a reporter in the worst kind of trouble, and he doesn't know how to wriggle out of it.

Usually I picture him slumped in a chair, staring at a phony needlepoint sampler on his wall that says, "Cubicle Sweet Cubicle." Along with a jumble of empty Styrofoam cups, the debris of another ill-starred project litters his desk: documents that now seem irrelevant, notes on uninformative interviews, jottings on half-formed thoughts.

He can't say what this snowdrift of material adds up to, if it adds up to anything. Having read through it, he's only sure that too much still is missing. Lacking a fix on his story theme, he can't begin to write because he doesn't know where to start. So, hagridden by angst, he waits for lunch and a brighter afternoon, only to find—again—that time is his enemy, not his friend.

Is there anyone in the writing game who hasn't been in his shoes at one time or another? I've certainly shared his depression and anxiety, his belief that he won't be able to do justice to the story before him. And in teaching hundreds of other reporters and writers I've seen the syndrome again and again.

Granted, there's always pain in good writing; if you're not hurting, you're not stretching. But that pain is supposed to buy, at the end, the deep satisfaction that flows from a creative task well done. The sorrowful thing is that so many writers know so much suffering and so little satisfaction.

This book aims to reduce the pain a little, and increase the pleasure a great deal, by offering a new kind of systematic, progressive instruction in how to tell true stories well. It is adapted from an internally published manual used by feature writers of *The Wall Street Journal*, particularly those doing the major features appearing on the paper's acclaimed front page. But it has nothing to do, really, with business writing (only a couple of the examples cited are business stories) or with the unique difficulties of *Journal* reporters. It's more concerned with the central problem that faces everyone who wants to write nonfiction—newspapermen, magazine and book writers, you and me.

How can we make the truth as interesting to others as it is to us? That's the nut of it. Some of us roam, as I have, over whole nations or regions, doing stories wildly different in topic or character. Others stay at home and specialize. But all of us share one frequently neglected responsibility: We're supposed to be tellers of tales as well as purveyors of facts. When we don't live up to that responsibility we don't get read.

In this, our interests are interwoven with those of every story-teller who ever lived. We're modern, well educated, computerized—and still no different from those men who wandered from one rude village to another in ancient Greece, enchanting people with tales of an Odysseus driven by storm and the gods' caprice across Homer's wine-dark sea.

From their time to ours, the challenges of the trade have never changed. What elements make a story intrinsically interesting? How can the attention of the audience be seized instantly? How should the tale be shaped to hold that interest, and what can be done to nail it into the memory?

Journalism students learn too little about all this. They learn reporting and editing, but not much about the country around and between, places pretty much left to fiction writers. Once on the job the journalist may gain some knowledge of this territory, but only in bits and pieces gleaned over many years. Too often he learns nothing at all about it. No wonder poor Bookstein agonizes so; he's unequipped to do his life's work well, and knows it.

We can learn a great deal from fiction, and this book makes at least a modest start at connecting some techniques of fiction to the work we do. But it differs most from other writing books, I think, in two other important respects: It denies absolutely the presumption that writing can be taught without considering reporting, and it treats the whole effort as a flowing process and not a series of discrete steps that can be analyzed in isolation.

Reporting and writing can't be divorced. All the instruction available in how to bang sentences together gracefully (and there's a powerful lot of it) will produce nothing but glitz if the right material, and a pleasing variety of it, is missing—or if it's been collected without regard to what readers like and need. So while there is little in this book about the techniques of reporting, there is much about the nature of the material a reporter should strive to get, as well as the way he ought to present it. (In referring to the typical reporter, I use the masculine pronoun only out of convenience and tradition; the contributions women have made to journalism are beyond counting.)

As for reporting/writing as a flowing process, that idea still hasn't gained full currency in teaching. But what good writer can deny it? He knows that what he's done before powerfully influences what he can do now, and that what he does now governs to a great extent what he can do next. Decisions made early, when his idea is being shaped, wind through all the rest of his work. As a whole, that work can no more be divided into tidy, discrete steps than the waters of a river can be sorted according to their tributary sources.

This book reflects that indivisibility. It's meant to be read from beginning to end. I suppose a reader could pluck out useful items here and there by hopscotching through certain chapters and sections, as he might even more profitably do in other writing books. But I don't recommend it. He'd miss a great deal of the material needed to put his fragments into proper perspective. More important, he'd miss the whole idea of writing as a process, one that begins with the first flicker of an idea in the reporter's mind and ends with the last jot of self-editing.

We'll move through that process, using *Journal* stories as illustrations. They're good stories as newspaper pieces go, but none is perfect; each was picked because it illustrates one or more teaching points, not because it's a paragon of journalism. Much of the work cited is mine. That's because the method I teach stresses a lot of hard thinking about the story during its development, and I don't know how other people think when they work.

Throughout, the book emphasizes the ingredients, structure and craftsmanship that make stories a pleasure to read. The reporter/writer, not his editor, carries almost the entire burden of providing these. Editors can smooth, shorten and clarify, but they can't supply the qualities that make a piece vivid and truly alive, that transform it from superficial chatter into a tale with the power to strike deeply into a reader's consciousness. Yes, that reader does require specific information, and our first priority is to provide it. But he has deeper and more universal needs that have to be met at the same time or he'll flee. Nothing is easier than to stop reading.

We often forget about those needs, if we knew them to begin with. And if we do acknowledge them, it may only be with bare scraps of so-called color (most of it irrelevant) dropped willy-nilly into our stories as we scurry to finish them, our attention fixed on the immediate perceived demand of the reader for information. So we fail to heed the unspoken commandment that undergirds all others, the only common demand of readers everywhere: For Pete's sake, make it interesting. Tell me a *story*.

That first and greatest commandment is what this book is all about.

CHAPTER 1

RAW MATERIALS

Bereft of new ideas, a reporter spies his boss approaching with glittering eye. The editor presents him with an idea. It's a terrible idea, but the reporter is stuck with it because, having nothing better to offer, he is so enfeebled by guilt that he can't argue forcefully against it. So he drags himself out of the office in pursuit of a grail whose existence he doubts to start with. The prognosis for the story is poor.

The feature writer who doesn't have two or three projects bubbling on his own stove is doing only half a job. As the party closest to the action, he and not his editor has the primary responsibility for generating ideas. Yet many reporters are chronically starved for them or pursue vague, hastily formed notions that fall apart during the reporting or writing stages; a mountain of effort produces a molehill of a story or nothing at all, and before long the reporter is being force-fed assignments like a Strasbourg goose. He has lost control of his most important creative function. He is not having much fun, either.

In generating ideas a vivid imagination is a big help, and if our unfortunate reporter doesn't have one we can't supply it. But most of the time something else is wrong, something than *can* be fixed: he doesn't do enough thinking or reading, and he doesn't talk to the right people. He is suffering the journalistic equivalent of sensory deprivation.

"Rubbish!" our man cries, ticking off his regular reading—
Time and *Newsweek*, the *New York Times*, one or two local
papers, *Forbes, Business Week*, several trade publications on his
beat (if he has one). And when he isn't reading these, he adds,
he's talking to people, hordes of people. His Rolodex is full of
people. What more can he do?

A lot.

Besides those few people who see story possibilities everywhere, anyone who hopes to maintain a steady flow of ideas has
to be an omnivorous, gluttonous reader, including in his diet
publications few others read. It's not enough to scan mass-
circulation papers and magazines; they keep a reporter abreast
of events and the competition, but their coverage of a story often
kills or limits his chances of doing anything similar.

Usually the best he can hope for in pursuing the story is a
piece that might be more complete but that still has a staleness
wafting from it, or one that develops only a secondary angle of
the main story others are running. Straining at this gnat, the
reporter may pump it full of hyperbole and phony portent to
build up its importance. The editors usually aren't fooled. If they
are, most readers won't be; they know a short beer in a tall glass
when they see one.

One way out: Pick broad subject areas that interest you, that
appear to touch the lives of many readers, and that the paper
covers sporadically or barely at all (religion and family relations,
perhaps, two areas undercovered by practically everybody).
Identify and read publications that cover them—professional
quarterlies, association newsletters, academic, think-tank and
foundation reports, and the emanations of government agencies
involved.

These may be excruciating reading and much of their contents
dross, but such publications are not competitive, meaning we
can steal ideas from them with impunity, and they often carry
the latest developments and most original thinking long before
the general press.

When reading, make quick notations of possible stories that
the material suggests and file these with the clips; data may be
stored in the brain for later recall, but inspiration disappears

like the morning mist. Without notes, you may reread the clipping months later and wonder why you kept it.

Without an organized system of files, you may not be able to find it at all. A feature writer needs idea files, and he should cull them regularly. How the files are set up depends on his subject area and his tastes, but each system should include a tickler file. Into this go ideas hinging on events that will happen at specific times in the future, or ideas that just look hot—meaning that if they cannot be done quickly, the opportunity will disappear or very likely be skimmed off by competitors.

In doing these things, you are voluntarily creating a beat where none existed before and beginning to cover it the way a beat reporter should. For further instruction, let's peer into the Rolodex file of the fellow who has trouble getting ideas.

As he said, there are hundreds of people in there: platoons of PR types and an impressive array of sources at or near the tops of their power pyramids. New names go into the file with every story he does, names of more and more topsiders.

Fine. They belong there. But a closer look reveals a shortage of another type of source, the middleman. He is not at the top of the heap, but close enough to know policy. He is not at the bottom, but close enough to know about what is happening on the ground.

Sources at high levels are certainly useful, but that utility often is limited by their rank. They may be so high above the pavement that they can no longer see what is happening there, so busy (or swell-headed) that they have little time to educate the grubby minions of the press, and too protective of their own positions and organizations to give honest and complete appraisals.

Conversely, middlemen often are better able to provide specifics that bring stories to life or to guide reporters to them. They are less apt to be suspicious; indeed, many are complimented when interest is shown in their work, and respond well to reporters. Finally, some middlemen get to be top men, and they remember old contacts.

Finding these and other sources, a reporter may file and forget them until another story they can help with somehow materializes. This is what our man has done. He hasn't talked to most of his non-PR sources more than once or twice, and some haven't been called in years. If he phoned them today they might not know him from the Fuller Brush man. He has lost access through neglect.

"But I didn't have any *reason* to call," our man whines. Like so many others, he has been counting on plucking ideas out of the air through some kind of immaculate conception. When this divine event occurs—and he has no doubt it will—*then* he'll plug sources into the idea. But this is backward thinking. He should be using his best-informed and most cooperative sources—the Wise Men, whom we shall meet again—to help him *originate* those ideas. He gnaws a tuna on rye at his desk, congratulating himself for his frugality and long hours, when he could be sharing a sole Veronique and an interesting chardonnay with someone better informed than he.

This sort of cultivation can be more productive than an interview on an idea already developed. The latter is a commercial transaction: The reporter wants information that will advance (or preserve) his career while the source, faced with seeing what he utters in print, must decide whether it is in his interest to cooperate or obfuscate.

The chemistry changes when the reporter explores general ideas with a source who knows he is not being dragooned into a story just yet. The reporter now is a student, the source a guru; the object is not to squeeze pellets of information out of him but to create an idea with the help of his special knowledge and insight. This transaction is an intellectual challenge, and the reporter's interest now is flattering rather than threatening. This kind of flattery will get you everywhere.

Having greatly increased his flow of raw material for ideas, our man must now think about that material in ways that will produce those ideas. A few possibilities:

EXTRAPOLATION

An event occurs that may not be worth a feature story in itself. By applying extrapolative reasoning, the reporter may be able to infer that beyond the event lies a broader, more significant story. For example, let's inspect that old chestnut, the story about how well the local United Fund drive is going. The piece says contributions are far above targets, and there is much back-patting and hosannas for the energy and vision of those responsible. This boilerplate seems to promise nothing more.

But the story fails to note that a big income-tax cut will occur next year. This means people have reason to give most heavily now, to get maximum tax deductions under the current higher rates. This may have more to do with the fund drive's success than the quality of its leadership. It further suggests that next year the United Fund people may have to sweat bullets to bring in less.

In extrapolating, the reporter asks himself two questions:

1. What is the probable principal *cause* of this single development? It may be apparent, it may be played down, or it may be omitted entirely, just as the background about the tax cut was left out of the United Fund story.

2. Is it logical to think that this cause is a *common driving force* likely to create similar effects in other places on other people and organizations? In the United Fund story, the answer is yes, because the tax cut applies to everyone everywhere. It's probable that a wide variety of charitable organizations, from museums in Bangor to churches in Bloomington and rescue missions in Seattle, will benefit.

The reporter should spot-check his reasoning with some phone calls before touting a cosmic story about charity windfalls nationwide. Sometimes events don't follow logic, or something else is involved that the reporter didn't or couldn't foresee.

But logic prevails more often than not, and the reporter who trains himself in extrapolative thinking adds a sharp tool to his kit. Using it, he can begin to shape major stories out of seemingly innocuous, isolated events.

SYNTHESIS

The reporter adept at synthesis sees and exploits the thread unifying several developments that to others appear unrelated. He assembles promising story ideas from what looks like a junkpile of spare parts. He does this by staying alert to *possibilities of commonality* in the material he reads and discusses with sources; he thinks of events as being potentially linked and tries to spot the connections that will provide a story. G. Christian Hill did that in preparing this 1974 story about San Diego, which was going through a particularly bad period.

SAN DIEGO—If awards were given for civic embarrassment or bad luck, a number of candidates would spring to mind. There is Washington, home of Watergate, or Detroit, home of the troubled auto industry. Or that perennial front-runner, Philadelphia, home of Philadelphia.

Then there is this beautiful seaside town of 771,000, the long-suffering victim of a whole string of bumblings, scandals and disasters that make it seem almost a city accursed. The problem has gotten so bad that Doug Porter, ex-editor of an underground paper named The Door, now refers to any noteworthy job of bungling or failure as "typically San Diesque."

Take, for example, the problem of daylight saving time, which became mandatory nationwide last January as an energy-saving measure. In San Diego, however, there may be some baffled residents still walking around two hours behind the rest of the country. That's because the San Diego *Union* urged them to set their clocks back an hour instead of forward an hour. How could the paper have made such a mistake? "I have no comment, and don't quote me on that," says City Editor Al Jacoby.

The muddle over the time is nothing compared to what has happened to the leading elements of the business and financial community—or what is left of them after a wave of scandals and failures. The crash of collapsing companies and the cries of fraud recently led the San Diego *Tribune* to comment that the town has seized a leading position as "West Coast distributor of flimflam men and holder of the national record for suede shoes per capita."

The story then proceeds to list the more spectacular business scams and failures (even the owner of the building housing the bankruptcy court went belly-up), which led to both the largest IRS tax lien ever filed anywhere and the biggest chapter 11 reorganization ever attempted. After that Hill dwells lovingly on the heroic incompetence of the San Diego Padres, whose furious owner seizes control of the P.A. system at a game and castigates his butterfingered employees, and the NFL Chargers, entangled at the time in a drug case. Noting the squad's 2–11 record, a sportscaster figures the drug has to be formaldehyde.

The story finishes by noting that none of this has done much to enhance the image of San Diego, which was not exactly famous as a dynamic power center to begin with. A critic describes it as "a body of land surrounded on two sides by water, on two sides by mountains, and on all sides by apathy." (For full text of this story, see Appendix 2.)

The unifying element in this confection was a *common location*; all the action was in San Diego, so the theme adapted was that of a city that seemed cursed by bumbling and bad luck. The events were different, their causes varied, but they all operated in one place.

Sometimes the events will differ and the locations will differ, but there will be a *common cause* behind all. Spotting it, the reporter gathers the disparate story elements under this umbrella. Are there alarming rises in juvenile epilepsy, truancy and petty theft? Maybe growing teenage addiction to video games has something to do with that. Are steel companies trimming inventories of sheet while glass companies are slowing production of safety glass? Maybe the auto industry is planning production cutbacks.

Finally, locations may differ and causes may differ, but a *common class* of people, institutions or places is involved in a similar way.

In the 1970s, a big natural-resources boom was creating tens of thousands of new construction, mining and energy jobs in remote areas. At the same time, blue-collar retired persons began seeking new homes in towns with cheap housing and little or no crime. Also, younger families began fleeing deteriorating city schools and living conditions to seek better lives elsewhere.

These different migrants were moving for different reasons, but the net effect on one common class—rural towns and their inhabitants—was the same: After decades of steady population loss, they suddenly confronted all the problems and promises of overheated growth. Focusing on these towns, the writer could tie together the diverse streams of the migration.

By helping to broaden story themes and unify scattered developments, extrapolation and synthesis can give the reporter a jump on competitors who are lolling about, waiting for news to jump up and bite them. But opportunities to be original are limited. "There are no new stories, only new reporters," the saying goes, and some truth lies behind the cynicism. Too many of our rivals do not loll about. They are imaginative, energetic and out to beat us to stories. Often they do. Then the challenge is not to retell a twice-told tale, but to expand it, freshen it or change its character.

Some ways to do that:

LOCALIZATION

Thinking big, a reporter who has been grouping small events to create a broader idea is distressed to find others already at work on his big picture. He can still profit by reversing course and thinking small. Let them be muralists. He will become a miniaturist.

His rivals are using most of their space and effort to establish the scale and importance of the story. Their copy is full of statistics, commentary by august experts and lists of people and places affected. These elements are all necessary, perhaps, in staking out the farthest boundaries of the development, but they are hardly the kind of materials that readers identify with emotionally.

Readers can see the magnitude of a change in Social Security law when told that 1,143,000 pensioners will have $6.3 billion less to live on this year. But they cannot feel the meaning behind it; the people are faceless units, the numbers too large to be visualized. The information is abstract. It becomes concrete only when the reader is taken, for instance, to the porch of a decaying old hotel in St. Petersburg and introduced to a few elderly residents who despair because they can't buy food or pay the utility bills on $40 less a month. The reader learns nothing about magnitude from this, and everything about meaning.

So the miniaturist nods in gratitude toward his colleagues, who have proved that the story is important, and goes off to St. Petersburg to breathe life into it. They have left him the chance to do a piece of a different character on the same subject, and he snatches it. A free lunch is hard to find.

In putting events under his magnifying glass, a reporter needn't limit himself to doing only those stories hooked to broader developments. An event may have no such connection but make a marvelous tale in itself because it has some of the values that make good fiction: a protagonist struggling with an antagonist, lots of action, drama, mystery, humanity.

Many of these little passion plays occur down the street from the newsroom, but a reporter's instincts may be so dulled by familiarity that he misses them.

Marilyn Chase didn't miss, and produced a funny, touching 1981 story about an unusual park in San Francisco. A few excerpts will give you the flavor of it (for the full text, see Appendix 2):

San Francisco has long been toasted as one of the world's easiest places to get drunk and stay drunk. It has the requisite amenities: relatively cheap liquor, a temperate climate, and legions of tourists who are easy marks for a practiced panhandler. Now, to these attractions is added another: a park dedicated exclusively to winos. . . .

Wino Park, officially called Sixth Street Park, is a transformed sandlot tucked amid the transient hotels, pawn shops and liquor stores of the city's tough South-of-Market area. There, a wino can recline with a bottle of Thunderbird or Night Train Express wine, build a bonfire, cook a meal, sleep, loiter or play a game of sodden volleyball without being arrested. A brass plaque commemorates famous people who liked their drink. The winos like to read it aloud, like a roll call of heroes: "Honoring: Winston Churchill, Ernest Hemingway, W. C. Fields, John Barrymore, Betty Ford, Janis Joplin, Dylan Thomas. . . . ," they intone. . . .

On a mild and sunny afternoon, they are among the three dozen regulars who congregate in the tiny park. To an outsider, the first sensations suggest that this is some kind of crazy, landlocked beach party: blowing sand from the arid planters, the smell of woodsmoke from a midday bonfire, outdoor cooking, the blare of a radio tuned to soul and gospel music, and people drinking from styrofoam cups.

S.Q., 60 and gray-bearded, is the park's elder statesman. He occupies a chair next to the bonfire and despite the balmy spring day wears a fake Persian-lamb hat. It is adorned with a button that reads, "I'm alive," the slogan of Glide Memorial Church. "Winter was rough," he says slowly, "but it's all right now. All right." Hogshead, glowering and blind drunk, sits alone in a corner. He is the park's wood gatherer.

Ben, about 50, assumed the leadership role from S.Q. He is a robust black man with salt-and-pepper hair, a print polyester shirt and a vest with a nametag reading "Glide staff. My name is Ben." He surveys the park with a proprietary eye and says the winos are holding their ground in perpetual turf battles with drug traffickers.

"I be here every day, seven days a week, from 6:30 in the morning. If I pick up a broom, everybody here will do the same," he says with an expansive gesture.

Ben's steady lady is Peggy, 34, a plump, freckled, toothless, ponytailed bacchante attired in fuzzy slippers and a shapeless plaid shirt. Her conversation indicates that somewhere, there lurks a proper, middle-class upbringing. She asks a reporter for a stock tip, and when none is forthcoming, explains: "My broker is in Connecticut, and anyway, I don't trust him. But if I were investing, I'd buy Kimberly-Clark, because of the Rely tampon scandal. . . ."

* * *

Mickey, 36, is a merchant seaman with a wife somewhere that he dotes on. He's trying to go straight for her and has been dry for one day. "I'm afraid of getting the shakes, Fran," he confides to Mrs. Peavey, "But so far, I'm feeling okay. I'm eating and drinking a lot of water." Last winter, when an outsider brought in lice, Mickey obtained a half-case of delousing agent from a nearby clinic and took his friends up to his apartment and bathed them.

Mrs. Peavey points to such acts as vindication of her idealism. "If you had lice, would your friends bathe you?" she asks. "Mine wouldn't. . . ."

* * *

The winos know well that their park hasn't attained its ideal state. But to keep their goal in sight, they have designed a mural that will depict the park looking as green as the Garden of Eden, and themselves looking like exemplary stewards.

"Then we can always look up," says one wino, "and say: This is the way it's supposed to be."

The story of Wino Park had been beaten almost to death by the Bay Area press, but this didn't deter reporter Chase. She knew that while her piece in *The Wall Street Journal* might not be read by the tiny fraction of the paper's readers who live in the Bay Area, the millions who don't live there would find it new. She also gave the story freshness and humanity by telling it through the park denizens, while others had stressed the controversy the park had generated. A moral emerges: When doing miniatures, try setting up the easel in your own backyard first. It saves airfare.

PROJECTION

Perhaps the most useful of all story-development tools. Declining to follow the media sheep to a pasture already overgrazed, the reporter adept at projection can move past them into new territory. He does this by passing up detailed coverage of the central development itself and fixing instead on its results. He anticipates.

It's important to remember that many stories unroll in stages over a period of time, roughly in this fashion:

1. Central development. Something begins to happen. It may be a single concrete event, a more subtle trend or societal development, whatever.

2. Impacts. As the development advances, it begins to affect people, places and/or institutions in specific ways. Its impress is being felt by them, for good or ill.

3. Countermoves. As the impacts become more apparent and more forceful, those affected may try to slow, halt, deflect, mitigate or enhance them, depending on whether they benefit from those impacts or are harmed by them.

Now, terminology: When a story is just beginning, when impacts and countermoves haven't had time to take concrete shape, that story is a *juvenile* story. When they have had the time to jell, the story is *mature*.

Keeping this in mind, a reporter who comes late to a story can often break new ground anyway. While his competition is clustered around the main development, he can move on to some of the impacts they haven't had to time or vision to cover, or he can jump all the way into countermoves.

During a surge in mineral and energy development a few years ago, for example, the press generally remained fixated on the so-called boomtown syndrome, the enormous strain felt by some small communities near new oilfields, mines and power-plant sites. Since the competition was already covering the boom and one of its principal impacts, *The Wall Street Journal* jumped ahead to countermoves. What was being done to alleviate the problem?

A great deal, it turned out. Towns and counties that once were pathetically grateful for any new jobs that came along had stiffened up and were forcing companies to pay in advance for new schools, roads, sewage-treatment plants and policing. Many other companies were voluntarily aiding towns with grants and creative financing, because they had learned that degraded living conditions for workers prompted high turnover and low productivity. And taxes by states on extracted oil and minerals, previously low, had been jacked up and more of the increased cash flow channeled to affected areas. The inescapable conclusion: This boom would cause far less damage than those before it, an important thing for the reader to know. Coverage of the subject had been stretched through projection.

That broad story was mature: Enough time had passed to allow both impacts and countermoves to form. When a story is still in its juvenile stage, the reporter who has no appetite for copycat coverage of the main development can always wait in the weeds until they occur.

He also can use the elements of projection to shape multistory treatment of that happiest of discoveries, the mature story that the competition hasn't yet discovered. His first major piece might dwell on the development itself, his second on its impacts and his last on what was being done about the impacts. The progression is natural and easy, not strained.

VIEWPOINT SWITCHING

Think of a story scene as a piece of terrain with varying topography. Over there, in the thickets to the west, workers are striking a key industry; the good reporter travels there briefly to tell part of his tale from their turf. To the east, in the city on the plain, managers are plotting countermeasures. The reporter visits, again briefly, to tell us what they see from their office windows. The rest of the time, which is most of the time, he spends on the snowy summit of Mount Objectivity, apart from the action but able to view it widely in a general way. He can also discuss matters with Olympians who live there full-time and share his wide view—labor consultants, union presidents and field marshals of industry.

This is the time-tested way most good stories get told. But if a latecomer finds the high ground occupied, it only makes sense that he move to another, different vantage point from which to work. George Getschow did so in this outstanding 1980 piece on immigration from Mexico. Read it carefully, for it will be referred to in other contexts later.

NAPIZARO, Mexico—An astonishingly effective U.S. trade program is operating in this rural hamlet of 1,200 people—but Uncle Sam knows nothing about it. He wouldn't like it if he did.

Napizaro has street lights, new brick homes with TV antennas sprouting from their rooftops, a modern community center and infirmary, and a new bullring named "North Hollywood California." It is a fitting name. The money for the bullring and all the rest came from North Hollywood in exchange for Napizaro's main export: its male population.

For decades this town has systematically sent its men north to work as illegal aliens in small plants and businesses in the California community, and for decades they have sent their pay home, part of it earmarked for civic improvements.

"Our town is a monument to our workers. None of this would be possible without them," says Augustin Campos, a 61-year-old town elder and an early migrant himself. It was Mr. Campos's success in North Hollywood (the first year he went there to work he earned $4,000, or more than all the Napizaro villagers combined) that attracted all the others to North Hollywood, where they now work in a number of factories, including one started by a Napizaro villager.

The price of the new-found prosperity is high. Napizaro is a town of children, old men and lonely women. More than three-quarters of its 156 heads of household are in the States, and they return only briefly for the town festival in January if they can come home at all. After many years of such separation, they will finally return for good to houses built with their savings, some of them stunning homes with landscaped courtyards and even saunas. "The boys want nice places to retire to," Mr. Campos says. In Mexico, a nice place to retire to can be built for $8,000.

Napizaro's wealth is an anomaly in poverty-stricken rural Mexico. It stems from the town's unusual system of self-taxation and the willingness of its men to spend so much of their lives away from their village. But the extent of its migration is no anomaly. It is the norm. Pushed by poverty, pulled by the lure of jobs that pay at least 10 times what they can make here, men throughout rural Mexico are going north in numbers that may even exceed the highest estimates, about five million crossings a year, with some men making several crossings in the course of a year.

A journey through central Mexico shows town after town almost stripped of working-age males much of the year. In a country that on the whole can't create enough jobs for its people, so great has the rural migration become that farm fields lie untended and local businesses suffer severe labor shortages. Now some skilled workers from the cities, lured by U.S. pay scales, are joining the northern migration too.

The Migrants' Plight

Most of the workers, however, are poor peasants who trek north because they must. Otherwise, they face lives so wretched that few Americans can imagine them.

One such migrant is Teofilo Gomez of the village of San Nicholas de los Agustinos, 250 miles northwest of Mexico City. He, his wife, Teresa, and their 10 children live in an adobe and log hut 10 feet wide and 30 feet long. There is no stove, no heating system, no plumbing. Their only possessions are two broken-down beds, three chairs, a picture of The Last Supper and a skinny chicken that combs the dirt floor for crumbs. Seldom are there any to find.

The 39-year-old Mr. Gomez is better off than some in the village. He has work. Twelve hours a day every day, he milks cows and cleans stables at a nearby farm for a salary of $40 a week, enough to buy beans and tortillas but little else. "Hunger is something we have learned to live with," he says, dispatching a son to scavenge a nearby potato field for anything the harvesters have missed. His wife has been ill and a loan to pay her medical bills hangs over his head. The children are half-starved. It is time to go north again.

A 1,500-Mile Journey

He has made the 1,500-mile journey 14 times in the past 12 years, pushed always by necessity. It is lonesome away from home, but in California he makes more in six months picking vegetables than he can get in four years milking cows here. To Mr. Gomez, a small, soft-spoken man, the U.S. is simply the difference between meat and milk for his family a few times a month or a diet virtually devoid of protein, and between rags and clothing.

"If I didn't go north we would live in worse misery than we do now," he says. His son comes back from the potato field empty-handed. This means the chicken won't eat either. It isn't fed when the children are hungry.

There are millions of campesinos, landless peasants, like Mr. Gomez. They are living testimony to the failure of Mexico's land-distribution programs, a failure that day by day drives more rural Mexicans over the border. Agrarian reform, which was supposed to provide every Mexican peasant with his own small farm, has collapsed under the onrush of the nation's rural population growth. There just aren't enough arable acres to go around.

Government efforts to control the birthrate have met with some success in urban areas, but the rural rate of about 5% a year has been altered hardly at all. Many peasants are illiterate and cannot read what the government tells them about avoiding pregnancy. The women who can read, one Mexican population expert says, won't go against the teachings of the Catholic Church by taking birth-control pills. So new generations of the landless are born in poverty and move eventually to the border.

Contrary to common belief in the U.S., they aren't quite the bottom of Mexico's barrel, economically speaking. "The poorest of the poor cannot afford to migrate," says Jorge Bustamante, a migration specialist at Mexico City's Colegio de Mexico. These are called the *morosos*, "those without hope."

They don't have the will, the energy or the money to go north. The *coyotes*, smugglers who transport groups of migrants to the border and slip them across, often charge several hundred dollars, an impossible sum for many. So those without hope struggle on in the towns where they were born, or drift to the teeming slums of Mexico City in search of work. Every day, 1,400 more arrive there.

Most of them who can migrate—some estimate 80%—come from the six central states of Michoacan, Zacatecas, San Luis Potosi, Guanajuato, Jalisco and Queretaro. These states have a dark and bloody history of conflict among government, the church and landowners, a conflict that devastated the land in the revolution of 1910 and again in the late 1920s, sending countless peasants fleeing all the way to the U.S. There they found new opportunities, and a tradition of migration began.

Ironically, the migration was helped along by the U.S. government. In 1942 Uncle Sam began the Bracero Program to bring in Mexican laborers to relieve wartime manpower shortages. Under pressure from agricultural interests enamored of the cheap farm labor, the program was extended until 1964. Some migrants who received their "green cards" to work in the U.S. during that era continue to use them legally today. But most migrants must sneak across the border, with or without the help of the coyotes. Many get to the border town of Juarez from the central states on a train nicknamed "The Wetback" because of the large number of illegal migrants it carries.

The roots of the migration are apparent even today in such places as Yotatiro, a decayed village of 550 people brooding in the mountains of Michoacan. As dusk falls on a recent evening, Padre Poncho Amaya celebrates Mass by candlelight for a congregation of women and children. During the sermon he implores the women, fidgeting on hard pews, to be "firm in their faith" even if their husbands aren't.

"The Church Is Our Cross"

Where are the men? Most are working in the States, Padre Amaya says after the Mass, and those remaining are "not religious." Outside, old men returning from the fields wearily ride their donkeys down a mud road lit only by moonlight (there is no electricity here). They have toiled all day on land they never owned. "Greetings," says the padre, but the men ignore him and hide their faces in the shadows of their sombreros. Later, a village elder mutters, "The church is our cross." His bitterness goes back more than 50 years, to an event that cut off the peasants of Yotatiro and many other villages from any chance at free land.

The event was the Cristeros Rebellion of 1926–29, a war between the government, then seeking to break up the estates of big landholders, and the church, which backed the landholders. The peasants were stuck in the middle.

In 1927 the conflict came to Yotatiro when Antonio Cortez, the owner of the hacienda embracing the village, was ordered to distribute his acres to local peasants. Their priest at the time told them they would be excommunicated if they took the property. Torn between the temporal and spiritual powers, the villagers, like many others elsewhere, obeyed the church—and lost their opportunity. The land was given to peasants from nearby villages who had backed the government against the supporters of the church, the Cristeros.

So today's villagers have no choices. "The priest told our parents they would go to hell if they took the land, so now we have no

means at all to support ourselves. We go to the U.S. or go hungry,"
says 40-year-old Fidel Rodriquez, who spends half of every year
working fields in California.

Anguish about Leaving

A recent stint in the vineyards brought him enough to restock the
bare shelves in the tiny grocery he runs out of his home. The money
was welcome, but Mr. Rodriquez says he is "full of fear and an-
guish" every time he must leave here. Both his mother and father
have died while he was away in California, and his wife has had to
bear two of their eight children alone. When he is in the U.S., he
worries so much he often cannot sleep.

Those left behind to wait in this flyblown hamlet fare no better.
Surrounded by her 10 tattered children, Julia Mendoza, 40 and
pregnant again, complains that they cannot survive on what her
husband sends back from the U.S. She has moved in with her
in-laws, but they too are impoverished and depend on remittances
from her husband and two other migrant sons.

"We have nothing but tortillas and water," she laments. As she
speaks, a rat creeps boldly toward a small pouch of corn on the
Mendozas' dilapidated porch. Her 69-year-old father-in-law grabs a
broomstick and smacks the rodent over the head. "One less mouth
to feed," he says.

Though hunger and deprivation in the villages remain the strongest forces stimulating migration, urbanites have joined the flow,
too. As a street urchin in Netzahuacoyotl, a squalid slum of 2.5
million people on the fringe of Mexico City, Jose Louis once scav-
enged garbage cans for food. He is still there—but now as owner of
a grocery store and a modern two-bedroom home full of appliances,
a color TV and a stereo system.

All this has come from regular trips to Oklahoma City, where he
picks up $15,000 a year painting cars by day and washing dishes by
night. Mr. Louis has learned English ("call me Joe"). His store is named
"Oklahoma City." He loves America. "I wanted a good life here, and
the U.S. has given it to me," he says. "The U.S. is a dream come true."

Home Away from Home

But he has no thought of moving there permanently, and neither
do an overwhelming percentage of other migrants. They are Mexicans first and always. Besides, why live in the States when the
dollar buys so much more here? Their feelings for the U.S. are akin
to those of a dairy farmer for a prize cow; he may have real affection
for an animal that reliably yields rivers of milk but feel no inclination to move into the barn with her.

Sheer economic opportunism, not poverty, is what brings a small but growing number of skilled and semiskilled Mexican workers to American cities. They can earn a decent living here, but 10 times as much up north. Some trained glass workers have left, along with many construction tradesmen; it is estimated that a third to a half of Houston's construction workers are illegal Mexican aliens. Meanwhile, the ICA Group, a big Mexico City construction company, is already having trouble finding enough skilled workers to meet the needs of Mexico's own rapid industrialization.

That buildup, based largely on the nation's oil boom, is helping Mexico in its long struggle to provide enough new jobs to keep its people working and at home. About 800,000 new positions were created last year—but that still didn't match the 1.1 million to 1.3 million newcomers entering the labor force. And the lure of the dollar, always seductive, now is more so; devaluation of the peso has given U.S. paychecks even more purchasing power in Mexico than they had.

Manpower Shortage

So the flow northward continues and expands, practically emptying the central Mexican countryside of its prime manpower. At the local slaughterhouse in Purpero, a Michoacan town of about 20,000, women and old men pluck chickens and slice the throats of pigs. There simply aren't any other men around to do the work, says a plant official. Even the oldsters, too aged and poor to migrate, must be bused in from neighboring villages. The local gas company, construction firm and hospital all report similar labor shortages.

Ironically, even prosperous little Napizaro is feeling the pinch now. So many men are going to North Hollywood that corn fields are left fallow and construction of a new water system—funded by several hundred dollars a week collected from the migrants—hasn't even started. To retain some of its men, the town has considered putting in a clothing factory, but the notion was dropped when elders sadly agreed that they couldn't afford to pay their own young men enough to keep them here.

The government has pledged to correct the economic conditions that lie behind the growing mass migration. President Jose Lopez Portillo says rapid industrialization is closing the job gap, and he vows that employment will stand at 4% in 20 years.

Economists are skeptical. Almost half the work force is jobless or underemployed now, they note, and there is an ominous bulge in the population of 68 million; almost half are 15 or younger. In coming years they will be pouring into the labor market in numbers so great that even a continuing boom economy may be utterly swamped by them. If so, pressure on the border can only increase.

Migrants' Factory

In such places as Napizaro, the migration to the north is already becoming institutionalized, ever more deeply imbedded in the life of the village. One prosperous migrant has opened his own clothing plant in North Hollywood, and he hires fellow townsmen at $5 an hour. The village offers prospective migrants an orientation course in life and work in America, and the school director is considering adding English to the curriculum—at the grammar school level.

But beneath the prosperity of Napizaro there is always a note of sadness. It is a town of leave-takings, a place where women must endure much.

Ricardo Campos, son of the village elder, Augustin, has just returned from North Hollywood to marry the girl he left behind nine long years ago. Like some, he has been unable to get enough time off to visit. There will be no honeymoon after the wedding. He must return to work. Tears welling in her eyes, his pretty fiancee says: "When he leaves, my heart will be full of misery."

Illegal immigration stories were all over the papers done secondhand from various peaks on the U.S. side of the border, when this piece was written. But Getschow's perspective from his base in the poor, arid villages of central Mexico gave his work a power and graphic value that overshadowed everything done by his rivals.

Spending so much time there, he also was able to see and tell elements of the broad story that others did not: the bitter legacy of the Cristeros Rebellion, the irony of depopulated towns and jobs going begging in a nation with, overall, a crushing labor surplus, the ambivalent attitudes of Mexican peasants toward the U.S., and above all individual lives so wretched we understand immediately and completely the reasons for migration. A mountaintop would have provided a wider view, but from there we could not have seen the faces of the people.

So often we simply must see their faces, hear their voices, in order to really be convinced of the truth of what we are being told—and so often we do not because the reporter has failed us as a storyteller. He has not been sensitive to what readers *like*, to those high-interest elements that separate a good story—or story idea—from a tedious, unengaging one.

My own selective list of what readers like, in descending order of preference:

1. **Dogs,** followed by other cute animals and well-behaved small children. A reporter may do a skull-cracking analysis of talks on arms limitation and await the praise of an admiring readership. He gets one phone call from a nitpicker in a defense think tank who chides him for misstating the throw weight of the SS-20 missile. Meanwhile, a colleague tosses off a light piece on a three-legged collie that has rescued a child from an ice floe, and gets a sack of mail and 40 calls. Life is unfair.

2. **People/Actors.** Lacking a dog (and it's a shame how often we do) this element carries the most intrinsic reader interest, provided the people meet two criteria. First, by actors I mean people who are either pressing the buttons and pulling the levers, or those getting ground up in the gears. They are not the uninvolved: analysts, consultants—a consultant has been defined as a man who knows 123 ways to make love but doesn't know any women—researchers, lawyers who fight to the last nickel of the client's resources. Actors are those people who make things happen or who are directly affected by what happens.

Second, they ought to be doing or saying something interesting and germane. Some reporters shoehorn people into stories that don't lend themselves to personalization, or insert dullards whose testimony or experience fails to grip the reader. Having chucked a human being or two into his story, the reporter feels he has done his duty. But he's only genuflected to human interest, not served it. A piece about, say, warehouse inventories doesn't benefit by having a forklift operator drive through it. His presence makes the story appear strained, if not ludicrous.

If this is a sin, however, there is a graver one: Failure to get off the mountaintop and mix with the actors in a drama when the nature of the story idea cries out for on-the-ground reporting. I believe this is the greatest deficiency in newspaper reporting today. It is simply impossible to do a convincing piece on the root causes of, say, Mexican migration without going to the villages of the people who are driven north and *showing* why they leave—yet hundreds of writers have tried to do the impossible.

3. **Facts,** when they are relevant and move the story forward. Again, the distinctions are vital. Trivia and information of tan-

gential worth often get shoveled into the stories of reporters who are unconsciously or consciously trying to cover up story flaws—a lack of action, of direct human experience, of clear story theme. Such facts are clutter, not information, and only slow the tale.

4. People/Observers. Now we're getting into elements low on the reader-interest scale. As opposed to actors, these people don't have direct involvement in what's happening; they are the aforementioned consultants, analysts, commentators, lawyers, experts of every stripe, and what they do is talk. When Ronald Reagan invades Grenada, he is a high-level actor in that play. When he castigates the Russians for invading Afghanistan, he is only an observer in a different drama.

The insights and interpretations of observers are useful in many stories, but the reader regards them coolly. Other things being equal, he would rather hear a farmer talking about the damage boll weevils had done to his own cotton field than suffer the ramblings of a professor at the University of Arizona who offers the expert and painfully obvious opinion that the insect is becoming a threat to Southwestern cotton crops. The farmer has more credibility because he has suffered. He is an actor in the play.

This suggests that observers should be used sparingly and that sources with direct experience get prominence instead. After all, it is the sum of their experiences that *is* the story. But the opposite happens. The reporter inflicts upon his readers batteries of experts, but fails to illustrate the reality that these experts can only comment on second-hand. A high-interest element (the actor) gets replaced by a low-interest one (the observer), but the reporter sees only that he has put people into his story. The trouble is that they are the wrong kind of people.

5. Numbers, especially big numbers and comparative sets of numbers densely packed in consecutive paragraphs. This is cyanide to reader interest, but don't take my word for it; test the assertion by reading a story with a paragraph or two larded with statistics. Don't slow your reading speed when you come to them. Then try to remember the information. You probably won't be able to. You may not even recall the general meaning the swarm of numerals was meant to convey.

Big numbers are abstract, not concrete. Encountering them, the mind pauses, reflexively trying to translate the data into something it can picture. If too many abstracts assault it simultaneously, it gives up, and the rest of the story goes unread.

The moral of all this ought to be apparent, but too many of us remain far too dependent on a gross excess of statistics and expert testimony. It's time to jettison some of the numbers and the more gaseous effusions of the experts, replacing them with fresh factual information and the direct illustrations from life that hammer stories into the reader's memory.

These principles are most important in the reporting and writing stages of storytelling, but they must be considered in idea selection too. If a reporter has several ideas of roughly equal importance and topicality beginning to germinate, he should develop first those with most potential for introducing high-interest elements. And he should shy away from those likely to rely on statistics and a lot of gabble by experts.

He should prize above all those ideas with *action* in them. Something is happening, it is having specific effects, and perhaps a counter-action is under way. There is no substitute for such built-in movement in a story, and ideas centering on action are more likely to succeed than analytical thumbsuckers or static profiles. A reporter must do a superior job to make the analytical story interesting, but an idea with action in it can cover some sins of execution—especially if a relevant dog is present, too.

CHAPTER 2

SHAPING IDEAS

As everyone who lives there knows, the principal show-business product of Los Angeles is the Concept. Thousands are manufactured monthly and are bought, sold and optioned at parties and in bistros all over the west side of town. The fellow without one in his briefcase or his cranium—always a "viable Concept," which I suppose differentiates it from a dead one that nobody will buy—is poor indeed.

But few of these Concepts are viable enough to get made into movies. Laid on the anvils of the storysmiths, they shatter like glass at the first tap of the hammer. They are only vague notions, not fully developed ideas, and usually can't be forged into ideas. They simply don't work.

The same thing happens in newsrooms. Eager to get rolling, reporters armed with nothing more than Concepts waste time and energy discovering that there is no story after all, or that it is only a shadow of what they dreamed it would be.

Forethought is the missing ingredient here. Before flying out the door, a reporter should consider the range of his story, its central message, the approach that appears to best fit the tale, and even the tone he should take as storyteller. Mistakes in one or more of these can degrade the piece or put it on the spike.

Some common errors and suggested countermeasures:

RANGE

The reporter may think too small. The development he has chosen to treat may be limited and its extent easily defined in a few sentences. The reasons for its occurrence may be so apparent they are hardly worth mentioning, and he may fail to think past the obvious, initial effects of the development. He has come up short—but like as not he only discovers this when he sits down to write and sees that his grand Concept will resolve itself into only two or three pages of honest, tight copy. This will not do. Important stories don't get told in two pages, and a reporter's own idea never yields a story that isn't important. So he lards the piece with repetitive quotes, irrelevant facts, lots of numbers and other hokum.

Most of us, however, think too big. We try to embrace the circus fat lady, and only well into the effort do we find there is too much of her and not enough of us. The result is a piece impossibly long, or superficial, the reporter skipping frantically from point to point without dwelling on any of them long enough to illuminate and convince. The pace is frenzied, and the reader wearied by it. A limited tale well told has more impact and persuasiveness than a sweeping story that can't be adequately illustrated.

Solution: Subject the story's concept to cause-and-effect reasoning. This has two benefits: It helps identify in advance potential action elements in the story—the moves and countermoves that have high reader interest—and it helps stake out visually the story's boundaries. Having drawn what amounts to a rough map of the territory, the reporter can then carve out a section of it he can handle in the time and space available.

In this process, only action and reaction count. We're not interested in details, explanations, instruction or other elements that will appear in a finished piece. And the imagination should be given free rein.

Let's say, for example, that there is a nationwide shortage of physicians and that our reporter is trying to shape an idea about that. In using cause and effect, he treats the shortage not only as an event in itself but as the cause of another logically ensuing event. The latter, in turn, becomes the cause of still another event, and so on. On the following page is a graphic depiction of just some of the elements the exercise can yield. Inspect it briefly.

Now: Is anyone out there crazy enough to try wrapping all this into one backbreaking opus? I hope not; the impossibility of doing so in one feature story ought to be obvious.

Yet without the rough map logic provides, reporters *do* get lost in mazes like this one. White canes tapping, they stumble into byway after byway, wasting effort on material that only later they realize they have no room for. They get seduced by anecdotes and details that, under the harsh discipline of writing, turn out to be off the point. They labor too long covering too much, and so suffer lack of reporting depth in story sections that *are* important. All this happens because they didn't decide in advance what to leave out as well as what to put in. They had no fence around the story.

In drawing and analyzing his cause-and-effect map, the reporter must consider *time, distance* and *constituencies*. The farther an element is from the central development at the core of the story, the greater the chance that this element hasn't occurred. It may be logical to foresee a sharp rise in malpractice insurance premiums as one end result of a doctor shortage, but that may not be happening yet because the story hasn't had time to mature to this point.

Also, the greater the distance from the central development, the greater the chance that external forces have intruded to pollute logic. Maybe malpractice awards have soared as speculated. But perhaps insurance rates haven't, because the companies writing coverage are locked in a bitter competitive struggle. They are willing to accept minuscule profits, even losses, rather than raise premiums and risk losing their market shares to rate-cutting rivals.

So the reporter looks skeptically at the remote elements on his logic chains, and may choose not to chase them unless he has early evidence that they exist. This narrows his reporting, but he still has plenty to work with if he has considered all the

A Chain of Cause and Effect

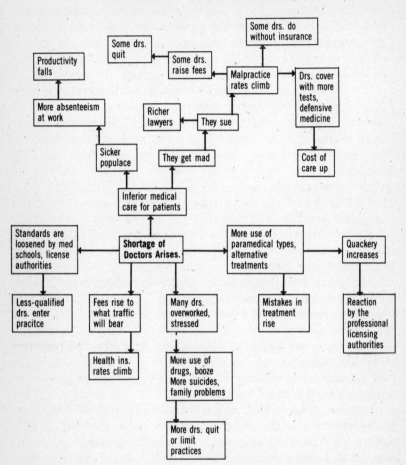

constituencies involved—the interest groups and institutions touched by developments. In our doctor story, physicians themselves are one obvious constituency, patients another. But we see what effects may be felt as well by medical schools, licensing authorities, lawyers and industries.

It almost goes without saying that cause-and-effect thinking, as well as other speculation, yields only *potential* story elements, things that *ought* to be happening. Burrowing into the story, a reporter must never hold inflexibly to his preconceptions, straining again and again to find proof of them where little exists, ignoring contrary evidence and passing up chances to explore fruitful areas that didn't figure in his early thinking. When he does so, he becomes a propagandist for his own logic, not a journalist. Events, not preconceptions, should shape all stories in the end. Only in the beginning is speculation useful—but then it's essential.

THEME

Cause-and-effect logic only gives our reporter a reasonable range of possibilities. If he doesn't select those he believes he can cover adequately, and then hammer them into a concise statement of what his story is likely to say when he is done with it, he still may lose reporting focus. Later, buried in material, he'll be unable to say what it adds up to, and if *he* doesn't know, it's a lot to expect of anyone else. Yet this sort of rambling, unfocused copy crosses editors' desks daily, and they're forced to pull the piece together for the person who has failed to. This is dangerous, and they don't like to do it. They don't like the reporters who make them do it.

Solution: Carve out a piece of the story map you've drawn and express it in a couple of simple, tightly written sentences. Concentrate on action—the main development, one or two of its likely effects and the logical major reaction to them, if any. Ignore all else. Tack this *main theme statement* up where you can see it. Let it guide your work. Let it reproach you, question you, when you stray too far from it.

I consider the main theme statement the single most important bit of writing I do on any story. It crystallizes for me the main action currents of my piece, at least as I foresee them going in. Later, when the reporting is done, I'll recast the main theme statement in light of what I've actually found, and use it then to guide the writing of the body of the story. Frequently, it's the basis for my lead.

A good main theme statement is brief and contains no details, but boldly and accurately sketches in the main movements occurring in the tale. If the whole finished story is an oil painting, the main theme statement is the initial quick sketch, the few but telling lines that delineate key shapes, from which the finished work eventually develops.

This main theme statement, incidentally, developed early in your work on the story, can also serve as the guts of your formal story proposal to editors. They want to know as precisely and concisely as possible the path you propose to follow. A well-constructed theme statement in your proposal will give them the clearest possible picture of the scope of your story.

The elements that should be stressed in a theme statement depend on whether the reporter is doing a *juvenile story* (where the central event itself is news) or a *mature story* (where the central event has been covered, perhaps, but not all its effects or the reactions to them).

Let's assume that our reporter has tumbled to the doctor shortage only because a colleague in rewrite has complained that he can't find a sawbones willing to take him as a patient and treat his gout. Doing his initial idea research, the reporter finds that doctors generally are in short supply, but that this has been reported thinly or not at all. The shortage is news. So his theme statement might simply be:

An acute shortage of physicians in many specialties is developing, and the quality and availability of medical care is being affected as a result.

This theme statement keeps the reporter near home base, the newsy central development, and only ventures into one generalized effect of it. The implied stress is on proving out and detailing aspects of the shortage—what specialties are most understaffed, what localities are most in need of doctors, what hospitals are suffering most, which health-care functions (emergency services? elective surgery?) are hardest hit. With the space remaining, the reporter will begin to deal with the broadest aspect of effects on patient care. But he does first things first.

Alternatively, let's assume that the shortage itself, as well as its general effect on health care, has already been recognized and covered by others. The theme statement in this case will instead stress some forward elements of a mature story:

The deterioration of medical care resulting from the doctor shortage is generating malpractice judgments that are pushing insurance rates through the roof. Some insurers are abandoning the business, and many physicians, appalled by rising rates, are going without coverage or forming pools for self-insurance.

Notice that the central event here is treated as a given; everybody already knows there is a shortage of doctors, so this only needs to be alluded to briefly, not proved out in detail. The deterioration in health care is similarly kissed off. The theme statement emphasizes the legal effects and the reaction of insurers and physicians. Looking at this statement, the reporter is constantly reminded of where his main reporting effort belongs.

DEVELOPING A PROFILE

A somewhat different technique can be used to shape a profile. These stories are treacherous. Because they seem by nature narrow in range, a reporter may feel that all he must do is find an attractive subject and launch himself into the blue. He tells his editor, "I'm doing a profile about such-and-such"—and promptly wades into a swamp of complexities he didn't anticipate.

John McPhee wrote an entire book about oranges without exhausting the subject, but most of us are allotted only a few thousand words to treat far broader topics. So it's imperative to ask, "What should I concentrate on?" By asking this, we are also asking by inference what sort of material we can or should omit—and we always have to omit more than we include. Editors like to talk about the "definitive profile," but there's no such thing in the newspaper business.

Broadly speaking, there are two kinds of profiles, the general and the microcosm. The **general profile** subject is chosen for its inherent interest, which usually depends on qualities that make it unique or unusual. So it makes sense in this kind of piece to pour most effort into detailing these qualities of *differentness*.

But the **microcosm profile** subject is picked because of its typicalness, its *similarity* to others in its class; we are using it as a vehicle to tell a wider tale, as a representative of other subjects that are going through the same experiences and having the same reactions to them. A story about one auto worker's family during an industry strike, for example, would stress that family's similarities to others, not its differences.

In preparing to attack either kind of profile, the reporter should again write a terse theme statement, this time identifying not action and reaction but those facets of his profile subject he plans to focus on. These should be concretely expressed, but not so narrowly that he has little reporting room, and they should be few.

Notice, for example, where the reporting emphasis lies in this general profile written by me in 1981 on big-tree logging. Pay close attention to this story, too, as it will be referred to several times later in this book.

KALAMA, Washington—Let us say that you work in an office building with 1,000 people and that every day at least two are hurt on the job. Some suffer such ghastly wounds—multiple compound fractures, deep cuts severing muscle, sinew and nerve, shattered pelvises—that they may never return to their old posts. And every six months or so, a body is taken to the morgue.

Almost anywhere, this would be called carnage, and a hue and cry would be raised. But in the big-tree logging woods of the Pacific Northwest, it is simply endured with what logger-writer Stan Hager has called "proud fatalism," and few outside the loggers' trade even know of it. Miners trapped behind a cave-in draw national media attention, but in the dim rain forests men fall singly and suddenly. There aren't any TV cameras.

Increased stress on training and safety in recent years has helped. But death and injury rates still are extraordinarily high—in part because loggers are an almost suicidally prideful and tradition-bound group, hooked on danger and suspicious of new equipment and techniques.

Resistance to Change

"There's tremendous macho, and I can't imagine any group of men more resistant to change," says Joel Hembree, the safety coordinator for local 3-536 of the International Woodworkers of America, which represents loggers and mill-workers in southwest Washington. The union, he adds, is thus in the awkward position of pushing measures that many of its own members oppose. "We're a bunch of dirty S.O.B.'s for trying to jam safety down their throats," he says.

In the forest, a few loggers sit in a bus reeking of old socks, wet wool and tobacco smoke, grousing about safety. "They've already got us decked out like Christmas trees," growls Howard "Spider" Mason, a 36-year-old Weyerhaeuser Co. "timber faller," or cutter, displaying a pair of heavy water-soaked leg protectors the law now says he must wear. Another logger recites a poem about the idiocies of the safety people that concludes, "Who's going to protect us against our protection?"

Even if the loggers did festoon themselves with every safety gadget available, the forest has a hundred treacherous ways to get them anyway. "To you the forest is a pretty place," says a union staffer. "To our guys it's dark, it's scary and it's out to hurt them." In the woods men are crushed to death by trees that simply fall over without being touched. Some are speared through by broken branches that fall 250 feet on a windless day. Others are maimed by rocks bouncing down hillsides.

The forest also is unforgiving of error, and a moment's carelessness can wound or kill. About 15,000 men are usually working in the Washington woods; over the past three years they have suffered a total of almost 28,000 injuries and 75 deaths. "It's you against the trees," says a veteran woodsman.

This toll is viewed with stoicism. Spider Mason, tall, dark and talkative ("Spider wore out two pair of lips before he was 18," says a co-worker), keeps his buddies laughing at his banter, but he is serious about the hazards of the job. "You go to work every day knowing death is in the trees," he says. "Your family knows it; my wife doesn't want to hear anything about what I do. But a logger has to *enjoy* danger or he isn't a logger."

Generations of the Mason clan have gone into the forest and, as with so many other families, the forest has made them pay for their fascination with it. The forest has killed Spider's uncle, grandfather, father and brother. The forest has reached across the country to exact its price from the town of Hayesville, N.C., population about 300; Clarence Stamey, woods business agent for the IWA local here, comes from Hayesville and can think of 10 fellow townsmen who have come to the Northwest woods to die. He may have forgotten a name or two, he adds.

The trade-off for all this? Membership in a fraternity.

* * *

At 4 A.M. bedroom lights go on in Kalama, Longview and smaller lumber towns—"the three-house, two-bar places," one logger calls them—buried in the green spires of the Cascade Range. A little later, the sleepy men board their "crummies," the aptly named crew buses that take them to their camps. All wear a uniform that hasn't changed in decades: caulked boots, heavy trousers cut off near the tops of the boots, work shirt, suspenders (no logger wears a belt), and usually a full beard or a brushy mustache.

By dawn the chain saws are snarling in the woods. The loggers won't get back home until dark—or well after dark as the days grow shorter. In between, they do some of the hardest physical work in American industry. Toiling "in the pit," at the bottom of infernally steep slopes, choker-setters struggle to fit 100-pound collars around logs to be dragged uphill on one-inch cables grinding overhead. Laden with 50 pounds of gear, the timber fallers crawl up and down hills clogged with man-high brush to find their trees. In summer there is heat exhaustion, in winter the sheer misery of constant rain or snow.

It is the ability and the will to endure such work that bind Northwest loggers together. To them the loggers of the Southeast, where the trees are smaller, the land flatter and the climate benign, are mere woodchoppers. "*This* is logging," brags one foreman, indicating a virgin forest where monster Douglas firs eight feet in diameter and 250 feet tall can still be found. Nine miles east, Mount St. Helens rises like a white wall, its shattered summit banked in mist.

This is a male society. Few women apply for work requiring such great upper-body strength, and those who do confront a relentlessly macho atmosphere. At one camp men chose lots to sit next to a woman choker-setter on the crummy so they could harass her on the way home; she quit. A logging supervisor says, "The idea that a woman possibly could do what they do—well, it just kills them."

Few blacks work in the Northwest woods, either. Many loggers are from Southern families, and deeply ingrained racial attitudes persist. An old logger, arms covered with chain-saw scars, says earnestly, "A while back, they tried real hard to get some of those niggers up here to work, but they didn't stick. I don't know why."

Everyone who enters the woods is hazed crudely and unmercifully. Does he have big ears? He is Dumbo forever. Is he a newlywed? Slip some dirty pictures into his empty lunchbox so his bride will find them. Put rocks in his gear bag, give him grueling, unnecessary chores to do, test him. "The tender young boys don't last," says Spider Mason. One called Dimples so displeased the veteran logger he worked with that the latter picked him up overhead and threw him uphill with instructions never to return. He didn't.

In work so dangerous, it is vital to cull the unfit and the incompatible. A streak of meanness in the hazing often is the first sign that a man is on the way out, says Jack Coady, the superintendent of Weyerhaeuser's District 6, comprising 142,000 acres of forest east of Kalama. The victim may have his lunch destroyed or his clothes set afire; then another man may invite him behind a tree for a faceful of knuckles. Finally the hook tender—the boss union logger—may simply say, "Go on down the road. We don't want to see you anymore."

If a man is a good worker but cannot get along with his fellows, Mr. Coady will bluntly tell him that he is fouling up and that if he can't adjust to his next crew he will be run off. Bluntness is always the loggers' way. "It's good, clean communication, one on one," he says. "No dancing around, no politics. Logging is an open society, and that's one reason I like the industry so much."

The woods are full of men who have repeatedly quit the miseries and dangers of that industry, but who keep coming back. The open, rough camaraderie, the knowledge that they can do work others quail from out of fear or weakness, forges a sense of community they cannot find outside.

Greg Kruger, a strapping, fair-haired logger, says, "The beauty of the woods is that if you can do a damn good job, you can be any man you want, you can wear a clown suit or a tuxedo to work if you want. You'll get razzed to death—but you're accepted. You belong."

In 1974 a basketball-sized rock glancing off a canyon wall crushed Greg Kruger's left side. (One of the men who carried him out quit on the spot when he saw the wounds.) Now Greg's arm is a mass of scar tissue, and a piece of shattered pelvis still floats around inside him. Partly disabled, he works in the office at South Camp, the headquarters of District 6.

Work is somehow found for many men hurt seriously on the job—even though this may involve violating contract rules that require filling slots by seniority. Union representatives and company supervisors just look the other way; it is more important that the fraternity to which both belong takes care of its own. As for Greg Kruger, he wishes he could set choker again. But it is enough just to be here, still a member in good standing.

* * *

Thirty of the 210 men at South Camp are in a little contest. Divided into three groups of 10, they have been promised that if any group goes six months without an injury, the men and their wives will get a free dinner. "Shoot, they'll never collect," mumbles one logger. Three men on two of the teams were hurt within days after the list had gone up, and so had to start the six-month cycle all over again.

The 30 are South Camp's crack crew of timber fallers, the loggers who bear the greatest risk of death. This camp hasn't lost a cutter in many years, but every old-timer on the crew knows someone who has been killed at this exacting craft. Conversation with fallers is a litany of tales about crushed skulls, broken backs, legs half-severed by chain saws. They also suffer scarred eyeballs from wood particles flying out of saw cuts, permanent hearing loss from saw noise far in excess of maximum federal standards, and damage to the capillaries and nerves of the hand because of vibration, damp and cold.

Safety Record

This is called white hand, and Roy Palmer has it badly. At times his hand turns a corpse-like white and he loses feeling in it, a dangerous thing that Roy and the others shrug off. "You just clamp your fingers on with the other hand, and once in a while you burn it on the muffler (of the chain saw) till your glove starts to smoke," he says cheerfully.

At 62 and near retirement, Roy is still one of the most productive cutters. He went 27 years without an injury, an incredible record. Men have died around him, and once a partner, immobilized in front of an oncoming log when his foot got stuck, screamed to Roy to cut his leg off (he cut him out of his boot instead). But Roy himself escaped until recently.

He tore his hand on a running saw last year and this past July had another accident while he was cutting a fallen tree into log lengths. When a tree is lying on uneven ground, it is full of areas of tension and compression called binds. After these are cut through, the sections can writhe like snakes or swing uphill or down, pivoting on rocks or stumps and crushing anything in their way. Roy Palmer fell as a tree moved, and his saw cut through muscles near his ankle and halfway into the bone.

There are scores of ways that loggers can die from a single mistake, and they are acutely conscious of the need for total concentration. Gary Trople, who is going through a divorce, says his production drops when marital troubles are on his mind because he won't touch a tree without having his entire attention on it.

Like others, he has a love-hate relationship with his job. Even at six, he wanted to be a timber faller. "I'd take a hatchet and beat on some of those little-bitty pine poles till they fell down," he recalls.

But four months after he started in the woods, a snapping cable threw him against a stump, crushing his ribs, fracturing his skull and breaking his back in three places. "I swore I'd never come back," he says. "Five months later I was back. I went in the Army for four years and swore I'd never come back. Here I am."

Value of Narrow Escapes

Not long ago he felled a tree that brushed another tree in its descent, bending it like a 220-foot catapult. The tree sprang back to fire a deadly hail of broken limbs at him, but he escaped with lacerations. "Most of the time that would kill you," says his supervisor, a ginger-bearded logger named Jack Davis. But he adds that without close calls a faller can be lured into a false sense of security that may prove fatal. Jerry Baldwin, a young cutter, listens dubiously. "When I have a close call," he says, "I just go home and shake for a while."

For this extra ration of danger, fallers get some of the top pay in the woods—$30,000 in a good year for an hourly paid union man, more for a good "gyppo busheler," a cutter working for a nonunion contractor and paid by the amount of wood he can lay on the ground.

Their psychic income is the satisfaction that comes from conquest of the great forest giants, and fallers always remember their biggest trees. "Lay one of those big dudes down just where you want, save it all, and you've done something damn few men anywhere can do," says one. A bad job that splits or breaks a tree can destroy 90% of its lumber value.

"Uphill! Uphill!"

In a virgin grove, Elmer Osborne and Paul Cline are working on a tree that was growing before Columbus sailed. It is about seven feet thick and 240 feet tall. After making the undercut, a thick wedge of wood removed in the desired direction of fall, Elmer cuts through the other side until only a thin slab of "holding wood" supports hundreds of tons above. Its equilibrium altered, the tree creaks, the wood tears away, and Elmer yells, "Uphill!" (No one yells, "Timber!" anymore.) The fir falls slowly, striking with a mighty *whump* that shakes the earth. It is a perfect fall, saving intact about $6,000 in logs and much more in lumber value at retail. "I'll take that one. That's a good one," Elmer says with a broad smile. It doesn't matter now that an hour earlier a 160-foot dead tree falling the wrong way almost wiped him out.

Such scenes grow rarer. On the private lands of the big timber companies, the enormous trees of the virgin forest are quickly disappearing. In their place are strange, monotonous woods that seem almost dead by comparison—filled with trees of the same height, thickness and species, all planted by men. They will never be allowed to reach the size of the old giants because that would be uneconomical. Harvesting them will be far safer than working in the virgin forest, with its treacherous rotting trees, snarls of interlocking top branches, and leaning trees. But much of the glamour of logging will fade with that natural forest, too.

"That's why I've got pictures of the biggest trees I've cut," says Jack Davis, the supervisor. "For the kids, so they can see what it was really like. The day is coming when men in these woods will laugh if you tell them there were really trees 10 feet thick here."

I stressed only two main elements in my theme statement for this story:

—Logging is one of the most dangerous of all jobs.
—The men who do it have created an unusual work society shaped by those great dangers.

The reader learns little or nothing from this story about the fine points of woodcraft, about loggers as rounded human beings with wives, kids and mortgages, about the logger's place in the whole forest products industry, about a dozen other things that could be considered germane. But by omitting or treating briefly all these, I was able to detail more fully those aspects of logging that make it unusual or unique—the full ration of danger and death men face in the woods, and the specific values and codes of the strange work fraternity they have formed. If this story has power, it is because of that concentration of effort into just two channels.

APPROACH

A tale of two reporters: One, an opportunist with a lazy streak, always looks for the easy way to tell a hard story. Faced with a feature opportunity about some development, he reflexively tries to tell it as a microcosm profile. A few phone calls to bring in a smattering of outside material, a few days spent hanging around his profile subject, and he will have his story nailed down.

His colleague is a less facile interviewer and writer, but a more dogged and thorough reporter, a fact man. He is comfortable with a classic roundup approach that lets him bring in many sources from many locales without forcing him to give detailed attention to any. This fits his journalistic personality.

Some stories of these two reporters turn out well. But others don't, because the approach each habitually uses doesn't fit every story. The nature of the tale itself, rather than a reporter's preference, ought to dictate the approach to it.

Solution: Weigh the story idea against the advantages and drawbacks intrinsic in each approach. Then use the one that gives you the best chance of success, not the one that makes you feel cozy.

Some advantages and drawbacks of the two approaches:

The Profile Approach

It offers the chance to involve the reader deeply. By focusing on a single subject, the reporter can resolve complexities and abstracts into concrete, pictorial examples the reader sees and grasps. And the subject is seen in the round; the reader can get to know a man, an institution or a place in a way he never can in a roundup approach. Finally, profile approaches are easier to organize, having a built-in thread (the subject) to tie disparate elements together.

But—and it is a big but—the profile approach can yield ghastly results if the subject is uninteresting. There are decent, capable men so dull they put their own wives to sleep. There are places and institutions that anesthetize even their own inhabitants, to say nothing of the stranger. Stuck to one of these tar babies, the most artful reporter seldom escapes with grace.

Even if the profile subject is a suitably jazzy fellow, he may be the wrong fellow. A Chicago reporter, let's say, wants to do a piece on how farmers must be suffering because of removal of price supports on milo. A source at the Farm Bureau assures him that this suffering is real and widespread. Smelling a good microcosm profile, our man seeks sources in Kansas who can lead him to a few affected farmers. After a couple of days he is finally able to reach a handful, and he picks the one who seems most articulate and cooperative. Sure, the reporter can visit, booms this agriculturalist. The more folks learn about how the poor farmer is taking it in the chops from the bubbleheads in Washington, the better. He promises chapter and verse in his own case.

Practically salivating now, our man sketches out the story for his boss and gets approval for a trip. He books a flight, fills out expense forms, draws money and tells his wife. This shoots his afternoon. The next morning, he drives an hour and a half to O'Hare and waits as long again because the flight is late. Finally arriving in Wichita, he wrestles his bags into a Hertz rental and drives 200 miles to the milo capital of West Bumstead, where he collapses in the Ramada Inn. The next morning, he arrives at the farm of his profile subject. It looks like the set for "Giant."

A pillared mansion stands in a wheat field, a few Angus browsing nearby at the base of an oil pumping unit. A Mercedes sits in the drive and a Cessna out back. The owner of this spread strides out to greet him, shod in $450 lizard-skin boots.

He is charming, outspoken, a mine of information about milo, and rich as Croesus. His own milo crop has indeed been a loser, but the price of wheat is holding up, his condo development venture is looking good, oil is a nice thing to have on your land, and his shopping-center deal is throwing an airtight tax shelter over the rest.

This is suffering? This is privation? Goodbye, story.

The lesson is clear: Profile subjects have to be thoroughly vetted to ensure not only that they won't bore people to death, but, in the case of microcosm profiles, that they represent what the reporter needs them to represent. Half the work in doing profiles can lie in finding just the right subject, and there are risks even when much care is taken.

These risks dwindle if the reporter can use a hybrid form, the **collective profile.** Instead of betting the whole pot on one farmer, he might instead have chosen as his subject West Bumstead itself, a small farm town in the milo belt. He is sure to find other area farmers better suited to his theme, and he can bring in a few other aspects as well—the impact on the local economy and on the civic mood, for example. The reporting stage is still small enough to give the reader some sense of intimacy, but the chance of failure is diminished.

The Roundup Approach

This belt-and-suspenders method is safer yet, and has other qualities to recommend it. The writer has maximum reporting room, making it more likely that the story will contain real meat. The technique also gives the piece a faster-paced, newsy flavor that is appealing; the reporter can move from farm to farm, town to town, bringing in varied elements in rapid succession. Properly executed, these stories have punch that profiles often lack.

But the development treated had better be broadly based or the reporter will run out of gas, and it should have a variety of effects and counteractions to avoid being repetitive. If consumers have cut their consumption of pork and a new virus is decimating pigs at the same time, swine raisers obviously are in trouble. But if they haven't had time to react yet, a roundup may produce a repetitive, monotone piece amounting to little more than a nationwide laundry list of dead pigs and sick balance sheets. A microcosm profile might be preferred. If swine raisers are reacting, however, by quitting the business, marching on the Agriculture Department, or breeding superhogs with immunity to the virus, a roundup would be a better fit, because it is unlikely that one swine raiser would be doing all this.

TONE

A story with the wrong tone gets posted on bulletin boards or passed around so the author's colleagues can snigger at it. Sometimes it even slips into print, to the merriment or pain of the reader. The following is a desperate attempt by *The Wall Street*

Journal to cover in its own fashion the blossoming national story of the Boston Strangler, who was murdering and sexually violating women in the Massachusetts Bay area over 20 years ago.

The headline tells it all:

BOSTON STRANGLINGS
MAKE PEOPLE WARY
OF DOOR-TO-DOOR VENDORS

Fuller Brush Sales Decline;
Insurance Men Turned Away;
Taxis and Locksmiths Busier

The *Journal* probably was led into this grotesque by its aversion to covering transgressions of the flesh. The paper long maintained that almost nothing occurring below the waist is newsworthy, a position that changing standards have eroded but not obliterated (years after the strangler piece appeared, a queasy editor removed from a story about the popularity of vasectomies the passage describing what the operation was—leaving any totally uninformed reader to guess at what part of the body might be involved).

The *Journal* was only trying to get a fresh slant on a story that gripped the national attention. But in straining for a different angle, it only succeeded in turning a dramatic and tragic crime tale into a small-bore business piece that opened the paper to ridicule. Nothing is wrong with trying to give a fresh turn to a heavily covered story—unless the idea denies or distorts the inherent drama of the development by turning tragedy into comedy, the cosmic into the mundane, the sweet into the sour.

A more prevalent mistake, however, is lack of any tone at all. When this happens, and it happens too often, the story is a dead fish. Facts, numbers and quotes are present, but the reader has the nagging feeling that he might as well be perusing the encyclopedia. The reporter has failed to see and develop points of *drama* that might dictate the tone of the story, or has been reluctant to take a stance, an attitude, toward developments he is writing about. I don't mean editorializing, which involves the taking of sides. I mean empathizing, the reporter briefly putting himself in the shoes of sources on both sides of an issue so he can write with a bit of their feeling showing.

Solution: Approach your story idea as a novelist might, looking for potential elements of comedy, tragedy, irony or conflict that can be stressed in the reporting and writing. Look particularly for tension between protagonist and antagonist, remembering that these need not be individuals. In the logging story, the typical logger was the protagonist but his foe was the malevolent forest itself. Seeing the forest this way, I was naturally led to depict it as an active, living thing. The result of the struggle between the two forces is drama. If the forest had not been treated this way, much of that drama would have been missing.

And always consider your own feelings about the story idea before you start reporting, and throughout. If you are amused, skeptical, outraged by the development or major aspects of it, try to identify what makes you feel that way. Hang on to your emotions, remember your analysis of them, and your reporting and writing will be guided toward values they may not have included before. If you can't muster a shred of passion for your own story or the people in it, you can't expect the reader to care, either.

Finally, cultivate a spirit of healthy skepticism toward people and institutions that are taken too seriously by almost everyone. This stance is invaluable in covering the citadels of business, finance and government. If a reporter is too earnest in approaching these, he may get cowed by the importance of it all and begin producing stuffy, prolix copy that makes what is happening seem more complex than it is, that dwells on insider aspects useless to the reader, and that obscures the humanity lying just below the glass-and-granite skin of every institution. If instead he approaches them with irreverence, he'll be more likely to reduce unnecessarily complicated material to clear, simple form and demythologize his subjects. Most of them badly need it.

We can all learn from Stan Freberg, the comic-turned-adman who made his living spoofing his own clients' products. Criticized by his peers for denigrating Sunsweet prunes in one campaign, he said: "It's just a prune, for crying out loud. It's not the Holy Grail. So why not entertain a little?" The wise storyteller takes this as a motto.

CHAPTER 3

STORY DIMENSIONS

Someone once said that the ideal *Reader's Digest* story would be titled, "How l Had Carnal Relations with a Bear for the FBI and Found God." Not bad. The story certainly promises a lot of high drama, and we've just learned how much that can help any piece.

Alas, there just aren't enough Bear/FBI stories to go around. If they're lucky, reporters can expect to handle only a few stories in their entire careers that contain really riveting drama. But there are other story dimensions that they can rely on far more often to help them add interest to their tales. Let's consider some of them now, in a general way; in the next chapter, we'll try to build them into the reporting plan for stories.

TIME

One of the most neglected dimensions. As journalists, we dwell in the present and generally that's where we belong. But there are times when the past and/or the future plays a sizable part in our tales, and are neglected. When we can develop them, such stories gain a depth that is pleasing to readers. Standing in a time tunnel of our construction, they can look backward to the origins of an event and forward to its possible influence on our tomorrows.

In some stories the past is so important that it governs the reporter's attitude and thus dictates the tone of the piece, as in this 1979 story of mine on a modern-day mountain man:

ROCK SPRINGS, Wyo.—In 1906 Henry Reese Mitchell left a tiny Missouri farm and struggled west with his family across a rolling sea of sage. He had bought, sight unseen, 160 acres north of here on which to make a new life.

But the rich farmland of his dream proved to be just more arid, scrubby desolation. His Son Finis remembers that when his mother, Fay, saw it, she wept. "Reese," she pleaded, "Let's go home." And he said, "Cain't. You ain't got no home."

So they toughed it out there, under the blue ramparts of the Wind River Range, living with the country, going to the foothill forests for timber and taking elk for food. On a hunting trip with his father in 1908, young Finis climbed his first peak, a hill really, to scout game. Suddenly he could see deep into the majesty of the Wind Rivers, 2.25 million acres sprawling along 100 miles of the Continental Divide. "I fell in love with the mountains right there," he remembers.

Time Grows Short

Over the years the fascination grew into obsession. He vowed that someday he would climb every major peak in the range, Wyoming's highest. Decade after decade he used his weekends and vacations to climb, disappearing into the wilderness with up to 76 pounds on his back for as long as 17 days at a time, conquering almost 200 different peaks in more than 250 ascents.

He is almost 78 now, silver haired and bespectacled. He has a bum knee, and time grows short. But he is still at it—fading into the mountains again and again, traversing glaciers with ice axe, crampons and rope, talking to his friends the elk and bighorn sheep. Retirement in 1967 from a railroad foreman's job gave him more freedom for what he sees as his real occupation: mountain man.

Mr. Mitchell is a peppery fellow with a rich past, strong opinions, and no reluctance to declaim at length on both. (Sometimes Emma, his wife of 51 years, tells him, "Finis, you're blabbin' again.") Asked to write about himself for an outdoor magazine, he cranked out a manuscript so hefty the editor had to tell him he didn't have the whole magazine to play with. But when he talks about what still draws him to the peaks, it is different.

"From the first time I saw them I felt they were my real home," he says simply. "Where else can a man get so close to heaven, to his Creator, with both feet still on the ground?"

Finis Mitchell is part of a unique line of men stretching back to the early 1800s, when trappers and explorers like John Colter, Jim Bridger and Jedidiah Smith first penetrated the cloud-capped Western ranges—and found there a beauty and solitude that bound them in spirit to the high country all their lives. That line continued well into this century with men like Norman Clyde, who spent most of a solitary life in the Sierra Nevada under a backbreaking pack exceeding 100 pounds, including a portable library in Greek and other languages.

Part of the Scenery

Mr. Mitchell doesn't read Greek. He never saw the inside of a high school because he was too busy greasing rail cars for 17 cents an hour. He was never a true mountain nomad; he journeys to the Wind River from a small home, filled with memorabilia, here where Emma was born and raised. But few mountain men have put such an indelible stamp on one set of peaks as Finis Mitchell has on the Wind River Range.

The still-husky, barrel-chested six-footer, clad in wide-brimmed hat, red wool shirt and bib overalls, is now part of the scenery through which he has hiked some 15,000 miles. In 1975 he wrote an authoritative guide to the mountains, and hundreds of hikers seek his counsel, keeping him busy writing letters all winter.

A scientist for the U.S. Geological Survey calls him "the leading authority on Wind River geography," and at the survey's request he has named glaciers, peaks and lakes in the region—as well as moving one mountain from its erroneous location on the old maps to the place where it belongs. Anglers in the Wind River today catch the descendants of 2.5 million trout he and Emma lugged into the high country in the 1930s, when the Depression temporarily cost him his railroad job and he opened a fishing camp.

He has used up more than two dozen cameras taking more than 106,000 pictures—Mr. Mitchell keeps careful track of his statistics—that have adorned outdoor magazines and government publications. Many are of forest-fringed meadows golden with wildflowers, but he takes them mainly because other people like them.

He personally prefers the jagged, cold austerity of the lands far above timberline. It is a bare world, done in blues and grays, where the glaciers creak and groan and only the glacier lily, blooming in the melt at the fringes of the vast ice rivers, is a reminder of the flowered fields below. This is where he feels true contentment. "Suits me from A to Z," says the old man. "You can really appreciate your own insignificance up there."

It is also unforgiving and treacherous. In 1975, on a glacier, he twisted his knee so severely in a snow-covered crevasse that he had to cut his clothing away from the swollen joint and half-crawl back to timberline, where he hacked crude crutches out of two young pines and hobbled out 18 miles. Another time, rotten rock crumbled under him and he fell 200 feet into a soft tongue of snow that spilled him far down Dinwoody Glacier—unhurt. It was the only time he ever felt real terror in the mountains.

"But I learned from all that," he says, "and now I feel my decisions and judgment in the mountains are waterproof." He also brags about his physical condition, never touching alcohol or tobacco, avoiding spices and not eating food much above body temperature. "The tongue is the guardian of the stomach and I don't put anything on it that makes it uncomfortable," he declares as a once-hot Chinese dinner congeals on his plate.

The payoff is a resting heart rate of about 50, one sign of an athlete's ticker that lets him play sly games on younger mountaineers. Leading the way, he will stretch out the periods between rests, getting a little ahead, moving on quickly when the others catch up to stop. Finally he is way ahead—where he conspicuously and gleefully waits for his panting colleagues.

He scorns freeze-dried food ("costs four times as much as it should"), hundred-dollar boots and the other accoutrements of wilderness chic. His boots are J.C. Penney. He doesn't cook on the trail and relies on the corner grocery for all his food. He isn't fussy about campsites. "Fella once asked me where he should make camp every night," snorts an exasperated Mr. Mitchell. "Now how can you tell a man that? Wherever the sun goes down, that's your home." Sunset has frequently found him on a ledge too small to lie down on, and he sleeps sitting up.

Advancing years bring him more honors and less solitude. He has a mountain named after him now, and an honorary college degree. Strangers show up to go hiking with him, and he is often asked to speak about his beloved mountains. He does it all without charge, taken aback by the notion that he could collect fees for his services.

"What, show people the wilderness that belongs to them and make them pay for it?" he asks. "I want them to come, all of them. Had a couple of hikers from Illinois and when they came down someone had written in the dust on their car, 'Go home and stay.' That's selfish, selfish."

He is also saddened and angered by the uglification he sees around him. Rock Springs, a major mining center, has been badly scarred by the energy boom; heavy trucks raise plumes of dust, power transmission towers march over bulldozer-scarred buttes and plains, the aluminum boxes of trailer camps sprawl over barren acres. "Our quaking aspen isn't the same bright green," the old man says, looking out his window. "I used to be able to see 100 miles over the desert; no more. The white man is accelerating his own extinction."

High in the glacier country he loves it is the same as it has always been—but how long can he keep climbing there? What if something happens to him, far above timberline? Emma Mitchell, who does not climb and who long ago got used to sharing her husband with a mountain, is fatalistic. "I used to worry," she says, "but if the Good Lord wants him up there, I guess he can have him."

Mr. Mitchell concedes that he is slowing down noticeably now, that the slopes are steeper than they were. But he is convinced that the Creator wouldn't play such a dirty trick on him, not now anyway. "I figure I'm good till about 90," he adds. That would give him 12 years. There are 20 peaks still to go.

It would have been easy to treat Finis Mitchell as a crank pursuing a bizarre obsession. But his own history, and that of the pull that has drawn men to the mountains since the first white trapper saw them, dictated a different outlook. Mitchell is not an aberration. He is part of a historical line unbroken for generations. To have omitted that element might have left him depicted, however subtly, as a nut case, a characterization not only insensitive but inaccurate.

Pertinent historical data also amplify our understanding of current events, as in the Mexican migration story. We cannot fully grasp the impetus of the flow northward without knowing about the Cristeros Rebellion of more than a half-century ago, an event whose consequences still propel the landless over the border.

Finally, a good story lead sometimes can be dredged out of historical material, as illustrated by this one on a piece about the Colorado River:

BLACK CANYON, Nev.—More than a century ago a young Army officer named Joseph Christmas Ives sailed up the Colorado River to explore it. Stopped near here by deep gorges and wild water, he later reported: "Ours was the first and doubtless will be the last party of whites to visit this profitless locality."
Lt. Ives was a lousy forecaster.

The profitless locality has become Las Vegas, and the story goes on to show how an entire modern desert civilization now depends on a river resource unable to handle more growth.

If the past illuminates the present, the future can give a story the flavor of suspense and anticipation. By simply asking actors and observers what they think will happen next, we can project the reader into realms of possibility.

Opportunities to do this are often missed because the reporter, unable to get a formal projection from a think tank, government agency or other expert, goes no further; he assumes that if professional forecasters haven't spoken, there is no reportable future. He is mistaken. The experts have no corner on crystal balls.

So, instead of just asking a demographer and economist at the Agriculture Department about the future of small farmers, ask a small farmer what he thinks his own future is. Knowing his own problems and opportunities better than anyone else, he has ultimate credibility within this range.

When it's possible to do so, developing the future aspects of a story gives the writer another considerable benefit: Move than any other kind of material, it provides good endings for stories, as we shall see later in this book.

SCOPE

We've learned how to cut a sprawling, multifaceted story down to size by building a fence around part of it. Now we have to think about how to handle the developments that lie inside the fence. When I refer to scope in this context, I mean the extent to which a reporter must go, the considerations he must address, in order to fully and convincingly treat those developments. In a nonprofile story about some happening, that involves factors I label *quantity, locale, diversity* and *intensity*.

When a reporter addresses quantity, he tries to give the reader some idea of the proportion of the development, sometimes in numbers but also in quotes or factual statements bearing on size. He seeks to answer a common question in the reader's mind: How big is this, anyway?

In addressing locale, the reporter tries to sketch out the extent of the field on which the development is being played out. Is it local, national, global? Is it industrywide or only companywide? What is its breadth? The reader questions he is trying to answer here are: Where is this happening? What is its sweep?

Most of us deal adequately with quantity and locale. If there is indeed a shortage of doctors, we immediately try to discover how many are needed overall and how many in specific specialties. We seek the regions, states, towns or facilities most affected. Or if we don't, some editor quickly tells us we should have.

The last two factors, however, often get skimpy treatment. In addressing diversity, we want to show the different *ways* in which our development reveals itself, and in addressing intensity we seek to illustrate the *degree* to which people, places and institutions are involved in or affected by it. To do this, we must often rely on the experiences of primary actors, people at the lowest level of the story action.

In the piece about Mexico, for example, we get a fuller idea of the scope of the migration when we see a small city so denuded of working-age males that oldsters have to be bused in from the country to staff businesses. We see the scope of the poverty that drives migrants northward, not in general statistics about income but in the life of family members so poor they cannot afford to feed their pet chicken. Taken together, these and other such snapshots provide intensity and diversity.

The notion of scope in a profile seems a contradiction, but given a broader meaning it is not. The subject may be a single person, place or institution, and we will be treating only a few of its many aspects—but we still have to report those in a way that brings out the full extent of each.

In the logger story, the danger of the job was one major aspect. Look at all the ways it was defined: How men can be hurt and killed through sheer accident, how they can be hurt and killed if they make one small slip, the statewide toll of death and injury, the tragedy of one family and one town, occupational diseases, exhaustion factors, and so on. All these define the scope of the danger-death aspect by showing how dangerous the work is (intensity) in how many ways (diversity).

VARIETY

This story quality can be enhanced in two ways:

1. *Providing different source types.* The greenest cub knows he must seek sources on both sides of an issue, but he may give little thought to the level of those sources—whether they are actors or observers, and, if actors, their distance from the action. Without such consideration, his story is apt to become a talky, tiresome squabble among desk people—officials, pols, executives, think tankers and others who are involved at a level a bit too far above the street or not directly involved at all. He should use a few of these, certainly. But if he dips down lower for additional sources on both sides, his piece gains a gritty, streetsmart quality desk people never give it. Hal Lancaster did so in the following story on insurance fraud:

LOS ANGELES—The man at the bar is a personnel officer for a large concern. He is well-scrubbed, well-groomed and as anonymous-looking as a glass of water. All this helps him in his sideline business, which happens to be bilking insurance companies by filing fraudulent claims.

W. T. Stead (a pseudonym he has borrowed, for this story, from an unfortunate passenger on the Titanic) is very good at his avocation. He figures he has netted about $60,000 in settlements over the past few years on 15 staged pratfalls and induced auto accidents. He is not contrite. "I am in every sense a communist," he says. "If you've got a wealthy insurance company out there that will pay out so many dollars, then people should get it."

Is there a grape on the floor of the supermarket? Mr. Stead will slip on it in front of a horde of witnesses and suffer lumbosacral strain; a generous check from the store chain's insurer alleviates it. Is there a distracted mother with a station wagon full of kids on the Santa Monica Freeway? Mr. Stead will abruptly change lanes and swerve in front of her, trying to induce a rear-end collision. A mild collision, of course, but his whiplash injury is just terrible.

Down for the Third Time

Insurance-fraud artists like Mr. Stead have plagued the industry since at least 1730, when a London woman faked her own death three times to collect the insurance money. The toll of such fraud is enormous. While no one knows exactly how much is lost to "scammers," as con artists are called here, various insurance sources estimate that up to 30% of all claims are inflated or fabricated, and that up to 20 cents of every insurance premium dollar subsidizes fraud. This means that the honest policyholders ultimately pay the bill. . . .

Lancaster then establishes the astonishing range of fraudulent practice. Among other things, we meet one chiseler who tried to collect for a knee injury, claiming it hindered his full participation at mass (he turned out to be a Methodist), and we are taken to "Nub City," a Florida town where some 50 people collected a bundle from the supposedly accidental loss by gunshot of various appendages. "They always seem to shoot off the parts they need least," says one insurance-company cynic.

The story then goes into industry attempts to catch big-time rings of scammers, and cites the difficulty of getting insurers to fight smaller claims in court instead of rolling over and paying them. Fighting them is too expensive, the companies maintain, and juries' sympathies are almost always on the claimant's side anyway. The con man encountered in the lead is then heard from again:

Expert scammers like the larcenous W. T. Stead are well aware of this. "You just tell the adjuster that if he doesn't pay, you'll see him in court. He pays. I've never had a case go to trial yet," he says.
One reason is that Mr. Stead is careful to get corroboration for his claim, sometimes from a cooperative doctor. After one staged pratfall, he says, he saw this physician; the latter gave no treatment and never saw the "victim" again, but presented him with a bill for a whopping $800. To Mr. Stead this was not highway robbery. Both he and the insurer knew that if a case came to trial and the insurer lost, the jury would be likely to make a pain-and-suffering award based on a multiple of the doctor's bill. The more their doctor charged, the larger the likely award. The insurer coughed up $8,000 in an out-of-court settlement. . . .

Shortly afterward we meet another actor, a long-suffering insurance gumshoe who says that successful prosecutions are hard to come by even when the insurer does press a case:

"The police aren't really interested, the DAs aren't interested, and if you ever do get a prosecution the guy is apt to get off with a light sentence," complains Joe Healy, a fraud investigator for CNA

Insurance Co., a unit of CNA Financial Corp. (He is still smarting over one case he developed against a ring of scammers in Philadelphia; they were convicted, but the judge gave them all suspended sentences.)

Mr. Healy, a loquacious 240-pounder, logs 100,000 air miles a year for CNA, a job not without its hazards. Once, investigating the death of a young man, he was held at gunpoint for 10 minutes by the nearly berserk father of the victim, who demanded to know who had killed his son. Another time, tracking a man who had faked his death, Mr. Healy found himself in a Mexican saloon, surrounded by thugs. Breaking off the ends of beer bottles, he and a companion bluffed their way out.

Mr. Healy does win a few, but not often:

He estimates that less than 10% of his cases are prosecuted and a still smaller percentage result in convictions. He must often be content with what he calls "preaching the gospel"—letting fraudulent operators know that he is on to their game, even if he doesn't have enough evidence to support a prosecution, and that they had better desist.

A recent case involving a ring of scammers in Los Angeles is a typical one. Knowing he didn't have enough for a prosecution, Mr. Healy assembled the members of the ring. "Hey, you guys—we're not fools," he said. "We're not going to keep paying." (CNA is already out about $10,000.)

The scammers took the news with good grace. "It was a very convivial group," Mr. Healy says. "We all knew what was really going on. One of them even asked me if I knew any good companies that *would* pay." Mr. Healy says that if the claims dry up, which he thinks they will, he'll close the books on the case. "I know it's not perfect justice," he says, "but it's a solution. . . ."

The insurance fraud story is a hardy perennial at *The Wall Street Journal*, and with reason. It has cops and robbers in it and it never stops happening, so every new generation of reporters takes a shot at it. I think Lancaster's effort would have been a decent one in a crowded field even without scammer Stead and flatfoot Healy, but their voices lift his story above the others I've seen. W. T. Stead is the ultimate credible source on one side, Joe Healy his mirror image on the other. Street people both.

2. *Providing Different Internal Proofs.* When a reporter wants to establish a point in a convincing way, he often starts by

making a declarative statement. Then he seeks to support it by citing authorities, offering facts or expert opinion, and giving examples from life. Each of these snippets serves as proof for his statement, but the reader may find the passage tedious or unconvincing if these proofs are not properly deployed.

Repetition is the hammer in the writer's toolbox, but used clumsily it only flattens interest. Try to prove something to a reader by throwing three sets of figures at him, and he drops you and turns on the tube. Give him three quotes in a row by Authoritative and Informed Sources, and the same thing happens. He may even grow restive if you give him a long string of examples drawn from the direct experience of primary actors in the story. Too much of a good thing all at once is still too much, and the string of illustrations lacks perspective.

But give him one of each of those elements mixed together and you've got him. He's convinced, and his full attention is still engaged, because you have provided a *variety of internal proofs*, a quality important to both the persuasiveness and conciseness of your story. Knowing this in advance, you plan to report points from various angles, seeking out quantitative evidence, quotes, and examples instead of piling up one class of material like this:

"There is a growing and critical shortage of doctors in many specialties," says Dr. John Thighbone, president of the American Medical Association. Adds Dr. James Hipbone, chief of surgery at the Cedars-Sinai Medical Center in Los Angeles: "The quality of medical care is suffering." At Minneapolis General Hospital, medical director Dr. Edward Anklebone says, "We could use five more obstetricians right now."

Let's see how this could have been handled using different elements of our interviews with these three healers:

Authorized midwives now deliver some babies at Minneapolis General Hospital because a shrunken staff of resident obstetricians can't handle the load. Scores of elective surgeries have been postponed for months at Cedars-Sinai Medical Center in Los Angeles, where the Chief of Surgery, Dr. James Hipbone, says: "The quality of medical care is suffering." Nationwide, 50,000 more doctors in specialties from internal medicine to radiology are needed, the American Medical Association says.

Better. The midwives give this passage tight-focus action. The AMA's Dr. Thighbone is snuffed out but leaves behind a broad, quantitative element more useful than his quote. The commentary from Cedars is retained but also tied to a pressing, specific problem there. This passage makes, through repetition, the same point in about the same space as the first, but the variety of proofs lends it more authority and interest.

Both of these paragraphs have three main elements of proof. For reasons I don't understand, the number three has a mystical, just-right quality, and I have noticed that good writers often use proofs in triplicate. Somehow, four elements seem to be too many, and the writer senses he is verging on overkill, while two seem to provide only threadbare backing. This *rule of threes* is worth keeping in mind when reporting for different values as well as in writing the story, especially when you are seeking evidence to support a particularly important point. Set it on a three-legged stool if you can.

MOVEMENT

Readers love action, any kind of action, and the story that does not move, that just sits there stalled while people declaim, explain, elaborate and suck their thumbs is justly labeled by some editors as a MEGO—My Eyes Glaze Over.

The most desirable kind of movement is the unfurling of natural story progression in the mechanism of development/impact/countermove. But all a reporter can do is recognize the existence of this progression when it is indeed occurring, and bring it out in his reporting and writing. He can't invent it if it isn't there. There are, however, other pleasing kinds of movement that he can provide himself. The most common one involves the alternation of opposite elements.

When doing this, the reporter constantly shifts the reader's attention back and forth from the abstract to the concrete, from the general to the particular, from the mural to the miniature.

The alternation of opposite elements is a writing technique, narrowly speaking, but we treat it here because the elements that make it possible have to be reported first. Few of us have much trouble scooping up generalities, abstractions and big-picture material, but most of us have a lot of trouble digging out the specifics, the concrete tight-focus material that ought to be interwoven with the rest. So we skimp on the latter and inflate the former. Only when we recognize in reporting the story that we *must have* this hard-to-get material are we goaded into getting enough of it to make internal movement work.

Notice that movement in these passages from the loggers story:

This is a male society. Few women apply for work requiring such great upper-body strength, and those who do confront a relentlessly macho atmosphere. At one camp men chose lots to sit next to a woman choker-setter on the crummy so they could harass her on the way home; she quit. A logging supervisor says, "The idea that a woman possibly could do what they do—well, it just kills them."

Few blacks work in the northwest woods, either. Many loggers are from Southern families, and deeply ingrained racial attitudes still persist. An old logger, arms covered with chain-saw scars, says earnestly: "A while back, they tried real hard to get some of those niggers up here to work, but they didn't stick. I don't know why."

Everyone who enters the woods is hazed crudely and unmercifully. Does he have big ears? He is Dumbo forever. Is he a newlywed? Slip some dirty pictures into his empty lunchbox so his bride will find them. Put rocks in his gear bag, give him grueling, unnecessary chores to do, test him. "The tender young boys don't last," says Spider Mason.

Flat generalizations about sexism, racism and hazing, each expressed plainly and briefly, are backed by illustrative, tight-focus material. The reader starts a distance away from the point, surveying the generalization, and suddenly is moved up next to it for close inspection. Then he is marched backward for another broad look at a different point, and taken forward again. (Notice also how internal variety is built in through inclusion of general observations, points of reasoning, incidents, and quotes by actors.)

In certain other cases, a reporter may slyly insert into his piece a few physical actions performed by a profile subject or other actors in his tale. He does not let his people just talk at us; he has them do something, anything. He knows that if he doesn't, they may be only plaster busts of themselves when they appear in print.

Relief pitchers, for example, spend most of their baseball careers sitting in the bullpen. Even when they do pitch, there is a sameness about the action: fastball, slider, curve, day in and day out. But Hal Lancaster, helped by sleight-of-hand, was able to give life to a reliever in this 1973 story:

TUCSON—It's a Sunday-night doubleheader, and the veteran relief pitcher is in the bullpen awaiting the call. He sits on a folding chair, arms draped over a low, wire-mesh fence. He fidgets. He picks up a ball, stares at it, rotates it in his hand, tosses it up and down. This is the reliever's time-killing ritual, the battle against boredom that goes on night after night.

There was a time when he was a starting pitcher in Yankee Stadium, Fenway Park, all the big parks of the American League. Now the park is Hi Corbett Field, the league is the triple-A Pacific Coast League, and he is relegated to the bullpen, such as it is. The pen here is a cramped place, where young curiosity seekers poke the players and giggle or grab their hats and race off with them. "A circus," the pitcher says disgustedly.

He suffers through the first game and two innings of the second before the call finally comes and he begins warming up in the 90-degree heat. The public-address announcer is rattling off an unending stream of promotions: the "royal family," a lucky group chosen by lot who get free tickets, Coke and peanuts; the archery exhibition, the Food Giant attendance-guessing contest (the winner gets $5 in groceries and free Green Stamps) and the "lucky-seat" winners, who get free bowling, free car washes and free child care.

It is all part of promotion-crazy minor-league ball, right down to advertisements on the outfield walls for everything from the Panda Steak House to Kile Jarvis Realty. Atop the left-field fence sit the golden arches of the McDonald's hamburger chain; belt one through them and you get $500. To the reliever, 30-year-old Lew Krausse Jr. of the Tucson Toros, the whole scene is just another galling reminder that he is now a world away from where he once belonged—the bigs, the major leagues.

Lew pinwheels his right arm, tugs at his sleeve, as he walks to the mound. . . .

We then learn something of the reliever's past, his frustration, his desperate attempts to get back to the majors. After that, the scene shifts:

The Toros' locker room is small, muggy, strewn with towels. Lew, a slim six-footer, wipes the sweat off his forehead as he assesses a career that is seemingly slipping away from him. He puts most of the blame on himself. "If I'd worked harder, I'd have made more money and I'd still be in the majors," he says. "When Catfish Hunter (a star hurler with the A's) came up in '65, he was only 19 and he was already working on throwing curve balls to spots. I was still just trying to gun the ball past people. I still do. Some guys are like that."

Though he blames himself, he can't escape some bitterness; reminders of the vast differences between the majors and the minors are everywhere. Metal cleats click on the floor as Lew pulls off a sweat-stained sweatshirt and pulls on an equally aromatic one. "That's the minors," he says. "Torn shirts, shoes that don't fit. Do you know the trainer on this club is a first-semester college student? And that we get $7.50 a day meal money on the road compared with $19.50 in Oakland? Up there you wear $300 suits and alligator shoes; here it's jeans and sandals."

Lancaster goes on to detail more of the differences between the bigs and the minors: the terrible grind of travel, the tight-fisted owners, the insecurity of veterans who, because the future of the big club depends on developing youngsters, will be the first to go when cuts are made. A league official and former manager says: "I've had to cut players like that. Some of them cried. But it's the best thing; all they had ahead of them was to become baseball bums."

After that, the reader suddenly finds himself on a road trip. A couple of bits and pieces:

SUNDAY: Lew has just pitched 3⅓ scoreless innings against the Phoenix Giants and is happy. "Last time I couldn't get the ball over at all," he says. "I got so mad I tore this uniform right off my body and threw it into the beer cooler." His temper is fierce. In Little League, he recalls, a deep fly ball bounced right off the skull of his centerfielder and over the fence, costing young Lew a game. "He took one look at me and jumped the fence," says Lew. "I chased him all the way home." In later years, Lew would lay waste to several clubhouses, rip phones off walls and brawl in bars. . . .

* * *

TUESDAY: The team is on its way to Phoenix by bus. The inevitable card games are under way, and the Latin players are singing and playing guitars. Jose Morales, a catcher (later to be called up by the parent club for the first time in a 10-year career), says the quality of bus travel in the PCL is infinitely better than in the Texas League. "Sixteen hours between Amarillo and Memphis," he says with a moan, "bouncing all the time. . . ."

* * *

FRIDAY: A morning flight to Albuquerque, a town the whole team dreads. "There's nothing to do after you see the skin flicks," groans Chuck. At the airline terminal Lew does his specialty, "the old pro," a relief pitcher coming in for his thousandth appearance. Legs stiffly straight, back bent, upper torso leaning so far forward he seems to defy gravity, he struts past bewildered passengers while players lean against posts, howling. . . .

The story ends after a Saturday game in Albuquerque:

In the clubhouse later, Toro pitcher Randy Scarbery, a reported $50,000 bonus baby in his first season, is talking about how he'll invest the money. Lew listens. Though far from destitute, he has blown almost all his own bonus on cars, clothes and booze, besides paying about $40,000 in taxes on it.

What will he do if he quits? "I don't know," he says. "I've got some money in a used-car dealership, and I've got a real estate salesman's license. I could try that. But I'd really like to be a pitching coach."

For the week, Lew has piched 9⅓ scoreless innings but doesn't have a win or a save to show for it. The season is drawing to a close, and his hopes for a reprieve from the minors grow dimmer. "I guess it's all been for nothing," Lew says. There are three more games in Albuquerque, and then it is home to Tucson for El Taco night.

We see Lew Krausse fiddling with a baseball, tossing warmup bloopers, pinwheeling his arm, tugging at his sleeve, wiping sweat from his forehead, dressing, and doing a comedy routine at the airport. In the clubhouse, metal cleats are clicking on the floor. On the bus, players are singing, plucking guitars, playing cards. Small things, yes. But they make a difference in a story without much action in the idea.

Lancaster also uses a structural device to gain more action. He sets his players in collective motion by building part of his story around a road trip. Sometimes entire stories can be reported and written by putting main actors in transit and tracking them from place to place, task to task, time to time.

To use these tricks effectively, a reporter must be a keen observer of the innocuous. He must notice almost everything about his surroundings and his actors and be able to recall these details when he needs them. Again, what first appears to be a writing technique has its origins in a reporting value.

It's a value, however, that shouldn't appear in all stories. If there is real, built-in action present in a development/impact/countermove mechanism, if principal actors are taking dramatic and significant steps, it only weakens the story to salt it with trivial action and hocus-pocus. Even the best magic act is an unwanted distraction when the theater is on fire.

There are no tricks in the following story about Walt Disney Productions by Earl Gottschalk. A single cardinal virtue made it go, although the idea seemed shaky at the start.

Disney was not one of the great whales of the entertainment business in size or as an innovator others might copy. It occupied a special niche, and what was happening there didn't really apply elsewhere. Strike one: The reporter's scope will be limited. Worse, nothing much was happening at Disney when the story was done in 1972. There were no new directions, policies or big gambles. Strike two: minimal story action. This is how Gottschalk overcame these weaknesses:

BURBANK, Calif.—In a buff-colored building at the corner of Dopey Drive and Mickey Mouse Boulevard, there are two rooms in which time has been suspended, by executive order, for more than five years. This is where Walt Disney dreamed his dreams.

Nothing has been changed in these offices since the co-founder of Walt Disney Productions Inc. died of lung cancer in 1966. His last notes lie on the low black desk, and the scripts he was reading are pigeonholed in the rack behind his desk, where he left them. In his outer office is the piano on which musicians would play tunes for his approval. On it stands a tiny wind-up toy—two birds in a gilded cage—on which he based his idea for audioanimatronics. This is the process by which models of everything from pirates to presidents are made to move and speak in an eerie imitation of life.

Once asked to state his greatest accomplishment, Mr. Disney replied: "The fact that I was able to build an organization and hold it." The shrine made of his office symbolizes the strong grip he still has on his company. His photo smiles down from the walls of every office in the Disney Productions complex here. Mickey Mouse clocks tick away incessantly, Mickey Mouse watches adorn many an executive wrist, and the supreme accolade for a good piece of work is "Walt would have liked it."

Following Walt's Dreams

His corporate heirs remain harnessed to his ideas. "We took advantage of Walt's concepts, but we haven't gone in any new directions," says E. Cardon Walker, president. He and other executives make it clear that they don't intend to make any radical departures; instead, their goal is to skillfully manage those of Mr. Disney's dreams that are already reality and to develop those that aren't—including a planned city in Florida crammed with new technology that Walt Disney hoped would be a test for a better urban life.

All this makes Disney Productions a striking anomaly in American big business. Usually corporate chieftains, even founders, depart without leaving a lasting imprint on corporate policy, let alone on the individual values and attitudes of those who work for them. The new bosses pay lip service to the old, wait a decent interval, and then try to make their own marks with different products, management techniques and goals.

But no new brooms are sweeping away the old ideas at Disney Productions. Everyone makes it clear that Walt would *not* have liked that. And neither would his brother, Roy, who died last December after serving as chairman and chief executive officer since Walt's death. Considered by far the shrewder of the two as a businessman (he was primarily responsible for raising $262 million in public offerings to build Disney World in Florida), Roy, too, devoted himself to developing Walt's ideas.

Is It Time for a Change?

To some critics, however, a change in the Disney way would be welcome. They view the empire as one huge, multi-spigoted dispenser of schlock culture—from amusements, architecture and art, to movies and music. They feel that the Disney influence has been too pervasive already. In his book, "The Disney Version," critic Richard Schickel says:

"Disney's machine was designed to shatter the two most valuable things about childhood—its secrets and its silences—thus forcing everyone to share the same formative dreams. It has placed a Mickey Mouse hat on every little developing personality in America. As capitalism, it is a work of genius; as culture, it is mostly a horror."

Disney officials respond. Gottschalk then goes on buttressing his theme: Disney's newer movies, continually profitable, are all cast in the old mold Walt favored. Disneyland and Disney World reflect his rage for order, control, cleanliness, his propensity to create unreal worlds. EPCOT in Florida is another fulfillment of his dreams by his successors, who seem to have no dreams of their own.

Disney has been shrewd, Gottschalk notes. Instead of fighting TV as other studios did, the company embraced it, sponsoring its own show. Instead of selling its film library, it held to Walt's precepts, retained total control, and made a fortune rereleasing classics for each succeeding generation of children.

But there are disquieting signs that the company, lashed to its founder's values and practices, is falling too far behind the times. Its animators are aging, their work dated. Some erosion is visible in its more recent movie productions. Attempts to impose a dress code for park visitors are a failure. Labor problems are surfacing, and Brer Bear goes on strike. These things, however, seem to matter little in the hermetically sealed Magic Kingdom Walt brought forth, and the story ends this way:

> But these are minor ripples on an otherwise placid surface. Disney Productions is loaded with people who have worked nowhere else, and most seem totally attuned to the "Disney Way." This concept is being preserved in part by a Disney archivist, and is continually reflected in training courses at Disneyland and Disney World "Universities." Though these are mainly for the young people who staff the parks, even veteran employees return for refesher courses in Traditions I, II, III and IV—in large part a compendium of Walt's ideas and philosophy. A young Disney instructor shows a visitor a series of placards illustrating the "Disney Ways." The first says: "What do we do? We create happiness."

This story proved prophetic. In the years after it was written Disney did indeed fall so far behind the times that its fortunes suffered, and it underwent a management upheaval. Now the company makes a lot of money producing movies Walt definitely would not have liked.

There are no bells and whistles in this piece, but the reporting is insightful. There is a smattering of conflict as a dramatic element. Gottschalk sets up the obvious protagonist–antagonist face-off between the company and critic Schickel, but also develops another and more subtle one: Disney, harnessed to values and standards fixed many years before, versus the force of social-cultural change. Its animators want to work in more current styles, its customers have hair that is too long, and it is having trouble finding squeaky-clean movie vehicles at a time when writers were wallowing in their new freedom to fill bookshelves and theater screens with sex and violence.

Above all, however, we get forceful treatment of an imaginative main theme, the facet of Disney that reporter Gottschalk chose to stress—how the company is being run from the grave by a founder dead for six years. This is seized on immediately, developed and threaded throughout the piece. The shrine made of Walt's office, the accolades given good work ("Walt would have liked it"), the vows of continuing fealty to his dreams, the keeping of these promises in the construction of EPCOT, the teaching of his maxims—all show the scope of the dead founder's influence and the intensity of his grip. The concentration of reporting and writing effort on this unusual facet is what made the story work.

Other aspects of Disney's *differentness* are emphasized as required in a general profile. Chief executives, even founders, leave few marks on their companies because their successors wipe them away—but not at Disney. Most movie companies, fearful of television, fought it; Disney embraced it. Most of them sell or lease film rights after theatrical runs; Disney retains total control and makes a potful of money on rereleases.

Finally, Gottschalk puts an ending on his piece instead of letting it trail off in a whimper of weak material. All in all, a good tale—and one that might have been a disaster without the values developed by the storyteller's skill.

Some people maintain that this skill is inborn and can't be taught. I don't believe that, and in teaching reporters I've seen proof that it isn't so. But the nagging question persists: If it can be taught, why are there still so few storytellers in a business whose product is stories, where editors have been crying out for better copy for years and spending much time educating reporters, where good work wins quick recognition and praise?

One answer, I think, is that too many reporters don't see themselves as storytellers but as something else.

Some are lawyers, in effect. They believe their job is to convince people of the rightness or wrongness of things as they've determined it, so their copy has a didactic or shrill tone. Fixated on ideas, they lack humanity in their work. They may talk down to the reader or talk at him, but they seldom talk *with* him as the storyteller does. They try to make their points by battering their victims with numbers, studies and multiple quotes from experts and topsiders. It doesn't occur to the lawyer that "little people" with direct experience can be more important, more convincing, than his certified Somebodies.

Lacking variety in his reporting, the lawyer uses repetition like a club and is given to circular organization, pounding across essentially the same message in different parts of the story. He's hurt and angered when the desk demands more material or puts his legal briefs through the mixmaster; it was all so clear, so persuasive to *him*.

Other reporters are scholastics who, against all reason, try to learn everything about a subject before writing anything. Lacking a sense of scope, they report and report and report until their desks are hidden under stacks of papers and notes. They become prisoners of their stories. One, I'm told, staggered home every night under the weight of a double wooden orange crate slung over his shoulders with ropes, and filled to bursting with research matter.

When the scholastic finally starts to write he is, of course, overwhelmed, and spends eons producing stories that are far too long. His prose usually is stuffy, he often pays unwarranted attention to petty matters of interest only to insiders, and his epics lack highlights on major points because these are so deeply buried in drifts of irrelevant or marginal material. Editing him is like smelting a ton of ore, taken spoonful by spoonful, into a single ingot that often turns out to be lead. Luckily, he produces few stories.

A third type, the objectivist, has a less obvious problem. He turns out a fair volume of work in good time and it appears to be sound and reasonably well structured. He doesn't try to save the world by bending it to his will, and he doesn't strive to become the ultimate authority on his story topics by researching them to death. But his work seldom sticks in the memory, either.

That's because he sees himself as a fact funnel. He writes flat prose; colorful expression might let the reader sense his presence in the story, something he regards as uncomfortably close to editorializing. He shies away from making firm conclusions dictated by plain sets of facts. Instead he gives us timid, weaselly ones or, more often, drags into the story a source who will state the obvious for him. After all, if he jumped in, that too might be seen as a cheeky intrusion. He fails to highlight intrinsic drama because it makes him queasy; someone might accuse him of hyping or sensationalizing the story.

Bullfeathers. As storytellers, we are in the drama business. And we can't be totally objective, at least as I understand the word. By the act of selecting what material to use and what to omit, by deciding what to stress and what to downplay, we forfeit any claim to ultimate objectivity. The best we can be is fair, going on the evidence and not on our prejudices, and fair we must always be. It is a commandment.

But it doesn't allow us to run away and hide from the reader. The reporter who does so writes stories without tone because he has left out the last and most important story dimension—himself. A feature story without the reporter in it, without his strong presence in interpretation and conclusion, without his calling a spade a spade instead of bringing in someone from Harvard to solemnly declare it a long-handled personal earthmoving implement, is a weak, flaccid story. The reader *expects* the reporter's presence and misses him when he's absent.

This most emphatically is not a defense of so-called personal journalism, which, it seems to me, is nothing but arrogance. Wallowing publicly in his own feelings, the personal journalist assumes the license to filter reality through them and presents without shame a picture of the world as reflected in a fun-house mirror. By contrast, the honest storyteller responds emotionally to what *is*. Facts and events govern his attitude. His attitude never governs them.

Within these bounds he still has great freedom, and he uses all of it. He steps in to make conclusions that cry out to be made. He gives cant and self-serving puffery short shrift. He summarizes crisply instead of dunning the reader with multiple testimonies that say the same thing. He may make observations of his own from time to time because he is the reader's agent, his man on the spot. He controls absolutely the telling of the tale, never letting it run away with him.

When all this is done, the reader gradually becomes conscious of a guiding intelligence within the story working for his benefit, the close and warming presence of a fellow human being conversing with him in print—not that of a bloodless entity lecturing him from afar. And he responds.

The above suggests that good storytellers have to have guts, and if some reporters fail at the art because they misperceive their roles, others fail because they are hamstrung by fear.

We don't like to talk openly about this fear because it makes us too vulnerable in a craft that still operates in a swaggering, tough-guy climate. But more than a few of my colleagues have told me privately of its effects on them, and I've seen its tracks in the work of others. Many a reporter hunched over a beer at the local pub proves to be a fine storyteller; he's witty, wise, incisive, a natural dramatist. Later, when I read his raw copy, I can't believe it was written by the same person. It is wooden and timid, without a trace of the author in it. The reader, instead of sensing a personality and guiding intellect, gets only a whiff of fear.

This type of reporter often is confident and facile at turning out difficult news stories on deadline. But he's tied in knots by major feature stories that depend on complex undercurrents rather than single events, that don't force on him the discipline of producing a story immediately, that leave so much to his own initiative and judgment.

When he approaches a major feature, phantoms crowd around his desk. The bureau chief is there, the page editor is there, maybe the managing editor is there, too. Especially if the reporter is a new kid on the block, the whole weight of *The Wall Street Journal*'s importance and reputation settles over his shoulders like a cast-iron yoke. This is no simple newspaper story he's attempting. This is not just tomorrow's kitty litter. This is the tablets of Moses, and if he fails to satisfy all the important entities clustered around, he'll be judged unworthy.

He's acutely aware that failure is a real possibility in feature writing, while only a remote one in the handling of breaking news. One victim of feature fear told me: "At least when you do a story about a billion-dollar deal for tomorrow's paper, you know they *have* to print the damn thing."

Buried under a truckload of anxieties and self-imposed expectations, our man never does struggle to the surface and take charge of his story. He has been too busy striving to please others, seeking to puzzle out what all these editors and bureau chiefs like and don't like, magnifying their quirks and prejudices into commands, trying to pin down the elements of the so-called *Wall Street Journal* formula so he will have a safe, approved chart to follow. At the end, he can take little joy in his work because so little of him is in it.

I wish I could assure you that this fear always fades with time, but that hasn't been my own experience. My work has generally been well received and lightly edited. I have little reason to be afraid—and yet I feel the same degree of crushing insecurity in facing every major project today that I did when I first stepped into a newsroom in 1961. An insidious voice whispers to me that maybe this time my luck will run out. Maybe this time the editors will hold their noses and pick up my story with tongs and drop it into the round file. Maybe this time I will make an ass of myself and fail the reader.

So feature fear has to be beaten down again and again. I don't know how others manage this. In my own case, I first try to remember that 20,000 parakeets will be heedlessly demonstrating their contempt for even my best work shortly after it's printed. This provides humility and perspective; I am *not* chasing the Holy Grail or chiseling out the Ten Commandments.

Then I get belligerent. My story may be so much avian toilet tissue, but it's still my story. No editor will be as close to it as I will, none will know as much about it as I will, and so no ghostly editorial presence will be allowed to meddle in the shaping and telling of it. All phantoms, with your quirks and prejudices, begone.

This act of banishment gets easier when a reporter learns what the paper and its editors are like, and sees that trying to please them instead of himself is impossible foolishness. For one thing, there is no *Wall Street Journal* formula, at least as the mechanical contrivance some reporters have made of it. They take too seriously the jargon of editors who refer to story components as if they were items in a hardware store: nut grafs, however grafs, and, in other lexicons, hoo-hah grafs and hammer grafs.

Captured by this nonsense, a reporter may in time see his job as bolting prefab components together according to an all-purpose blueprint drawn up in heaven. Content then becomes a slave to form, and everything he does reads as if it was extruded from a sausage machine.

But that said, isn't there a formula? Isn't there a *Wall Street Journal* Way? Well, we do try to engage the reader's attention immediately. We do try to give him a clear idea of what we're up to early on. And we do try to prove our assertions in detail throughout. If these add up to a formula then I suppose we have one. But it offers the reporter enormous latitude, and it's the same one successful storytellers have used for centuries.

The individual pecularities and prejudices of editors, too, all disappear when someone slips them a good story. This is all they really want, and I've never known an editor to butcher or reject a fine piece of work because it violated a few of his minor canons. It's the whole effort that is judged—and, far from being wary of the reporter who experiments and who shows courage, the judges only wish that more of his colleagues would do likewise. Editors are readers too, and want to sense the reporter's unique presence in shaping what they read.

There's a tale about an old teacher—I forget his name but it was something like Korlev—who lay dying. Knowing he was a man of faith and unafraid of death, the young men who were his pupils gathered by his bed to question him about this last mystery. "Teacher," asked one, "What do you think God will say to you when you see him?"

Korlev reflected for a moment before answering. "First, I know what he *won't* say," the old man finally replied. "He won't say, 'Why oh why, when you were on earth, did you not strive to be more like Me?' Instead he'll say, 'Why weren't you more like Korlev?'" Confronted by timid, wooden copy, a lot of editors could rightly ask the same question of the reporters who produced it.

CHAPTER 4

PLANNING AND EXECUTION

Writers are crazy people when they write, engaging in strange rituals that would earn anyone else a trip to the Rubber Room at the nearest mental hospital. They are obsessive about the paper and notepads they use, about pens (I take notes with one kind, draft copy with another, write letters with still a third), about the placement of items on their desks.

Some behave queerly long before they are ready to assemble a finished piece, and often before they begin reporting it. This behavior, however, usually signals more than quirk or superstition. These writers are thinking far ahead, doping out what their story might be, how much emphasis to give certain parts of it, and how it might string together when finished. Watching them, a fellow writer may have no idea of what is actually running through their minds but he understands their central purpose, however oddly it is manifested.

As a beginner I worked with a colleague who laid out eight blank sheets of copy paper on a table before reporting a story. He then blocked out the elements of his tale as he'd preconceived them, assigning each a varying amount of space and a specific location in the layout. This mapmaking, this physical visualization, served him well as a rough reporting and writing guide.

Later, I worked beside another reporter who seemed to have no plan at all. Unlike most of us, who report first and write later, he did both in short, alternating bursts, following no pattern I could see. After reporting for a few hours or a day or two, he laboriously wrote one or two perfect paragraphs (not necessarily related ones) and dropped them into a basket on his desk. When the slips of paper reached optimal depth, he taped them together. Amazingly, this seemed to work for him; he apparently carried a detailed story map in his head and didn't need a physical one.

Neither of these approaches may work for you. They certainly don't for me. But the specific techniques you employ aren't important. The only important thing is that you have a plan, however loose and informal, and use it to good effect. The good writers I know always do some kind of planning before they report and again before they write. The people who rely on divine inspiration to carry them from interview to interview, from sentence to sentence, usually turn in gibberish or are found sitting, stumped, before their VDTs long after the planners go home.

What follows is my plan. It's not an outline, just a guide; I don't believe in strict outlines, which tend to murder spontaneity and creativity. You're welcome to try it entire, to adopt only parts of it, or to dismiss it as unsuitable. It doesn't work for every story and I'd be suspicious if it did. Something has to be wrong with a system that invariably turns out stories like so many cans of peas. But it works for an amazingly high percentage of the pieces I do, makes them better, and helps me work much more efficiently than I would otherwise.

This guide nags me with questions about six different aspects of every story I do, both at the beginning of the reporting and later, when I write. Let's see how the guide applies to the reporting phase of the most common type of story, one that centers on some kind of occurrence and its consequences. We'll discuss profiles later in this chapter, and learn in the next how to use the guide in organizing the writing of the story, too.

Step 1: Noodling Around

My story idea is shaped and approved. I have a little information on hand, though probably not much. Now I look at my idea and at the six-part guide and ask this: How important, relatively speaking, are each of these six things likely to be in this particular story? Usually only one or two of them need to be fully developed in reporting and later in writing, with perhaps one or two others getting brief attention. But I start by considering all of them. They are:

I HISTORY

    A. Does my main theme development have roots in the past? What are they?

    B. Is it a clean break with the past? How?

    C. Is it clearly a continuation of the past? How?

    D. If history seems a potentially relevant part of my story, are there any historical details that I can use to lend authenticity and interest? Can I relate them *briefly?*

We're seldom interested in the past for its own sake, only in how it relates to the present, but we've already seen how vital this linkage sometimes can be. Without material on the unbroken line of mountain men, we can't see that Finis Mitchell is a continuation of the past and not a throwback. Without Lt. Ives viewing the howling desolation of the Colorado Plateau and judging that the white man will never come that way again, we lose, when we look at Las Vegas today, the sense of a total break with the past he lived in. (We also lose the chance to catch a forecaster with his pants around his ankles, and that's always fun.)

In the last item, D, we seek the little things that add glitter points of contrast. A modern cowboy's lunch of steak and beans may be a mildly engaging detail to those who always have salami on onion roll, but it gains interest when we're also told that a century ago he would have been having son-of-a-bitch stew instead. We can see that his life has changed in this small way.

II SCOPE—How widespread, intense and various is my development, the event or current of events that is at the heart of my story?

    A. Quantitative Factor:

        1. Can I partially define the scope of my development with numbers or other expressions of quantity? If so, what numbers would be most meaningful?

    2. Can I define it with comment and observation?
B. Locale Factor:
    1. What is the physical range of my development? Is it international, national, regional, local?
    2. Where are the hot spots?
C. Diversity/Intensity Factor:
    1. In how many *different ways* is my development likely to show itself? to what *degree* are people, places and institutions involved in it?
    2. Is my development waxing or waning, spreading or contracting?
D. Perspective factor:
    1. Do other developments bear on mine? Do they magnify its importance or temper it?

This last factor puts the story in wider context. For example, if the U.S. is losing prime farmland at a rapid rate, the importance of that single development is *magnified* if we also are told that per-acre crop yields are flattening out; that pressure for farm exports is soaring; and that the warehouse of new agricultural technology is almost empty. Against this background, the loss of land is more ominous. If instead we learn that export demand is down and new high-yield grains are on the way, the importance of land loss would be *tempered.*

Obviously, the scope section gets stress when the central development itself is newsy. But even when that development is *not* the focus of the piece, if we're concentrating instead on impacts or countermoves, we still will use the factors of scope to help define those other action sections. So in one place or another, scope is a consideration in almost every story. Notice the variety of elements it includes: We are trying to come at the reader from several angles, not bash him over the head repeatedly with the same class of material.

III REASONS—Material that shows why something is happening *now*.
    A. Economic. Is there money in this? Where does the money trail begin and end?

B. Social: Are changes in culture, custom, morals or family life likely to be affecting this story? How?

C. Political/Legal: Are changes in laws, regulations or taxes affecting this story? How?

D. Psychological—Are such things as ego, vengeance, wish fulfillment apt to be major driving forces in this story? Does the personality of a major actor bear heavily on it?

I treat reasons separately because many of us get so wrapped up in story action that reasons may be forgotten or dusted off too lightly. Item D is neglected most often; emotional motives are difficult to dig out, and when they exist are usually hidden behind a screen of other reasons erected as justification.

Look closely for emotional motives and personality factors when some action does not, on analysis, make convincing sense. Company A, say, is trying to take over company B. It swears up and down that the two will make sweeter music together than they ever could separately, and that all shareholders will benefit. But Wall Streeters are scratching their heads; A is already overextended and the other company's businesses don't seem to fit into A's operations that well. This mystery is solved in part when we can show that the chairman of A has a Napoleonic complex and detests the chairman of B to boot. Hard material to get? You bet—but necessary in a story like this.

Sometimes an entire tale rides on this one element. In 1976 Roy Harris convincingly showed that the rise and fall of Rohr Corp., a humdrum but profitable aviation subcontractor that transformed itself into to a leader in urban mass transit and then failed in that business, was traceable to the mesmerizing personality of its CEO, Burt Raynes. Highly intelligent, a genuine visionary and a man of enormous magnetism, Raynes exerted such a powerful influence on those he worked with that they became blinded to the faults in his thinking and failed to challenge it.

The story detailed this process and emphasized the irony of what happened in the end: Raynes' great vision, imagination and leadership ability, qualities much prized in executives, helped shatter his own dreams for his company because he had these gifts in such abundance. It was a case of too much of a good thing.

IV IMPACTS —The consequences of a development.
 A. Who or what is likely to be helped by what is happening? How? What is the *scope* of that help? (See section II and apply it here.)
 B. Who or what is likely to be hurt? How? What is the scope of the damage? (See section II again.)
 C. What is the *emotional response* of those helped or hurt?

The last is missing from many stories in which it should appear. You can bring it out by asking actors in the tale how they *feel* about what is happening as well as what they *think* about it. The answers may be very different in character and intensity.

A woman in Detroit, let's say, running a federally funded preschool for ghetto kids, has to close it because her funding has been eliminated. Ask her what she thinks about the closing and she may say she wishes the government's priorities leaned less toward weapons and more toward the poor.

Then say to her, "You said you've been doing this for 10 years; you must have a lot of yourself tied up in the school. How does all this make you feel, personally?" And she may reply, "It just rips my guts out. The day I heard there wouldn't be any more money I went home and cried for hours."

When we ask people what they think, many will automatically suppress emotional response or cloak it in reserved, reasonable language that doesn't fully express what's going on inside them. That's because we're showing interest only in their minds and not their hearts. When we ask them what they feel, we give them license to express that other side of their natures. The reader then gets a whole person, not half of one.

V COUNTERMOVES—The gathering and action of contrary forces.
 A. Who is likely to gripe loudest about what is happening? What are they saying?
 B. What actually is being done to offset, combat, change or deflect the impacts of the development? What is the *scope* of this effort? (See Section II and apply it here.)

C. How is this effort working out?

Countermoves is the last action element and one present only in a mature story. In gauging the likely importance of this section in his own piece, a reporter should give more weight to what is being done than to what is being said. Talk is cheap, action precious.

If the story is still pretty raw—i.e., the central development is fairly new and still building—often the only countermove element that has had time to develop is the grousing and handwringing of those opposed. By all means include one or two such lamentations, but keep it brief; if talk is all that's going on, your countermoves section will be of minimal interest. A lazy man could do well as an editorial consultant, even build a reputation as a guru, by scrawling the same criticisms on almost every piece of copy without bothering to read it, and playing golf the rest of the day. The criticisms: Less talk, more action. Fewer opinions, more facts.

VI FUTURES—What *could* happen if my development rolls along unchecked.
  A. Are there formal studies or projections that address the future of my development, and what do they say?
  B. What are the informal opinions of both observers and actors on the scene? How do the latter see their own futures?
  C. Can *I* indicate what the future might hold?

In C, note the use of the word "indicate." We have no business drawing flat conclusions about the future—but we do have a right and a duty to present material the *suggests* what may happen, particularly if there seem to be holes in the projections of others.

In the story about the Colorado River, for example, the weight of reporting showed that the Southwest was already overusing the river resource and that the problem would become critical if rapid growth of the desert civilization continued. A minority, however, treated the threat less seriously, maintaining that the Colorado's flow could be raised sharply through cloud seeding. I found the evidence for that less than overwhelming and closed the story this way:

> But what if there are few clouds to seed? More than 700 years ago the Classic Pueblo civilization reached its apex. Nourished by streams and rivers flowing from the mountains, the Indians irrigated land, built cities, and developed a culture. In 1276 a great drought gripped the region and this civilization withered, leaving behind only the empty, eerily silent pueblo cities nestled under cliffs.
>
> That drought lasted about 25 years. Today's desert civilization relies on the Colorado's two main reservoirs, Lakes Powell and Mead, to tide it over during drought. They hold a four-year reserve.

The conclusion is unstated but nonetheless clear: One flick of nature's tail and all the mighty dams and plumbing works along the river system, all the plans and projections, are junk.

The above guide is little more than an assembly of the kind of commonsense questions good reporters address in planning and executing stories. But considering these ordered, written questions in advance has helped to make me a more complete and efficient reporter. I can *see* what kind of material I probably will need, and I can check off the material as I get it. Above all, the structure of the guide compels me to consider and include where possible some of the most important dimensions of storytelling—time, scope and variety in particular.

As written, the guide applies to nonprofile stories. For **profiles,** I use a slightly altered version, as follows:

I HISTORY

    A. How has my subject's past shaped the nature of him/her/it today?

II QUALITIES (replaces scope)

    A. What are the qualities of differentness—personal, professional or other—that make my subject worth writing about? (Emphasize this in a general profile.)

        1. What kind of actions or behavior by my subject would reveal these qualities?

        2. How have these qualities affected my subject's fortunes and his life?

B. What qualities of *typicalness* does my subject have? How is he/she/it like others in the same class? (Emphasize this in a microcosm profile.)
   1. Do they share certain characteristics? Which ones?
   2. Do they share experiences? Which ones?

III VALUES AND STANDARDS (replaces reasons section)

A. What does my subject believe in most strongly? How does this shape the subject's actions in striving toward goals?
B. Are these beliefs different from or similar to those held by others in the subject's class? In what ways and to what extent?
C. Where did these values, standards and goals come from?

IV IMPACT

A. How does my subject affect those around him or other members of his class? What are these effects, both positive and negative?
B. How is my subject *being affected* by circumstances or those around him or other members of his class? Again, positives and negatives.

V COUNTERMOVES

A. How are others actually responding to my subject and his/her/its actions and attitudes? Show me in action where possible.
B. How is my subject responding to circumstances, those around him or members of his class? Again, show me in action.

VI FUTURES

A. What does my subject think his/her/its future looks like?
B. What do others think it looks like?

This profile guide stresses action and reaction. Without such reminders, the reporter may be seduced by an engaging and garrulous subject and produce an overly talky piece in which little really happens. The profile subject he found so charming then becomes just a windy bore in print.

Step 2: Setting Priorities

By now you may be thinking that all this seems a lot of fuss to go through in planning a newspaper story. Actually, it takes a great deal more time to explain it than to do it—I usually take no more than an hour—and the story plan arrived at is always a lot less complex and demanding than the guide might indicate.

I do consider briefly all the sections and questions in the plan, but at the same time I'm tossing out or deciding to play down those that at first don't seem particularly important to the particular idea I'm working on. What emerges from this priority-setting is a far simpler plan, focused on only a few essentials.

In a typical nonprofile, for example, I'll inspect the whole potential action sequence already described—development/ impacts/countermoves, but in my story plan will stress only the newsiest. If the story is juvenile, I know I'm going to have to pour maximum effort into detailing the central development itself, the concern of the scope section in my guide. Adapting the questions in that section to my story, I'll try to answer as many of them as I can. But if the story is mature, everyone may already be so familiar with the central development that I only have to mention it, not report it out fully. Instead I'll bear down on impacts and/or countermoves.

Read the following boomtowns story, which I wrote in 1981, and see if you can identify the section of the guide that gets the main emphasis:

WRIGHT, Wyo.—This is no Paris of the prairie. There isn't a sidewalk cafe in sight—or a doctor, theater, auto mechanic or pizza parlor. And outside this town of 1,600 people there is only the ocean of scrubland rolling to the horizons, scoured by a ceaseless wind.

Still, Wright is a noteworthy place. It is a custom-built boomtown, not a brick or board of which was in place five years ago.

Wright was planned and created by Arco Coal Co., a unit of Atlantic Richfield Co., to serve workers at Arco's huge Black Thunder mine nearby. By conjuring up a slice of suburbia in the sagebrush, Arco is seeking to keep its workers content.

Apparently they are. For a boomtown, Wright is remarkably sedate—dull, even. There is one bar, but it shares space in the glossy new shopping center with the family-style restaurant, and it's hardly the sort of place where patrons throw bar stools or fire six-guns into the ceiling. Tennis courts, a modern new school and a community center with an Olympic-size pool have been hacked out of the sage. There is Little League now, and yoga lessons.

If Wright is a bit on the quiet side, it is also a refutation of the fear that rapid energy development must overwhelm the West with the so-called boomtown syndrome—sudden, overheated growth that strains services until they break down, creates terrible housing shortages and promotes crime, crowding and social problems.

Better Defenses

Visits to Wright and other energy centers suggest that much of that fear is unjustified. For one thing, states have greatly expanded their taxes on minerals, funneling the money into boomtowns to ease the strain. In addition, experience with chaotic energy development in the early '70s has given state and local authorities more savvy in planning for the present boom, along with the toughness to demand that resource companies do a lot more to help.

The companies are responding by ladling out cash grants, lending a hand with financing of schools and other facilities, building housing and cooperating in joint planning efforts. "There's a whole new tone being taken by towns and counties, and the companies have been listening," says Burman Lorenson, the director of the Federal Energy Impact Office for the northern Rockies and Plains. Often they have to; some local and state authorities now require that mining, oil and power concerns agree to help before work is allowed to begin.

Scare Stories

This tougher stance grows out of the well-publicized troubles of places like Rock Springs, Wyo., which was the archetypal boomtown of the early '70s. Rapid development there doubled the population in four years, sent crime rates and housing costs through the roof and left the town one of the ugliest and most despoiled in the West. Other communities took note.

In recent years, they have been further alarmed by numerous Chicken Little studies suggesting that Rock Springs could be duplicated many times over in the current boom. Exxon Corp., for example, in a report speculating on the buildup of a $3 trillion synfuels industry in the West by the year 2010, figured that more than a million miners, plant workers and construction tradesmen might have to be poured into a few thinly populated areas. There wouldn't be enough water, so the Missouri River might have to be diverted to supply it.

To most experts, it now is clear that there will be a lot less development, spread over a longer period, than such studies suggest. Some proposed projects have already been delayed, canceled or scaled down, meaning that the West will have more breathing space to deal with the boom that is already occurring.

But existing growth is brisk enough, and in the effort to offset its ill effects, the turnabout in corporate attitudes has been striking. A few years ago, says an official of one power company, "Most outfits would say, 'Don't bother us with this impact stuff; take it out of our property taxes.'"

Now there is a growing conviction that cushioning the effects of a boom is simply good business. Companies are learning that unchecked development can so spoil a town that the skilled workers flee. As labor turnover soars, productivity sinks. In one Rock Springs mining operation, the entire work force had to be replaced in a year, and on one construction project turnover cut productivity to about a third of what was expected.

So there's less reluctance now to open the corporate coffers. Chevron USA, a unit of Standard Oil Co. of California, and Amoco Production Co., a unit of Standard of Indiana, have each given $500,000 to local authorities in southwest Wyoming struggling with a monster oil boom on the Overthrust Belt. Arco Coal has donated money for roads, land, and water rights near one of its Colorado operations.

That company also has spent $17 million building Wright. It figures it will be lucky to recover 75% of that through lot sales and other income. But it's worth the expense, Arco insists. To recruit and train a single heavy-equipment operator for Black Thunder costs $15,000; if he leaves quickly because he can't find a decent home for his family, the retraining costs and lost productivity hit Arco Coal's pocketbook hard. Thanks largely to the town Arco built, turnover at the mine is only 10% a year.

The lesson hasn't been lost on others. Exxon is building Battlement Mesa, a community eventually expected to house 20,000 to 25,000 people, near its Colony Oil Shale Project in western Colorado. And in Utah, Plateau Resources, a unit of Consumer Power Co. in Michigan, is building the uranium town of Ticaboo.

Resource companies also are using "creative financing" in helping some towns build their own facilities. One such town is Wheatland, Wyo., where power-plant construction by a consortium led by Basin Electric, a big co-op based in Bismarck, N.D., threatened to overtax schools. Already bonded to the hilt, the school district could do little to add space.

So the power consortium helped create a nonprofit entity separate from but controlled by the district, and that body issued the bonds. The power group then guaranteed them, making them salable at a rock-bottom interest rate. When the buildings were up, the district leased them from the nonprofit group—at rates scaled to the property taxes that would be collected from the new power plant when it was finished.

Communities currently being hit by development are studying towns affected earlier. A delegation from towns in North Dakota's Power Triangle, an area in and around Mercer County where huge power plants fed by lignite deposits are beginning to loom over the plains, took a hard look at Wheatland. One result: The town of Beulah, N.D., adopted stiff zoning measures for an area stretching for miles around.

Today's boomtowns also have more revenue sources. Before 1975, state taxes on production of oil, gas, coal, uranium and the like didn't exist or were too low to yield much; now they are expected to yield billions in income per year.

The Salvation of Zap

The taxes range all the way up to Montana's 30% levy on coal, which recently weathered a Supreme Court challenge by foes charging it was excessive. If anything, there is more pressure than ever to keep on jacking up severance taxes. Wyoming, for one, just raised its oil and gas levy to 6% from 4%, a move that by some estimates will add $95 million to its severance-tax take.

Some states, including Wyoming, Alaska and New Mexico, are aiming to build billion-dollar trust funds against the inevitable day when the resources run out. In the meantime, a varying but substantial part of the severance-tax money is being funneled into fast-growing towns for new roads, schools, police and a host of other necessities. (One Montana town used such funds to buy a street sweeper—and then came back for more money to build streets to use it on.)

To Zap, N.D., a town tucked into the hills of the Power Triangle, such funds make a big difference. "We've been studied half to death," says town auditor Chip Unruh, "when what we needed was money. It's the state coal impact office that has put up a good deal of the front-end funding we needed. They've been our salvation."

Delay and Disharmony

Neither state nor industry aid can completely insulate Western towns from the problems boom can bring. Planning can go awry, for one thing. Hayden, Colo., sold bonds to expand its water system in anticipation of a certain level of coal mining nearby; when it didn't fully materialize, neither did the revenue needed to meet the bond payments.

Elsewhere, there is less than complete harmony between localities and some of the companies that want their resources. Garfield County, Colo., commissioners recently voted, in effect, to withhold approval of a big expansion of Union Oil Co.'s proposed oil-shale operations nearby. They want Union President Fred Hartley or another executive with power to act to appear before them and give assurances that the effects will be mitigated. "We need someone with authority and a checkbook out here," says one commissioner. "Getting cooperation from Union has been like pulling teeth."

Sometimes action hasn't been taken until very late in the day. In the Overthrust Belt around Evanston, Wyo., some 35 concerns have joined the Overthrust Industrial Association to help local communities get funds, make studies and otherwise deal with superheated growth. But the association wasn't even formed until 1980, five years after the oil boom began. By then area roads were already crumbled by heavy trucks, housing was critically short, and services were overloaded.

"Now they're trying to apply Band-Aids to the problems out there," says John Gilmore, senior economist at the Denver Research Institute and an expert in the boomtown syndrome.

Making Growth Palatable

Overall, however, there is no doubt that the lessons learned from the past, together with the new tax funds and altered corporate attitudes, are taking much of the pain out of the current boom. "All this is substantially raising the threshold at which growth becomes intolerable," Mr. Gilmore says.

That threshold is still going up. Recently Rio Blanco County, in western Colorado, retained the heavyweight Washington law firm of Arnold & Porter to negotiate a sweeping and possibly precedent-setting agreement with Western Fuels, a coal operator wanting to develop a mine to feed a power plant just over the Utah line. Essentially, the agreement is constructed so that taxes and fees now paid by present residents won't go up a penny to meet the needs of the new population that will be living and working in the area, including the extra teachers, police officers and the like who will be needed. It is expected that this will cost Western Fuels $15 million to $17 million.

But even with the amenities supplied by corporate and tax money, and even with the jobs for local youths that energy development provides, there is a price for boomtowns to pay. The people of the rural West know it well. "The days when an old person who's lived here all his life could walk down the street and know and greet everyone—that's all gone," says a resident of Forsyth, Mont., affected by mining and power-plant construction. And on the open plains of the North Dakota Power Triangle, where shovels claw at the rangeland and draglines tower over hills of coal like giant black mantises, many ranchers lament the changes now occurring.

One is Werner Benfit, 50 years old, who has been ranching here all his life. Part of his spread is being torn up by power shovels now. "We fought them for three or four years, but we lost," he says. "I wish they'd never come."

Breaking this story down, we see that the *scope* section, as it applies to the central development (the drive for resources) is barely covered at all. The development is treated as a given. *Impact* is only sketched in briefly with a few generalized lines about the boomtown syndrome; there are no numbers, quotes, details, only terse statements that are just enough to put the reader in the picture.

Instead almost all the reporting effort is poured into *counter-moves*—what is actually being done to alleviate the impact, and how that is working out. There is a smattering of history, limited to what companies and towns have learned from past experiences, but the only detail given is about Rock Springs.

By contrast, George Getschow's Mexican migration piece has no countermoves element to speak of. It is powerfully centered on *reasons*, particularly economic ones, with history and local impacts as subsidiary elements. In the Colorado River story, the stress is on the *scope* of the main development—overuse of the river—and the *futures* of those dependent on it.

Deciding in advance of reporting what will be important and what will not is, of course, a risky, subjective exercise. We can't know enough at that stage to set most story plans in concrete. So the reporter must stay flexible and reassess his plan periodically as he works through it.

If this is done the advantages of a plan distilled into a few elements outweigh all uncertainties and risks. First, most thoughtful plans *do* work out well in execution; surprises occur, but they seldom are ones that dictate big changes in direction. Usually, one section the reporter thought might be moderately significant becomes a little more or less so, that's all. Second, what at first appeared to be a sprawling, daunting enterprise gets resolved into something simpler that looks doable and is doable. Finally, the reporter is apt to produce a better story in less time, one in which the main elements grow in power and importance because secondary ones have been stripped down or omitted. This contrast in emphasis gives the story strong highlights it might otherwise lack.

After finishing my stripped-down story plan, I add one more element to sections I expect to emphasize. I call it **focus points and people.** This element is my command to myself to descend to the lowest level of the action in those crucial parts of my story, my reminder that I can't really succeed if I don't, my accuser when I dog it or shy away from getting the material.

It's often hard to get, involving inconvenient and wearying travel and/or tedious telephone work. By contrast, experts who can provide sweeping overviews and statistical data are much easier to find because they're locked into a permanent symbiotic relationship with the press; we know who they are or can find out easily, and we publicly validate their credentials as authorities while we feed off them. They are accessible because it's to their advantage to be accessible.

But they are seldom the story, only assistants in its telling. The story is happening on streets where there are no PR men strewing palms in the reporter's path, no computers disgorging blocks of seductive statistics, and a lot of people who have nothing to gain from doing pirouettes for the press. This territory can be tough on strangers, but we have to go there to gather details and direct experiences that *show* the reader what we're talking about, that convince him of the truth of the sweeping assertions made by us and our desk people. Most of all, we go there to convince ourselves.

By the lowest level of the action, I mean the very lowest. Let's say a reporter is doing a story about how big cities are responding to a growing crisis in minority youth unemployment by sponsoring live-in job training centers for young men, many of whom have had scrapes with the law. Our reporter resolves—correctly—to spend time at a center or two and does so. He congratulates himself for getting to the nitty-gritty. His story describes the center, its clients and the routine they follow. It is full of quotes and information from the director and his trainers about how hard it is for these young men to break the cycle of failure in the ghetto.

Sorry, not good enough. The real story remains locked in the minds, hearts and life experiences of the sullen and possibly hostile young blacks and Hispanics who are the purpose of the center's existence. The information about them is secondhand. The director and trainers are close to the lowest level of the action, but not quite at it. Only the direct testimony of their clients carries maximum weight in this particular story.

Somewhere in his innards, our reporter (who is white, educated, fortyish and has never been without a job) knows this. But he's shied away from his primary sources, perhaps making only a stab or two at communication and giving up at the first barrier. By failing to give them first priority and by not persisting in trying to talk to them, he has left a credibility gap in his story. His readers may be informed but they won't be fully engaged.

Step 3: Reporting

To me, the most important part of reporting is knowing what you need to make the story go, and we've already been through that. Plenty of good texts cover the process of reporting, the how-to-do-it side of that black art, and there's no sense in duplicating their contents here. So we'll confine ourselves to a few pointers on maintaining order and priority in reporting, and on interviewing to get certain storyteller values into the piece.

The first people a reporter may want to talk to are the **Wise Men**, if he's lucky enough to have one or two qualified in his topic. We've already seen how helpful they can be in originating and shaping story ideas. Put to work as sources, they're equally valuable in providing leads for further reporting, insightful overviews of the topic and, above all, informed and dispassionate criticism of the reporter's early thinking. They may not appear in the finished piece, but they often influence its direction.

Wise Men are rare. To qualify, a source must have a broad range of knowledge about the topic; he is a student of it. He is unselfishly cooperative, interested in helping because he likes to see true stories get told about matters he's deeply interested in. He's able to tell us not only what events are but what they mean or possibly mean; he analyzes and speculates, but not wildly. Finally, he must have detachment and balance. The Wise Man may work for an organization that is partisan, and he may have his own feelings and opinions, but he is able to stand apart from them and examine the issue from all angles, including the viewpoints of people with whom he disagrees. He has the same power of empathy that the storyteller tries to bring to his work.

Depending on their positions these worthies may also provide documentation, but more often this comes from the next level of sourcing, the **Paper Men**. They work for entities that study and count things, and regularly disgorge masses of printed information about their findings. Some have little deep knowledge of their own and exist to facilitate the passing of the paper. We don't need to talk to them, except to request the names of others better informed. But it's a good idea not to talk to those experts, either, until we've seen their paper.

The reason is practical. A reporter doing a story about butterflies may consult a leading lepidopterist at the National Butterfly Institute or whatever and get a grueling, one-hour entymology lecture which he then has to puzzle over for another hour before he can make sense of it. Three days later, he gets a packet from the institute containing most of the same material in ordered, written form. So, read first and question later.

If the story is a profile, Wise Men and Paper Men may be of little help. The reporter needs a **Rabbi**. In the New York City Police Department, a Rabbi is a man with experience and good contacts who uses both in smoothing the career path of a young officer. In profile reporting, a Rabbi usually is a knowledgeable person at or near the scene of the action who gives the reporter helpful local background and leads him to others who can assist him. Often, he helps find and recruit the profile subject.

I view the above work as a preamble to the most important reporting—getting down to the lowest level of the story action and collecting the details, anecdotes and actors that give the piece life and power. I prefer to delay this until I have a grasp of the broader aspects of the story, because without that I may not know what to look and listen for when I'm on the ground. That isn't always possible, though, and if an opportunity suddenly arises to collect low-level material early on, I'll seize it. We always have to take what the story will give us when it decides to give it—or as my favorite politician, a cheerfully venal Illinois machine boss, once put it: "If you can't get a steak, take a sandwich."

It's true that some stories don't lend themselves to copious illustrations from life. It's equally true that a lot of others ought to include them but don't. And there is one class of story—I call it the hanging-around piece—that can't be done at all without focus points and people. One I've always admired is the following 1977 ground-level view of how the Agriculture Department works (or doesn't work) by Karen Elliott House:

WASHINGTON—Dalton Wilson has a nice salary, a long title and a clean desk.

Mr. Wilson, 52, is an assistant to an assistant administrator for management in the Foreign Agricultural Service of the Agriculture Department. The other day, when a reporter dropped in to chat, Mr. Wilson's desk top held a candy bar, a pack of cigarettes and Mr. Wilson's feet. He was tilted back in his chair reading real-estate ads in the Washington Post.

Exactly what, the reporter asked, does a man with that title do?

"You mean, what am I supposed to do?" said Mr. Wilson with a chuckle. "Let me tell you what I did last year."

It turns out that Mr. Wilson, whose annual pay is more than $28,000, spent the entire year trying to assess the adequacy and timeliness of the department's fats and oils publications. He says 1977 is shaping up as another slow year; he is planning another study, this one designed to justify the use of satellites to forecast crop production.

One Bureaucrat for 34 Farmers

Mr. Wilson's pace is typical of life at the Agriculture Department. With 80,000 full-time employees, the department has one bureaucrat for every 34 U.S. farmers. Now that President Carter is setting out to reorganize the government to make it more efficient, a close look at the Agriculture Department provides a vivid picture of the problems he faces.

As the number of farmers has declined in recent years, the Agriculture Department has turned increasingly to self-promotion and has adroitly managed to continue doing old jobs while thinking up new jobs to do. The result is a huge bureaucracy engaged in scores of dubious tasks and seemingly beyond direction.

"No Secretary of Agriculture runs the department," says Washington Democrat Thomas Foley, chairman of the House Agriculture Committee. "It's too big."

The department's full-time employees, plus 45,000 part-time helpers, occupy five buildings in Washington and spill out across the country into 16,000 others. Its employees direct self-awareness programs for women, write standards for watermelons and measure planted acreage for a dozen crops—even though government limitations on planting no longer exist.

Agriculture Secretary Bob Bergland, we're then told, will soon ask every employee to submit a written justification for his job.

But employees don't seem worried. "He'll never do it," says a young statistician, heaving his feet onto his desk. "He wouldn't have time to read them," a second man adds. A third man says, "Don't worry, guys—those with the least work to do will have the most time to justify their jobs."

Even a casual stroll through the department suggests something is awry. Throughout the main office building, old clocks are stopped at various hours as if time, too, had stopped. At all hours, hundreds of people mill about the corridors or linger in the large, sunny cafeteria.

Loafing became such a problem last year that the secretary's office sent a memo to supervisors requesting a crackdown on "significant problems of attendance in the Washington, D.C., complex." A second memo went to all employees warning that "tardiness, eating breakfast immediately after reporting for work, extended coffee breaks, excessive lunch periods and early departures" convey a "poor image to the public."

Today, laziness is still apparent and is a standard source of humor. Says a young man resting on a bench outside the cafeteria, "My only concern about work is breakfast, lunch, two coffee breaks, and being the first one out the door each evening." Sometimes the humor is unintentional. "I'd like to be sick tomorrow," a woman tells her elevator companion, "but I can't. The woman I work with plans to be. . . ."

Motivation is difficult for many employees because their tasks seem pointless. Paul Beattle in the department's Agriculture Marketing Service spent much of last year drafting a standard for watermelons, including sketches illustrating a good one. He concedes that the standard, which defines a bad melon in terms of its deformities and disfiguring spots, is rarely used by growers or retailers. Anyway, he says, most consumers know a good watermelon when they see one.

Ava Rodgers, the department's deputy assistant administrator for home economics, says she spends half her time traveling the country to coordinate activities of 4,000 home economists. Asked to describe a typical day in her office, Miss Rodgers says. "I've answered the phone a couple of times this morning. That's about it. It's a normal day." She is paid $33,700 a year.

Elsewhere in the department, 2,000 people are busily planning new dam projects even though there is a 10-year backlog of such projects already planned and awaiting construction. Secretary Bergland says he issued an order several weeks ago halting further dam-construction planning, but Joe Haas, assistant administrator for water resources, says he hasn't heard of such an order. . . .

And so on. This portrait of a bureaucracy of drones, running on its own internal momentum toward goals that are often senseless or hopelessly dated, would have been impossible to draw convincingly without these and other revelatory anecdotes House provided. She got them in the simplest way possible—by hanging around the department and asking people about their work.

There are too few hanging-around stories done, for reasons good and ill. The genre is risky; we can preconceive these stories all we want, but what if we hang around and nothing much happens? Who'll sign the expense account then? And these pieces are time-consuming. Even when they work, the reporter will have spent hours, days, even weeks of dead time waiting for something to happen.

Finally, these stories require a different interviewing touch than some of us are accustomed to. We're trained to collect data, and no one questions that ours is an information function above all. But this orientation can lead to a laundry-list interviewing approach; the reporter carefully drafts a series of specific questions geared to bring out facts and then fires them at his sources like bullets. If facts are all we're interested in, this approach may work. But it seldom works for the reporter doing a hanging-around story. He depends less on factual responses to specific questions than on his eye and ear for people and situations he encounters by chance. He must realize that he may get little good material at first because his sources must become accustomed to his presence, and overcome their suspicions of him and his motives, before they begin acting like themselves. If he barges in and starts firing pointed queries at them, he only confirms their stereotypes of the pushy newsman.

This is worth remembering in doing all sorts of stories. Good reporting means getting the facts, but good storytelling requires more. At the lowest level of the action, we get what we need only by showing genuine interest in the source as a fellow human being, not a lemon we are trying to squeeze dry in as few minutes as possible.

I know reporters who are chronically nagged by their failure to get good quotes. The people in their stories appear wary, blandly cautious in their statements, unwilling to show themselves. I suspect they're reacting to a quick squeeze by the reporter, who is conducting his interviews as cold, businesslike transactions when they should be conversations.

I don't enjoy conversing with people who aren't interested in me but only in what I can do for them. Story sources are no different, so it's often a good idea to try to form what amounts to a 30-minute relationship with the source. The reporter may introduce his business in an offhand way and, if the source is not too busy, express some interest in what he does for a living and in his setting—the town, the organization, the company, the issue in which the source is involved. This is not deceit. The reporter *is* interested, or should be, because this kind of talk can give him an idea of what the source is like, his degree of influence, his outlook on life. These are important in assessing what he says later.

The reporter's initial questions are broad, nonthreatening and designed to give the source a few minutes to size up the questioner and decide that he can be trusted. After this, the reporter gradually gets more specific and pointed. Usually, he'll get franker and fuller answers to these queries than he would have if he'd fired them at the source as soon as he entered the room.

I'm not suggesting that we strive for a bogus chumminess with sources. Most can spot this immediately and their wariness increases instead of abating. I'm only saying that storytellers must treat sources as something more than data banks. The reporter who can't or won't is probably better off programming computers for a living.

Other reporters talk too much. One chatty subspecies likes to put himself at or near the level of his expert sources by pretending to know a lot more about their subject than he does. He's afraid of appearing ignorant, when in fact he *is* ignorant and ought to confess it at the start. He's forgotten that by doing so, by approaching the source as a pupil does a teacher, he can tap the innate desire of experts to show what they know. By feigning knowledge instead, he usually gets one of two responses, both unfortunate.

The source may see quickly that the reporter is a phony and dismiss him, then and possibly always. Or, worse, he may fall for the reporter's act. Our expert may then begin talking jargon and referring to arcane background matters he assumes the reporter is familiar with; the latter, trapped, is reduced to mumbling acquiescences and making noises like the knowledgeable fellow he is not, all the while wondering what this man is talking about. The material gathered in such a fumbled encounter can be as dangerous as cobra venom if the reporter is stupid enough to use it in his story.

Investigative reporters sometimes feign knowledge they don't have to wring admissions or verifications from sources. Let's listen in on this fanciful exchange between one journalistic bloodhound and a union official he suspects of corruption:

REPORTER (who has no hard evidence): Why did you secretly drain $50 million out of the union pension fund and give it to Fat Louie (The Neo-Platonist) Benedetto?

UNION OFFICIAL (aghast): Geez, whereja get that? It was only $2 million. . . .
REPORTER: Gotcha!

This is the way it works in the investigative reporter's opium dreams, anyway. In practice the union official is unreachable. He's probably in Acapulco helping Fat Louie spend the pension fund, but we can't prove that either.

The reporter who has to fill the silences in his interviews with his own chatter blows chances to get good quotes. Let the source fill the silences. If you ask him a question and don't believe his answer is complete or really shows what he thinks or feels, just wait. He may start to get a bit uncomfortable. He may sense that he has somehow failed to satisfy you—and often he'll suddenly add something to his earlier statement or recast it. What he says at this moment often is more revealing than what he said at first.

Help him too much and you may get nothing. A reporter interviewing a cowboy, for example, wants an expression of the plainsman's feelings about his job. "Slim," he asks, "if the pay is so low and the job is so menial and exhausting, why do you keep doing it? What do you love about it?" This is a difficult question for anyone, and Slim, no orator, mutters something about liking the outdoors. This is not sufficiently dramatic, and our man rushes in to pin him down. "Tell me, Slim," he babbles, "is it the look of sunrise over empty land, is it the way of horse and cow, is it the rugged independence of the life?"

The cowpoke's gratitude is almost pitiful. "Yep," he says, much relieved. "That's about it." The reporter just did his work for him without payment. Make your sources do their share.

But when have you done your own share? When do you stop reporting and begin writing? Most reporters I know have to be torn away from the telephone because they're never satisfied that they've gotten all the material they need. Often that's because they don't have a story plan that allows them to see how the material they already have relates to what they require.

In reporting, I go straight at the jugular of the piece—the one or two or three (at most) sections I've identified as potentially most important. When I've done enough reporting on them to convince myself, and enough to give readers the varied proofs and detailed examples I know they require, I think about writing. Usually enough material on the secondary sections of my story has fallen over the transom while I've reported the primary ones, so starting to write becomes possible.

I'm frequently uncomfortable about starting, but I try to recall that all stories overwrite themselves and that probably I'll have to omit much of my reporting anyway, if the piece is to be kept within bounds. In all these years, I've never had a reporter tell me that he'd talked to everyone he could think of and had written a story that was too short. I've had plenty fret about the thinness of their reporting while writing page 11 of what should be a seven-page story.

Realistic deadlines help. Arbitrary ones plucked out of the air without thought of the individual story requirements, without allowance for unexpected interruptions, are no help at all. So inspect your story plan closely and gauge how much time the reporting and writing are likely to take. Make some allowances for work that looks difficult. Then add a few days more if the piece is a major one. This gives you no excuses for failing to bring it in on time.

If the story isn't hooked to some future event or isn't urgently topical, don't set a date for completion. Just give yourself a specific number of work days to finish it. This allows for matters you can't anticipate or control—an unexpected breaking story that you must spend a day or two working up, a bout with the flu, sitting in for a colleague who's out of town, or whatever. But every day you are at work and have no unexpected duties is a day you must charge against that story or any other you have in progress—whether you actually get anything done or not.

This system mercilessly ignores the usual reportorial work evasions. You spent the morning reading magazines, the early afternoon at a long lunch, the late afternoon conferring with colleagues (i.e., telling Polish jokes)? Fine. But it costs you every time and, with only a bit of bookkeeping, you will be able to see immediately what it cost you and how much time you have left.

As the days remaining dwindle, you'll be goaded into working harder at what you really need to do. As Samuel Johnson said, "When a man knows he is to be hanged in a fortnight, it concentrates his mind wonderfully."

CHAPTER 5

ORGANIZATION

We'll conveniently vault over the disorder that is the reporter reporting. One of his sources is shooting lion in Kenya and won't be back for a month, another hung up on him because a different scribe burned him on a previous story, and, seeking focus points and people, he spent two days marooned by a blizzard in a Nebraska motel with nothing to do but watch *Bowling for Dollars*.

In the end he emerges, as most of us do, with material that is less than what he hoped for. Reporters never deal in perfect, only in good enough. But what to do with the pile of good enough now sitting on the desk?

Asked to identify the most common fault in copy, most editors I know say, "Poor organization." But this is a symptom, not a disease. The disease is sloppy thinking, particularly in the earlier stages of story conception and shaping, and most of the book up to this point has been instruction in how to do that well. So, much of our organizational work has been done already, whether we realize it or not. This chapter addresses what remains in roughly blocking out a tale: sharpening the focus of the piece, segregating material properly, and settling on a narrative line that will work best in stringing the story together.

In doing these things, we'll be governed in a general way by the Laws of Progressive Reader Involvement, which I recently drummed up:

Stage One: *Tease me, you devil.* Intrigue me a little. Give me a reason for going on with your story instead of doing something else. Remember, I have no investment in you at all.

Stage Two: *Tell me what you're up to.* Enough teasing. What is your story really about? Please, no windy explanations, no details—just what's going on here.

Stage Three: *Oh yeah?* I'm from Missouri. You'll have to prove what you just said. Let's see your logic. Let's see your evidence. I've invested time in you by now, so I'll be patient—but you had better be convincing.

Stage Four: *I'll buy it. Help me remember it.* Make it clear. Make it forceful. And put an ending on it that will nail it into my memory.

We won't bother yet with Stage One, the lead of the story. To many reporters, this is heresy; they can do nothing else, they insist, until they get the lead. They're wrong. They can do practically everything else if they're willing to try, and there are some important reasons for putting aside the lead if it doesn't come to you right away. We'll examine those reasons at the end of the chapter. In the meantime let's get on with the work.

FIRST READING

Skim through all the interviews and documents. Read rapidly, not for mastery of detail but for the sense of things. Put aside material that is irrelevant or weakly repetitive.

Now give final refinement to your *main theme statement*, the most important part of your story plan. You first drafted this brief, stripped-down summary of what you thought the story would say before you started. It has guided your reporting throughout; now it will guide your organization.

As before, keep it simple, brief and centered only on the main aspects of the story. Always emphasize action elements if they are strongly present. Omit details and explanations. These will come later.

Take pains with these sentences, for you may be using the main theme statement not only as a writing guide but as part of the story itself. You want it to be a broad but accurate reminder of what you should stress in the body of the piece.

This refinement of the main theme statement helps satisfy the reader's command in Stage Two of his involvement: Tell me what you're up to here. Give it to me straight and quick and simple, written in plain vanilla. This exercise also crystallizes your thinking as you try to obey his Stage Three order for a complete, logical presentation that will convince him that what you say is true. Finally, the germ of a good lead often is imbedded in the main theme statement, as we will see later. So of all the writing you will do, this is the most important.

Editors frequently refer to the part of the story that contains this main theme material as the *nut graf*. Don't take this literally and become a slave to form. Yes, the main theme material may naturally fall into one neat paragraph—but it doesn't have to, and often it shouldn't. Sometimes a good main theme statement is a single sentence. In other stories it may cover several sentences, beginning in the middle of a paragraph and ending midway through the next. In still others several paragraphs may be needed to contain it. The important thing is the nature of the material and how clearly it defines the story, not the form it takes.

During the first reading, look also for *conclusions* that leap out at you, and jot them down. Buried in your research are bits and pieces of reporting that, taken together, point to things you can and should deduce. You have already concluded how your whole story will lean in drafting the main theme statement. Now you are pulling together the meaning of some of its parts.

In the logging story, for example, I reported the different aspects of the loggers' work society, but didn't see what the nature of that society was until I read through my materials. The loggers haze, they blackball, they exclude women; what are they but a fraternity?

The first reading is a good time to look for possible *endings*, too. They can be as varied as the stories themselves, but suitable endings, at least in most newspaper work, have one common characteristic: A copy editor interested only in saving space could scissor them off without damaging the factual soundness and completeness of the story. The result of this amputation may be aesthetically distressing, with the story ending lamely or in midair, but its substance will be untouched. The ending exists to fix the tale in the reader's mind; it should be expendable as a beautiful frame around an oil painting is expendable. The picture is complete without it.

This suggests that facts and illustrations with direct bearing on the most important sections of the story shouldn't be squirreled away for use at its finish; as concrete proofs, they are better used to buttress the points made in the body of the piece. We usually have too little of this material to afford the luxury of squandering any on an ending. This restriction aside, anything goes.

SECOND READING AND INDEXING

The pick-and-shovel phase of organization. During it you seek mastery of details ignored before by reading slowly and carefully through all your material. Then you index it, segregating it into certain key categories. These categories are the same ones employed in the reporting guide, and they were not plucked out of the air: There are reasons behind their selection, but these are better examined later, when we get to the section on choosing narrative lines.

I ought to note that you may not need to do much indexing, at least for shorter, simpler stories, if you have an orderly and retentive mind. Lacking one, I always index and would urge any reporter to do likewise when working on a piece involving many sources, documents and aspects.

I start by putting the reporting guide to a new use. Stapling a few sheets of legal-sized paper together, I write the main headings of the guide on them, leaving plenty of space between headings for my notations. I use all six elements—history, scope, reasons, impacts, countermoves, future (or their equivalents for a profile)—even though I know only a few will get any detailed attention in the particular story at hand. For the moment, I just want a place to put everything of possible interest.

Then, as I read through each interview and document, I assign it a number and log its contents under the appropriate headings of the guide, using my own shorthand. For example, suppose I have a productive interview on a story about efforts by cities to combat Indian water rights claims and appropriate their supplies. The interview happens to be the fifth one I log, so I give it the code T5, the letter T being my designation for interviews.

The source, the attorney for a tribe we'll call the Kokomo, has filled me in on a lawsuit he's just concluded. The tribe as complainant won a judgment against the nearby city of Boomsville, which had been wrongfully using the Indians' water. The lawyer also commented on how widespread the abuse of Indian water rights has become, saying: "If the cities had their druthers, they'd dry up every reservation in the country," and he showed me figures in a GAO report about water conflicts involving Indians. I took them down.

Then he compared the current climate with the one prevailing when he first became tribal counsel 20 years before. There was no conflict then because the city was only a town and the tribe had little irrigated agriculture, relying instead on sheep raising. There was plenty of water for both. Now the grass is gone, cropped away by the sheep, and the Indians want to irrigate 50,000 acres to offset the decline in their economy. But the town has become a metropolis with a vastly expanded thirst for a water supply that can no longer meet all needs.

I would log interview T5 this way:

Under **History**: T5—O. Kokomo econ 20, sheep.

This tells me that the material is an observation (O.) on the tribal economy 20 years ago, and reminds me it was based on sheep raising.

Under **Scope**: T5-q, druthers, dry up—nf ind wtr gao.

A double entry. The first part says that in interview T5 there is a good quote (q) bearing on my central development, the assault on Indian water rights, and reminds me of what was said by excerpting a few key words. The second part tells me that in the same interview I have national figures (nf) about Indian water issues by the GAO. If the attorney had given me the document or I had gotten it directly from the GAO, I would have given it its own number under a D (for documents) code.

Under **Countermoves**: T5-Ill. kokomo w/litig Bmsvl.

This says I have in T5 an illustration (Ill.) of how Indians are fighting back against cities—in this case, a lawsuit pressed and won (w/litig) by the Kokomos against Boomsville.

Under **Reasons**: T5-O. Kokomo-Bmsvl comptn: grwth v. ltd. sply.

This last entry tells me I have an observation on one reason for the conflict—the needs of both parties for growing shares of a limited water supply.

As I go on through each interview and document, the information in them is broken apart and gradually sorted into the six boxes I have provided; I am organizing not by source, but by the story aspect the material addresses. The boxes most important to my piece will have many entries; others will have few or none. If an item might be useful in more than one section—a quote, say, that addresses not only the scope of a development but also the reasons behind it—I'll log that snippet in both places. At the end, I can see how much I've got and, thanks to the coding, the nature of the material as well: figures, quotes, factual observations, illustrations from life.

That's nice, but why do this? Few interviews contain as much worthwhile material as the one hooked up above, but I won't kid you; indexing is hard, time-consuming work. I hate doing it. I do it anyway because I hate even more what happens when I don't.

Confusion happens. Multiple drafts happen. Because I cannot *see* what I have and what it says, I am apt to forget material entirely, or distort its specific meaning in my mind, forcing me to backtrack, rewrite heavily, insert or move paragraphs around. That's assuming I can write at all; without segregating the contents of my reporting I usually have to suffer several false starts before coming up with a sensible line of progression to follow. My research is a formless, intimidating heap, so I dodge out for a two-hour, two-margarita lunch, hoping all the confusion evaporates while I'm gone. It never does. Finally, I just wing it. When the dust settles, it's taken me twice as long to write the story as it should have, and I've had only half the fun I expected. Sometimes less.

Indexing eliminates most of this wasted time and pain by giving me an ordered picture of my story elements. Just as the proper shaping of a story idea focuses reporting on the most promising areas and makes the story doable, so indexing shapes the reported material and makes writing doable. There are other advantages too.

The very act of logging in details helps plant them in my less-than-leakproof memory. With greater command of my material comes more sureness in writing; I'm able to remember accurately exact numbers, quotes and incidents, and when I can't my notations refresh me. So I write off my index, mainly. Only later, after I have roughed out the piece, will I check what I have written against the original source material. Usually, I don't have to make substantial changes.

Writing off the index maintains spontaneity. When the work is going well and the Muse is whispering the right words into my ear, I don't want to break the enchantment by fumbling through a pile of papers for some vaguely recalled figure (do I really have it or just think I do?) on artichoke exports. I may find it, but by then the magic is gone.

NARRATIVE LINES

Every story is a river dammed at points along its course. Behind each dam is a reservoir in which the river seems to disappear; floating on the surface of one of these, we may not sense that it is more than a lake of still water. But the river current, though invisible, is surging far beneath on its path to the sea. Our task as writers is to keep the reader ever conscious that he is on a river, not a lake, that the current of story action and progression is always flowing beneath him. His vessel on the journey is the narrative line we choose in telling the story.

I use three of these lines. Now and then all of them may appear in a finished piece, but even then one predominates in the structure of the story. These lines are:

1. Block Progression Line

Now, a final and most important reason for indexing material into the six categories: They are the building blocks out of which a great many stories can be effectively told.

For years I examined pieces that seemed to me particularly well organized. I wanted to dope out why they were, and how they differed from others that seemed jumbled, confusing. The reason: Somehow the writer had succeeded in grouping material in the body of his story—the part after the main theme statement—into blocks of copy, each of them addressing a certain facet of the story. And those blocks corresponded closely to the six categories I've named and listed in the reporting/writing guide.

After establishing their themes, these writers would develop them fully in an orderly, powerful way. They might first group together almost all the detailed material dealing with the scope of the development itself, for example. Then they might do the same thing with the material bearing on reasons, and so on. They were following the first important principle of organization:

KEEP RELATED MATERIAL TOGETHER IN YOUR STORY

This means that the bulk of the material bearing on one section, as defined by the guide, ought to be assembled in one place when you write the body of the story—a job made much easier by your indexing. You can see exactly how much material you have that bears on, say, the impacts portion of the story, to name one category. You can see roughly what it says. And you can see its variety because you have identified the fragments as illustrations, quotes, numbers and factual observations.

The command to keep related material together applies fairly strongly to all elements of the index except history. Sometimes I use it all in one place, when it is a minor element requiring little space, but usually I sprinkle it in wherever it lends contrast, authenticity or deeper understanding of what is happening currently. Too much history in one lump draws the reader away from immediate events that are usually the story's main concern.

History excepted, the grouping of related material helps you meet the reader's demand for a clear, logical presentation that will convince him. It also gives the story punch. When material is scattered instead, both logic and force are diminished. If the problem is extreme, the story becomes a ball of fuzz and the despair of editors.

The idea of grouping related matter is a general principle only, not a flat rule. It will be impossible to keep every fragment of like material together in every story—though in almost every story it will be possible to keep the bulk of it together. This general obedience to the principle is enough.

Now, to summarize: You have a main theme statement that briefly touches on the most important segments of your story, and which links them together in a clear, conclusive expression of what the piece adds up to. You've assembled your detailed information into building blocks of related material that will reinforce the points you've made in the main theme statement. Your next concern is the order in which you lay them out.

The best clue to that order lies in the relative stress placed on these blocks in your main theme statement. The unit that has gotten the most emphasis there is probably the first one you will attack in detail.

For example, if the central development itself is newsy or otherwise important in your particular story, you'll probably attack the scope section first, linking it immediately with the main theme statement. Then, if the propulsive force behind that central development is of interest, you will write a reasons section. Following that, you could go to impacts and counter-moves, if any, finishing up with an aspect of the future.

This is one rather typical order of progression in a juvenile story. But let's assume that the central development is well-known, isn't news, and that the main theme statement reflects this by zeroing in on impacts and/or countermoves instead of scope. The writer can dismiss the latter as a given, or say just enough about it to put the reader in the picture with a general-ized line or two. His first block of *detail* will be about impacts.

In other cases, a central development seems to defy logic. Even if that development is newsy, the writer may want to delay outlining its full scope until he has told the reader the reasons behind it.

It's important to start well, but after that the order of sections you follow is less important. There's no one perfect fixed order, written in the stars, that a writer must puzzle out and follow for his particular story. One progression may be a little better than another, but several different ones may work fairly well when applied to the same piece.

Knowing this, the writer is free to tell his story with more spontaneity. He may move along in a natural way, letting a thought, a phrase, a place, a name, an event he has just written about suggest his next movement. This is better than writing tortured, empty transitional passages that warp the piece in a preplanned direction it doesn't want to follow. By all means think hard about what your first detailed section or two should be—but after that let the story tell you where it wants to go next. Don't preplan the whole order of sections before you write.

To see how the process works, let's dismember and analyze the text of a 1980 story of mine on the loss of prime farmland. It's a moderately complex piece, but it still boils down to a story that stresses three sections—scope, reasons and countermoves—with a secondary emphasis on the future. There is only a snippet of history and no impact section at all; the land losses haven't yet affected total farm output. However, the potential future consequences look so serious that people already are trying to stem the losses. We have countermoves occurring before impact is felt.

1. HOMESTEAD, Fla.—Tearing around southern Dade County in his pickup, tomato grower Rosie Strano points out parcel after parcel of land, sweetened by natural limestone and perfect for growing tomatoes. Now it is growing shopping centers and condominiums instead.

2. Mr. Strano himself recently lost a section of 640 acres that he had been leasing. The owner, more interested in development values than crops, subdivided it. "All gone," laments Mr. Strano, a bull of a man sweating in air that feels like hot, damp velvet. "Urbanization is going to force us all out someday—and you just can't replace this land."

3. Over the past 15 years Dade County has lost 55,000 acres of farmland to the concrete tentacles of greater Miami, snaking down

from the northeast, and to other development. Blocked off by salt marshes to the south and Everglades National Park to the west, growers are slowly being squeezed onto marginal land, or what's left of it: Almost all the unused agricultural acreage, once plentiful, is gone.

A garden-variety anecdotal lead derived from reporting focus points and people for the scope section. It helps that the general location—Dade County—is a hot spot. This lets us move from Strano's individual case to that of the county.

4. Much the same thing is happening across the country, from New England, where crumbling, empty barns are the only remnants of the farms about to be replaced by development, to the coastal valleys of California, now filling up with tract houses.

5. As global demand for U.S.-grown food keeps increasing, the country is losing, at a worrisome rate, one of its most important resources—the soil needed to raise this food. Awakening to the problem, states and counties are scrambling to pass measures that would keep their countrysides green, with mixed results. Meanwhile, bulldozers move on to more land that once knew only the plow.

6. Developers have been chewing up three million acres of farmland a year, according to the National Agricultural Lands Study, or NALS, a multi-agency federal team set up last year to assess the problem and investigate possible remedies. About one million of those acres are prime farmland—the richest, flattest soils capable of growing the most food and fiber at the lowest cost. The prime land lost yearly would form a corridor a half-mile wide from San Francisco to New York.

7. Up to now such losses have barely been noticed. Since World War II farmers have more than covered them with an explosion of productivity that has pushed total farm output steadily higher. Also, many farmers displaced by urbanization have been able to develop other land from the nation's reserves.

8. But now the squeeze is starting to hurt. The U.S. has about 230 million prime acres in crops, but the losses of past decades have cut to just 72 million acres the available reserves of the best land still unexploited. And there is evidence that the revolution in farm technology is rapidly slowing down.

9. The nation still has sizable unused stocks of fairly productive soil, although farming costs on most of it would be high. But the long-term outlook is increasingly bleak. "If we bank on technology and it doesn't come through, if we can't control urbanization and erosion, we will lose our options," says Robert Gray, executive director of NALS.

10. Don't count on a quick fix from new technology, warns Anson Bertrand, director of the Agriculture Department's Science and Education Administration. "We have used up most of our store-house of knowledge and applied it widely," he says. "But it simply isn't being replaced fast enough, and our crop yields are topping out."

11. The land is getting tired. Average gains in output per acre have drifted down from a sparkling 3% a year in the '50s to barely over 1% in recent years; yields for some crops in some regions have actually declined, despite increased dousings with fertilizer and pesticides. At the same time, foreign demand for U.S. food has been increasing rapidly. U.S. agricultural exports have shot from around $6 billion a year to more than $32 billion a year over the last decade, and are running 10 years ahead of earlier projections.

Scope section, with the main theme statement imbedded in it. We start in P4 with another *location* factor, showing that our development is nationwide. Notice that we show it pictorially, in terms of empty barns in New England and farm valleys in California disappearing under tract houses.

The main theme statement in P5 is an almost verbatim copy of the one I drafted at the beginning of the organizing process. It is general enough to embrace the important specific elements treated fully later. It centers on *action*—the land being lost, the scramble to do something about that, the bulldozers rumbling on.

In P6, we move to a broad *quantitative* factor about total losses. Again, we try to express this pictorially with the highway image. This is followed by a bit of history in P7 and by another and more specialized quantitative factor dealing with prime farmland only. We could have lumped this together with the data about total land loss, but this would have created a passage too dense with numbers.

At the end of P8, we introduce the *perspective* factor, the material that puts the loss of land into a context of other events. From there through P11, the end of the scope section, we see that the loss of land is magnified in importance by the slowdown in new farm technology, the beginning signs of soil exhaustion and the pressure of heavy demand for exports.

This scope section, including the lead drawn from it, has the dimension of variety. It uses many different elements to convince instead of overloading the reader with any one class of them. There are brief, separated quotes from sources ranging from top to bottom of the scale. There are three sets of numbers, also separated. There is one hot spot, one actor at the lowest level of the story, one line sketching out geographical breadth, and three instances of other events that add gravity to the central development.

12. With world population expected to rise 50% to more than six billion in the next 20 years, and with much of this increase expected in areas already suffering chronic food shortages, demands on the U.S. farmer can only increase. Even a tiny shift in global weather patterns could tip an already delicate balance, turning endemic malnourishment into the death of millions by famine, as is the case now in East Africa. Climatologists believe the weather through most of this century has been unusually favorable to agriculture.

13. "We are going to have East Africa in many more places than we have it now," says Mr. Bertrand. "There will be starvation, there will be many more refugees. Countries that now have surpluses with which to ease the pressure may not have them. We'll need all the land we have."

Future. Why this section here? Look back at the very end of P11, the last paragraph of the scope section, where the huge increase in U.S. food exports is mentioned. This raised the idea of foreign reliance growing even greater in years to come—a likely possibility (or so it seemed at the time), considering climatic factors and global population growth. So what I had written at the end of P11 clearly pointed me into my next section, a reasoned prediction of what the future might hold. This kind of natural transition is the best kind, and deserves a stated organizational principle of its own:

> LET WHAT YOU HAVE ALREADY WRITTEN
> SUGGEST WHAT YOU WRITE NEXT

This doesn't mean you ought to jump about wildly, leaping out of a section before you are done with it to follow some road sign in your previous sentence, and then jumping back. Stay within your sections until you clean them up. But use the principle to order related material within a section, and to guide you when you have finished it and want to move to a new one.

In P12, the reporter suddenly surfaces to seize control of a passage that might have galloped on for several windy paragraphs. Instead of hiding behind climatologists and demographers and citing studies and reports, I yank together their general findings in one paragraph and draw a conclusion from it that any prudent non-expert could make. This conclusion is then extended and reinforced by Bertrand's forecast of future famines.

14. Perhaps so, but to individual farmers there are many temptations to cash in and get out. Like money. Much of the nation's richest land is near its 242 largest cities, as well as around rural towns, and as urban sprawl approaches neighboring farmlands their value begins to soar. Land subdivided for development can sell for 10 times its value as a farm; one Dade County grower recently spurned $125,000 an acre for his place, but such offers are luring more farmers.

15. Another inducement to sell: The farmer may have no one to leave his place to. A Farm Bureau official in Northern California says the flight of farmers' sons to town jobs is widespread. "A kid is 20, he's getting paid three or four bucks an hour to work for dad, and his friends are getting $8.50 for checking the food he grows out of the supermarket. Hell, would you stay on the farm?" the official asks.

16. As one farmer sells out, then another and another; as a feed and grain outlet closes here and a farm machinery dealership there, remaining farmers who don't want to leave begin to suffer from the so-called impermanence syndrome—the growing conviction that before long the agricultural community will be no more, the farmer will no longer be welcome, the whole place will be developed. So more farmers leave, often after conflict with new residents who don't take to the noises and smells of farm operations next door.

17. The conflict is acute in places like Arizona's Salt River Valley, where residents of Phoenix and other towns coexit uneasily with a dwindling number of farmers. Some Scottsdale residents charge that pesticide sprays drifting from nearby farms have caused severe health problems. Cultivated acreage in the valley has slipped by almost a third since 1970, and towns and cities now cover more than half an area that once was 90% agricultural.

18. The impermanence syndrome also contributes to another kind of land loss—erosion. Sensing impending development, farmers abandon contour plowing and other conservation techniques, stop spending money on permanent improvements like terracing and more efficient irrigation systems, and wring as much profit out of their land as quickly as they can.

19. Increasing demand for food, moreover, is encouraging some to open up to cultivation hilly, marginal parcels that erode easily. From the Great Plains to the Mississippi Delta, farmers are tearing out windbreaks and shelter belts to gain a few more acres and create the longer reaches needed for most efficient operation of new giant-sized tractors—exposing more land to the sweep of the wind and the beat of storm-driven rain.

20. In many areas, including Iowa, west Tennessee, Missouri, and the Palouse, a wheat-growing region in the Pacific Northwest, the land is being worn away far more rapidly than it is being renewed. Because of the drive for more production, "land is being farmed that should not be, just to bring in a few more dollars," says Allen Hildebaugh, a soil scientist working with NALS.

21. While the Agriculture Department gives farmers funds and advice to control erosion, and tries to keep them down on the farm with liberal loan policies, other government actions only encourage land loss. The Environmental Protection Agency's drive for new sewage-treatment plants, for example, has given many rural towns more sewage capacity, which has stimulated their spread into the countryside.

22. In Florida, the National Park Service condemned and took over some of the best tomato land in the country, part of a 33,000-acre private parcel inside the boundaries of Everglades National Park, in order to return it to natural vegetation. But the land is now full of unwanted "junk" vegetation that was imported to Florida and took root. Growers are still angry over the seizure of the so-called hole in the doughnut. One is Mr. Strano, who in vain begged the owner of the land he worked there not to sell to the Park Service.

23. Like Mr. Strano, many other farmers have no control over what happens to the farms they work, because they don't own them. Often the farms are held by developers warehousing the property against future housing demand in the area, or by speculators who will cut them into building lots at the first flutter of interest. In Dade County, more than half the farmland is leased from nonfarm owners—including, it is widely believed, some of the cocaine kings of south Florida who stash illicit drug profits in real-estate investment.

Reasons. We deal in one place with all causative factors behind the withdrawal of land from cultivation. P14–15 treat briskly the obvious economic motive and a lesser social one. Notice the movement from general to particular; a sweeping statement about the subdivided value of farms is instantly followed by a local example. A general conclusion about farm inheritance is backed by a low-level source putting it in concrete terms people understand.

In P16–17, we learn how the development of farmland has a snowball effect; remaining farmers suffer the so-called impermanence syndrome and start to sell out too. Mention of that syndrome leads us to P18, where it is linked with another kind of land loss, erosion. And the mention of that leads us, in turn, through P19–20 and treatment of other factors bearing on erosion. Notice how one thought leads to another that is like it—and how this also helps keep related material together *within* a section of the story.

In P21–22, federal policies are treated as a separate cause of land loss. The first sentence of P21 is constructed to highlight a dramatic point of irony—the Agriculture Department sweating to preserve farmland while other agencies seem to promote its loss. The section closes with P23, where we see that many farmers are not owners. The latter often don't know a rutabaga from an artichoke and don't care; to them the land is just money in a different form. This attitude is clearly a contributory cause of farmland subdivision.

Look closely at P17. This paragraph is built around a *multiple element example*, the happenings in the Salt River Valley. This example could have been used to illustrate two different story sections—scope, because the valley is a hot spot where much land has been paved over, and reasons, because it shows the farmer-city dweller conflict that is part of the impermanence syndrome. I used it under reasons because that is where I needed it most, and because the conflict was sharp and specific in nature.

By keeping the Salt River Valley material in a single place I am giving the reader a more cohesive picture of that area and what is happening there. This leads us to the next principle of organization:

TRY TO ISOLATE MATERIAL FROM ONE SOURCE IN ONE PLACE

By isolation, I mean assembling all the attributed testimony of one person, all the events linked to a specific place, person or institution, at one place in the story. Note the use of the word "try." This is an even looser, more waffled principle than the others and can be violated frequently. In profiles, it can't and shouldn't be applied to the subject; that would be patently silly. Even in nonprofiles it ought to be violated when one source or set of events overshadows others, and is in itself an important story element. Finally, even in some stories with a broad set of sources and events to choose from, a single one may offer such helpful material for several different sections that they would be noticeably weaker without it. If so, ditch the principle and scatter the material. I did so with Rosie Strano in this story.

But hesitate before you decide to go your own way, for isolating one-source material is an aid to clarity and forces a bracing discipline on the writer.

It automatically discourages overquoting, a blight on many stories. Trying to keep one person's quotes together, the writer is more likely to pick the sharpest, most salient ones addressing the section that needs help most. This is all to the good.

It subtly builds up the importance and identity of the source, place or set of events in the reader's mind; these are diluted when the material about them is scattered. Most important, it prevents memory blocks that can be fatal to readability.

Say that our reader has met a rather colorless banker named Smith in the second page of some story. A distressing number of people are named Smith, and are easy to forget to begin with. This one, the executive vice president of Amalgamated Trust, compounds the felony by mumbling something innocuous about certificates of deposit and disappearing until page six, where the writer trots him out again by saying, "Mr. Smith of Amalgamated . . ."

The reader frowns. He has momentarily forgotten Smith. A lot has happened since they first met, and he has encountered other sources too. So he pauses, trying to remember. The story flow stops and the writer is in immediate danger of losing his audience. He can be sure of losing it if he treats several sources in this way; even if related material has been properly kept together in sections, the reader gets lost in the welter of names he must remember and gives up. Never rely on a reader's memory for routine details.

24. Florida, along with 47 other states, tries to preserve farms by levying lower taxes on agricultural land. The policy, however, clearly has failed, in part because it makes farmland even more attractive to speculators who can carry it at low tax cost. Most attempts at local zoning for exclusive farm use haven't worked well either, because of local politics and strong objections from landowners who don't want to be zoned out of big potential profits.

25. Oregon, however, is imposing what amounts to tough state-wide zoning that dilutes local protests. Its laws now require localities to inventory their lands and adopt plans for their use that set aside the best soils in enclaves for "exclusive farm use." Landowners within them get hefty tax benefits.

26. Some counties elsewhere are taking similar actions on their own. In Iowa, Black Hawks County uses a "corn suitability" rating system to steer development away from prime farmland. And Santa Cruz County, an important agricultural area on California's central coast, has put all its farmland into six different classifications for potential development, following a 1978 vote by residents to preserve the agricultural base. The top rating, 1A land, can't be subdivided at all. 2D land, often small parcels where there is conflict between farmers and other residents, is the lowest class and is open to development.

27. Farmers seeking reclassification of their land so they can develop it must go before a tough panel—a group of fellow farmers. At one recent meeting an orchardist pleaded that his property was afflicted by oak root fungus and was therefore no longer prime land. He wanted to subdivide. Openly skeptical, the panelists pointed out that the fungus is prevalent throughout the area and can be controlled. Petition denied. "It would take an act of Congress and three Hail Marys to convert one acre of 1A land," says Charles Barr Jr., president of the local Farm Bureau.

Countermoves. A straightforward account of some of the actions taken to control or prevent farmland loss. Again, I got into this section by keying off something I had written at the end of the previous one—a mention, in P23, of the cocaine kings of south Florida. Using the world "Florida" as a bridge, I crossed over into the tax policies of that state and others, beginning the countermoves section that way.

Smaller bridges connect separate items within that section. Mentioning the failure of tax policy leads us naturally into another failure, local zoning. The mention of zoning, in turn, feeds into Oregon's very different statewide experiment with it.

Then we move to other imaginative programs on the county level, finishing with a focus point in Santa Cruz County.

28. It is too early to gauge the effectiveness of these and other protective steps, and no one knows whether they will be adopted widely enough to check the conversion of farmland nationally. If not, says NALS, an area of prime farmland equivalent to the entire state of Indiana may be paved over between now and the turn of the century. The Corn Belt alone might lose land that could yield $1 billion in crops annually. Nearly all the prime land left in real-estate-crazy Florida will probably disappear, and California, the biggest farm state, will lose up to 15% of its best soils.

We end the countermoves section with a sentence that puts the efforts to reduce land loss into general perspective. The rest of the paragraph is a short subsection on the future. You'll notice that here I've chosen to break my own rule about keeping related material together; earlier in the story we had another short futures section. I divided the material because there was a natural cleavage between these two aspects of the future. The first dealt with the projected fate of the world's hungry, while the subsection above dealt with projections of continuing land loss. The division within the material let me get away with separating it.

29. In Dade County Rosie Strano drives out in his pickup to look at his lost land. He does this three or four times a year, and he gets upset every time. In Washington, Mr. Hidlebaugh, the soil scientist, keeps a poem from a professional journal on his wall. The last two stanzas:

> 30. *Beneath the sprawling shopping mall*
> *That shrouds a hidden secret pall—*
> *A field that cannot heed the call*
> *That's made by sun and rain.*
> 31. *Behold the suburbs and their yield:*
> *Beneath the web of streets is sealed*
> *The coffin of a fertile field*
> *The ghost of unborn grain.*

The ending, a circling-back that hammers home the main thrust of the story. We usually don't use poetry in stories and the author of the above is no Robert Lowell, but his verse was such a perfect reflection of what had been laid out factually that I could not resist. Notice the emotional content of this ending: Strano's anger and the sadness, edged with bitterness, of the anonymous poet.

In a story like this one, with moderate stress placed on several blocks, you don't have to be overly concerned with organization *within* each section. There will be few key elements in each, and you can rely on the road signs to carry you through. Even if you miss some, the results will not be disastrous.

But a lopsided story in which one or two blocks dwarf everything else requires extra organizational effort. The boomtowns story in the previous chapter, for example, has an enormous countermoves section and little else. In organizing it, I first asked myself: Who are the different movers at work here, and what are the different moves they are making? Three movers are each taking different actions, so I laid out the section around these movers—the companies, the localities, and the states.

In order, we see the companies ladling out cash grants, building whole towns, supplying amenities, and offering creative financing. Then we see, very briefly, how towns are reacting and cite one that has stiffened its zoning. Finally, we segregate all the actions of the states, which are increasing severance taxes, building billion-dollar trust funds and shipping money to affected communities. This cleans up, in an orderly fashion, what is happening. Then another subsection puts these countermoves into perspective—there are still some conflicts, some fumbled opportunities—closing with an assessment of how the whole effort is working out. The final paragraph of the section shows that such countermoves are still being extended and broadened.

This pattern can be used in laying out other kinds of sections that are formidably long. The general idea is to identify *differentness* and organize to exploit it. In this story, I organized around the movers because they were each doing different things. If they had been doing the same things—if states and localities had been building their own boomtowns along with companies, for example—I would have organized around the different *moves* instead of the movers.

The same idea can be used in treating a long scope section. In a reasons section, I would weigh the movers against the differentness of their *motives*, and for impacts the classes *affected*, versus the different *effects* being felt.

The block progression line can be followed in organizing a profile, using the alternative guide for such a story, but I don't find it a necessity most of the time. Block progression works best when there is no single character overshadowing the story and when it depends on multiple elements addressing move, impact and countermove—story action. Then this organizing line ensures clarity and power, minimizing possible confusion and giving the tale an ordered, marching quality. In a profile, however, the subject is threaded throughout, providing a natural, built-in unity. The writer still will want to keep most related material about that subject grouped according to its nature, and indexing helps him greatly in doing that. But he can take liberties.

2. Time Line

The body of the story, or a large part of it, is a simple chronology. The subject of a profile, for example, is followed from place to place and action to action by the clock or some other progression in time, as in the following occupational profile done by me in 1981:

1. RAFTER ELEVEN RANCH, Ariz.—The lariat whirls as the man on horseback separates a calf from the herd. Suddenly, the loop snakes around the calf's rear legs and tightens. Wrapping a turn of rope around the saddle horn, the rider drags the hapless animal to his crew.

2. The flanker whips the calf onto its back, and the medicine man inoculates the animal. Amid blood, dust and bawling, the calf is dehorned with a coring tool, branded in an acrid cloud of smoke from burning hair and flesh, earmarked with a penknife in the rancher's unique pattern (cowboys pay more attention to earmarks in identifying cattle than to brands) and castrated. It is all over in one minute.

3. Jim Miller, the man in the saddle, smiles broadly as the released calf scampers back to his mother. Mr. Miller is 64 years old. Born and raised nearby, he has been working cows in Yavapai County since he was five. He will keep on until he can't throw a leg over a horse anymore. "It's all I know, and I like it," he says.

4. The marks of his trade are stamped into his body: broken legs, a broken ankle, dislocated shoulder and elbow, a thigh torn open by a broken saddle horn. The fingers of the right hand are grotesquely broken, and he can't flex them fully. It is the roper's trademark, the digits that have been caught in the rope and crushed against the saddle horn, but Mr. Miller still wins roping competitions with that hand.

The lead is a rather tired, off-the-shelf item. I tried to do better but couldn't think of anything. It does have lots of action tightly related to the story and introduces the subject at work, where I want him to be.

5. Jim Miller is a cowboy. There are still many cowboys in the West. Some wear black hats with fancy feather bands, and tear around in oversize pickups with a six-pack of Coors on the seat. These are small-town cowboys, and the only horses they know are under the hood.

6. Others become cowboys at sunset, shucking briefcases and three-piece suits for designer jeans, lizard-skin boots and silver buckles as big as headlights. They go to Western nightclubs to see what everyone else is wearing. These are urban cowboys, and the only bulls they know are mechanical ones.

7. Finally, there is a little band of men like Jim Miller. Their boots are old and cracked. They still know as second nature the ways of horse and cow, the look of sunrise over empty land—and the hazards, sheer drudgery and rock-bottom pay that go with perhaps the most overromanticized of American jobs. There are very few of these men left. "Most of the real cowboys I know," says Mr. Miller, "have been dead for a while."

8. A big man with a ready laugh, he is both amused and exasperated by all the cowboy hype. "It almost makes you ashamed to be one," he says. "You've got doctors and lawyers and storekeepers runnin' around in big hats and boots." None, he intimates, would want to step into a real cowboy's place today; their image of the life is an illusion.

9. The typical ranch hand in this traditional cattle country, he says, is in his late teens or early 20s—so green he often doesn't know how to shoe his own horse—and must do all sorts of menial chores. Nobody can now afford the "horseback men," aristocrats of the saddle who spurned all ranch work, except branding, that they couldn't do from the top of a horse. Most hands are local boys who commute to work from nearby towns, as does Mr. Miller himself. With few exceptions, the bunkhouses full of "bedroll cowboys," wanderers from ranch to ranch over the West, are no more.

10. Some things haven't changed, though. Punching cows, says Mr. Miller, "is still the lowest-paid job for what you have to know and do." In the '30s in Yavapai County, cowboys made $45 a month plus bed and board. The standard wage now is around $500 a month without bed and board. There is Social Security and the usual state coverage for job-related injuries, but there are no pension plans, cost-of-living adjustments, medical and life-insurance packages, or anything else.

11. Mr. Miller is one of the elite. His salary from Fain Land & Cattle Co., the family concern that operates the ranch, is $1,150 a month, but that is because he is the cowboss. The cowboss is the master sergeant of the ranch; he leads by example, works along with his men, and is in charge of day-to-day cattle operations. At various times the cowboss, or any other top hand, has to be a geneticist, accountant, blacksmith, cook, botanist, carpenter, tinsmith, surgeon, psychologist, mechanic, nurse and a few other things besides rider and roper. "There just isn't any point in a young fellow learnin' to be a top hand when he can make so much more today doin' practically anything else,' the cowboss says sadly.

This section establishes what I set out to establish in my main theme statement. We've seen that in a profile this statement is not a summary involving action. It is a listing of perhaps two or three facets of the subject that establish its differentness (for a general profile) or its typicality (for a microcosm). This sort of theme statement can't be used as a part of the story, but its purpose is the same as those that can. It focuses the whole story and tells the reader why the subject is worth profiling, so it must be dealt with early.

My theme statement for this story was simple—the life and work of a real cowboy in an age of cowboy hype. This sentence told me to look for the differences, the contrasts, between the reality of cow punching and the illusion of it, and to set one against the other when I wrote. The paragraphs in this early section address those differences, letting the reader know why we are bothering to write about Jim Miller.

12. Then why do some still follow the life?

A natural question. I built up the pressure behind it by listing the drawbacks to punching cows for a living. Gradually taking this in, the reader begins asking with increasing urgency why some people actually like this job. So I empathize with him by echoing his question. This is one way the reader can be made to sense the human presence of the reporter, but it ought to be used very sparingly. Too many questions make a story look like a quiz show transcript.

Notice also that the question is not answered directly. The rest of the story is its answer, as the time line begins and runs its course.

13. It is early morning on Mr. Miller's domain, more than 50,000 acres of rolling semiarid dun hills and mountain slopes. The cowboss and two full-time hands work this country by themselves. They are going today to 7,800-foot Mingus Mountain to collect strays missed in the recent spring roundup. Mr. Miller surveys the land critically. Here and there the grama grass is greening up, but good summer rains will be needed to get the range in condition.

14. There is absolutely nothing that the cowboss can do about it except pray. The land is just too big. In almost every other occupation, man seals himself off from nature in factory or office tower, struggles to bend a little patch of it to his will, or tries to wrest away its riches by force. But the cowboy knows he is only a speck on the vast plain, his works insignificant, his power to really control the land almost nil; nature herself is the only manager of the Rafter Eleven or any other ranch. So the cowboy learns to bow humbly before the perils and setbacks she brings, and to truly appreciate her gifts.

15. A big buck antelope squirms under a fence and sprints over the plain, hoofs drumming powerfully. "Now, that's one fine sight," murmurs a cowboy.

16. The party is not sauntering colorfully over the hills on horseback. It is bouncing over them in a pickup. The cow ponies are riding comfortably behind in a special trailer; they, too, commute to work now. Though he grew up in the days of chuck wagons, line camps, bunkhouses and the great unfenced ranges, Mr. Miller is a strong believer in modern methods. He uses an electric branding iron because it is faster, and he will even use a trailer to take small groups of cattle from place to place on the ranch rather than drive them on foot. One pound sweated off a steer costs the ranch about 67 cents.

17. But he and every other experienced cowman draw the line at replacing the horse. There is a strange chemistry between horse and cow, a gentling effect, that he declares irreplaceable. "Some dummies around here tried motorcycles once. Didn't work worth a damn," snorts the cowboss. No machine, he adds, can ever duplicate the instincts and balletic ability of a fine cutting horse dancing into a herd to separate steer from heifer.

18. At Mingus Mountain the horses go to work. There is no glamorous dashing about on the plain, only a laborious, slow plod up a mountain canyon that is rocky, steep-sided, clogged with brush. Jagged tree branches jab at the riders. It is grueling, hazardous work, but a nice piece of high country is a valuable asset to any ranch here. In winter it is actually warmer for the cattle because the cold air settles in the valley below, and the nutritious scrub oak and other bushes are available year round and grow above snow.

19. In a high clearing fringed by oak, juniper and pine, 18-year-old Troy Tomerlin pauses awhile, chewing on a twig, to consider his future. He can operate a backhoe and could make almost twice as much doing that as the $500 a month he gets now. "But I don't know how I'd like diggin' septic tanks day after day," he says. "Here I can see animals, work with animals, move around a lot of country. In an office you can't see nothin' but a desk, and I don't like people lookin' over my shoulder. Jim tells us what to do, and how you do it is up to you. I like that."

20. Suddenly, dark clouds begin to boil up over the mountain. Last week the cowboys were pelted by hail the size of golf balls, but that is just part of the job. Lightning, however, is much feared by any mounted man caught on the open plain, and many cowboys have been killed by it. Last summer a bolt barely missed Troy and knocked him unconscious. Other cowboys have been killed or crippled when their horses fell on them and leaped back up to gallop in panic with the rider entangled in rope or stirrup. "I've had three real good friends dragged to death that way," Mr. Miller says softly.

21. The clouds pass over harmlessly, and 18 head coaxed out of the rocks and brush are driven toward the plain. Tommy Stuart, a fine rider with rodeo experience, crashes through brush again and again to divert straying animals. The men cry out to the cattle in a strangely musical series of yips, calls and growls. Tommy has to rope a balky calf, the only time anyone uses his lariat; the cowboy who does so frequently doesn't know how to drive cattle, Mr. Miller says.

22. The trick, he says, is to watch the way their ears are pointing and so anticipate their direction. Mr. Miller also rests cattle frequently on drives to let cows and calves "mother up" so they're more easily driven, or to calm trotty (nervous) animals. "If you don't rest them," he says, "they'll start to run, they'll get hot, then they'll get mad. Then there's no turning them. You've got to keep your cattle cool."

23. The fall weaning is a particularly sensitive time. Separated from their mothers until the maternal bond is broken, the calves, now sizable, are under stress that can cause pneumonia. When the animals finish days of bawling and finally lie down, the sound of a

car, a dog's bark, even the cry of a night bird, may set them back on their feet and running in stampede, mowing down fence, crushing each other in the pileup of bodies. This happened to Mr. Miller twice when he was cowboss on the big Yolo ranch.

24. Nothing untoward happens on this drive, and the riders finally reach the plain. No chuck wagon rolls up with a bewhiskered Gabby Hayes type ready to ladle out son-of-a-bitch stew—classically, a concoction of cow brains, tongues, hearts, livers and marrow, with a handful of onions thrown in to conceal the taste. Instead everyone rumbles back to the ranch house and the cowboss himself fixes lunch for his men: steaks, beans, bread smothered in gravy, and mayonnaise jars full of iced tea.

25. By tradition, the cowboss looks out for his cowboys and hires and fires them himself. Besides incompetence, two things will get you fired by Jim Miller: abuse of horses and bellyaching. The latter is a breach of a cowboy code still in force. For $500 a month, the ranch expects and almost always gets total and uncomplaining loyalty to the outfit. Unionism is an utterly alien concept to cowboys; if a man doesn't like his boss, his job or anything else, he quits on the spot.

26. Firing is as simple. There are no hagglings over severance pay, no worries about employee lawsuits. "I just tell them, 'This is it,' and they go," says Mr. Miller.

27. Once, when a cowboss needed good hands, he would just drop in at the Palace Bar on Whisky Row in Prescott. This was the hiring hall and water hole, full of men who had been on the range for months and were "getting drunker'n seven hundred dollars," as Mr. Miller puts it. He doesn't go there anymore. "Now it's full of hippies and such as that, people who don't know a horse from a cow," he says. Instead, cowboys call him at home when they need work.

28. Lunch is over, and the men get off their rumpsprung old chairs and go out to nurse a young heifer internally damaged when calving. If they don't get her up to walk, she will die.

The trail ride, and our time line, are encompassed here. I deliberately chose the mechanism of the trail ride (even though the only horses I like have tiny little men sitting on them) because it has such potential for action.

The construction of this long section follows another important organizational principle, one more rigid than the others:

DIGRESS OFTEN, BUT DON'T DIGRESS FOR LONG.

A digression for our purposes is any story element that doesn't have salient action in it. Observations, explanations, descriptions, and points of instruction or analysis are all digressions. The best quotes in a story are digressions, too. In brief, most of a typical story's content consists of digressions. The only elements that are not are those in which something is actually *happening* that pushes the story forward.

Accepting this principle honors the reader's liking for action above all else. If a story is indeed a river dotted by reservoirs, those still waters are the passages of digression within it. Floating lazily on them, the reader can forget the very existence of the river beneath and fall asleep in the sun. So hustle him over the lakes as rapidly as you can and get his vessel back into white water—story action.

This principle is my most effective policeman as I write. Every time I start a passage of digression I know I must get out of it quickly; this prods me to write more economically, slash repetitive material, select only the best elements, and pull things together instead of letting them sprawl. I digress because digressions provide variety and information, but the cop at my shoulder whacks me with his nightstick when I blather on too long.

You can see him at work in the trail ride segment:

P13: No action to speak of. We saddle up, but most of this unit is an observation by the cowboss.

P14: Still no action. Observation by the reporter.

We pause for another lesson. In this story I felt I had to distinguish cowpunching from other kinds of work, part of my job in continually stressing differentness. But how to do it? My cowboy can't tell me much because he has no frame of reference. A non-cowboy can't for the same reason. A cowboy sociologist might—yes, there are such people—but the reader will view such a noninvolved party with coolness. So I used my license as the reader's agent on the scene, an observer who has seen both worlds, and told him how it seemed to me.

P15–16: Mostly action, ending in explanation.

P17: Explanation by the cowboss.

P18: Action followed by observation.

P19: No action. Quotes.

P20: Action; the weather front moves in, launching us into observations about work hazards.

The story's road signs are being followed. The weather front slips us into a weather-related hazard, lightning. The very idea of hazard suggested another and different type of danger, being dragged to death. In previous paragraphs, the action of the horses commuting in a van gets us into digressions about modern ranching methods and the continued importance of the horse. The tortuous climb up Mingus led to an observation about the importance of high country to a ranch.

P21: All action, the men driving the cattle.

P22–23: No action. A digressive passage on the proper handling of cattle.

P24: Action. The riders reach the plain, rumble back to the bunkhouse, and have lunch cooked by the cowboss.

Notice the fragment of historical material—the mention of son-of-a-bitch stew and its loathsome ingredients. This lends a touch of authenticity and sets up a point of contrast between the past and the present.

P25–27: A passage of digression on cowboy personnel practices and codes, suggested by the cowboss cooking lunch for his men.

P28: Action, and the end of the continuous trail ride section. Next, I carry the time line a bit further with a visit to the ranch office, and maintain a progression by having the cowboss go home at the end of the day's work. The ending is a simple circling back to the main idea of the story, obtained by asking Jim Miller what his future looked like.

29. At the offices of the Rafter Eleven, Bill Fain has been told by his computer that the cattle he soon will sell will have cost about 68 cents a pound to raise and fatten. He expects to get 67 cents for them. That's the cattle business today, says Mr. Fain, vice president of Fain Land & Cattle and the third generation of his family on this ranch. And such thin margins make men like Jim Miller particularly important.

30. The cowboss is considered one of the canniest judges of livestock in the area, and buys the registered bulls and replacement heifers for the ranch. It is he, more than anyone else, who maintains the quality of the herd. He coaxes an 80% calf crop out of the 700 mother cows here, a good ratio. He does not overburden the land, letting it rest and renew.

31. "Our product isn't cattle. It's grass," says Mr. Fain, "and

Jimmy knows that. A lot of people can rope and ride and love the life, but there are damned few left who can do all the things he does."

32. Outside, cars whiz by on the road that crosses what used to be called Lonesome Valley. Some 6,000 people live there now because the Fains, trying to diversify out of an increasingly risky reliance on cattle, sold a piece of the ranch to a developer who built a town on it. The Fains developed another piece themselves.

33. This has made the cowboy's job harder. Cattle have been shot and cut up on the spot with chain saws by shade-tree butchers who throw the pieces in the back of a pickup and drive off, leaving head and entrails. People tear down cattle feeders for firewood, shoot holes in water tanks, breach fences to maliciously run down calves. "People and cattle don't mix," concedes Mr. Fain. "It's a sick thing," says Jim Miller, and there is icy anger in his eyes.

34. Meanwhile, the old family ranches are being sold, most of them to investors who don't know one end of a Hereford from the other and are more interested in tax shelter than running a good spread. This has driven ranchland prices so high that a young man who really wants to raise beef either can't afford to buy or has no hope of getting a return on his investment. "I really can't see much future in the cattle business," Mr. Miller says.

35. Perhaps not. But around Yavapai County the cycle of ranch life continues unchanged on the surviving family spreads. In Peeples Valley, cougars have taken 15 calves this year, and lion hunter George Goswick is tracking them through the Weaver Mountains. In the pastures, mares are heavy with foals; in time, some will find their way into the gentling hands of Twister Heller, the horse breaker. On the Hays ranch, owner John Hays is stabbing a wild-eyed Hereford bull in the rump with a needle full of antibiotics and fretting about the grasshoppers that are all over the property. There is too much ranch and too many hoppers, so he must simply accept them.

36. At evening, Jim Miller comes home to a house and five rural acres with horse corral outside Prescott. He and his wife, Joan, have lived here 10 years; for the first 27 years of their marriage they lived on the local ranches he worked, raising four sons and two daughters, teaching all to rope and ride. None have followed in his footsteps because there isn't any money in it.

37. Next year, when he's 65, Mr. Miller plans to quit as cowboss at the Rafter Eleven and start collecting Social Security. But he says he will never stop working. Few men around here who have spent their lives on a horse seem able to get off. Jim's friend Tom Rigden still rides roundup and castrates calves on his ranch, though he has been blind for almost eight years.

38. Mr. Miller doesn't expect any trouble finding day jobs on ranches. At a time when there are so few real cowboys left, he says, there is always work for a top hand.

In the entire trail ride section, the guts of this story, the reader is frequently taken off the trail but is not allowed to dawdle. Most disgressions range from one-half to 1½ paragraphs before something happens again. The longest digression, on cowboy personnel codes, is three paragraphs.

The action in this piece isn't particularly arresting and isn't as important in informing the reader as the digressions that enlarge upon and explain it. But it's all the action I have. Knowing how vital it is to readability, I use pieces of it to stitch the story together.

A time line imposes a natural order on a story, but keep in mind that it also imprisons the writer. If one element is far more important than others, if it has a core of news, he'll want to attack it early and highlight it. He often can't do so gracefully if he's trapped himself on a time line, particularly when the important element happens late. And I don't think time is a good line to use on a story that should place heavy stress on only a couple of aspects of the subject.

A time line works for the cowboy piece because the nature of the story—a real cowboy's life and work—implied a broad approach, a recitation of many little things that make up ranch work. No single event was of paramount importance. So I can meander through the day, noticing and commenting on those little things, because my purpose is to give the reader a general impression and not a specific, selected message.

3. Theme Line

This form delivers specific messages. Instead of trudging along by the clock, the writer ignores time and hammers instead at those few facets of his subject he has selected to treat. His main theme statement tells him what they are. He is free to play the most dramatic elements first, regardless of when they happened. He can weave the facets together, if they are related, or he can separate them and deal with each separately.

Scan again the loggers story in Chapter 2. You will recall that of all the aspects possible I chose to treat two: the extreme danger of the work itself, and the nature of the work society. I am not interested in giving a broad, rounded picture of these men; for this story I deliberately treat them only in terms of the danger they face and the code they follow. A time line might have forced me to include elements outside this restricted range, and to play them in order of time rather than importance. The message I am trying to deliver would lose power. So I organize instead around danger and death, and the rules and codes of the clan.

The first five paragraphs are true to my theme statement. They introduce both facets, first by translating numbers into a picture office workers can understand, and then by showing the reckless machismo that is one hallmark of the society of loggers.

I then separate the elements and deal first with danger and death in detail. Five paragraphs show the reader how dangerous the work is in how many ways; I am trying to back up the claim I made to begin the story. The next 12 paragraphs are devoted entirely to the fraternity of loggers. At the end, I weave both themes together in a treatment of a subclass within the fraternity, players in the most dangerous game of all, the timber fallers. The story ends with a look into a tamer, safer future—but one somehow tinged with a sense of loss.

The stories cited above were picked because each exemplifies one type of narrative line. In many stories, however, two or even all three lines may be used. In the piece about the relief pitcher, one line is thematic and interweaves two story facets: the pitcher's mounting sense of futility, and the differences between minor and major-league ball. But the writer also uses a time line when he follows the Toros for a week. The themes continue, but the structure changes.

Nonprofiles that follow block progression may employ one or both of the other lines, too. A story about warfare between two big companies, for example, could at one point include a time line covering a limited but significant chain of events. At another, it could include a thematic section about personality traits of one of the prime movers, if those bear on the action. The effect is that of a miniprofile only a few paragraphs long inserted into a development story.

Having plowed through all his organizational preliminaries, the writer finds his still-untold tale coalescing in his mind. He knows what the story will say and has already shaped a concise expression of what it will say. He has a rough idea of his narrative line structure and has identified a starting point for the body of the piece. His material has led him to conclusions that will also help him shape it, and he even may have his ending in mind.

So he sends the first photons skittering across his VDT—and runs into a brick wall. No lead comes.

He tries something and hates it. He stews. He tries something else and that doesn't work either. He wanders off to chat with colleagues, comes back, fails again. Before long it is time for lunch, a long lunch. . . .

After all the thinking, shaping, indexing and learning he's done, this seems grossly unfair. But it's also to be expected, if research into the function of the right and left sides of the brain is correct. And the trouble can be remedied.

According to that research, the left brain hemisphere is logical, obedient to commands, and linear in operation. It trudges from point to point along a line of reason, a plodder with no imagination but one that will work when you tell it to. It may feebly protest that it would rather be surfing, but you can always ignore this and lay your whip across its back. It will respond.

The right hemisphere, by contrast, doesn't give a hoot for reason. It is intuitive, emotional, creative. It is where sudden insights spring from unbidden, where flights of imagination take wing, where great pictures and symphonies and works of literature are conceived. It's where many good story leads come from, too.

But the right hemisphere is a willful infant. There are now an endless series of workshops peddling instruction in how to tame it, but I've never met anyone who could. The right brain performs only when it feels like it. This is why writers are blocked by leads even when they've done correctly everything described in this book. Almost all that thinking used the left hemisphere, which they control by will, but now they have to deal with an entity they can't push around.

If the brain researchers are correct—and I believe they are—then the writer who stubbornly forces the issue, who refuses to write anything else until he's got his lead, is at war with his own nature. He may get a lead, but he'll probably consume too much time and energy in the effort, and the rest of his story may suffer from hasty treatment.

So if you're blocked on the lead, let it lie. Ignore the unruly infant and turn again to the side of your brain that *will* obey you. Start writing the logical, orderly progression of story sections and elements foreshadowed in the main theme statement you have already completed. You know what that says and you know where it points you.

As you do that, the chances are a happy accident will occur: The lead will suddenly pop into your head. This often has happened to me, I've seen it happen to others, and I take it as empirical proof of something else the researchers claim—hemispheres can work simultaneously and independently on different things. Because you are a practical writer with a deadline, this is exactly what you want them to do.

But what if you finish the whole story and no revelation comes? If this happens, look again at your main theme statement; a fine lead may be hiding within it, as we'll see in the next chapter. In the meantime, you will have accomplished much.

This is important. Following your nature, you go home with something solid to show for a day's work and have every reason to look forward to tomorrow. Fighting your nature instead by insisting on getting the lead, you may go home with nothing but a string of failures, and a hollow feeling in the gut. That's too high a price to pay for stubbornness.

CHAPTER 6

HANDLING KEY STORY ELEMENTS

While writing we must make literally hundreds of small decisions in tailoring the material as we go along, and so every story poses a unique challenge to us as craftsmen. But though each set of writing problems and decisions is different when taken as a whole, each set also contains a few universals—important considerations that figure in every piece we do. Deft treatment of these alone can take us a long way toward a readable story, and each is worth talking about in some detail.

HANDLING THE LEAD

When someone pays $22.95 for a novel, he'll usually be willing to struggle through scores of pages of mush at the beginning. He refuses to concede that he's wasted $22.95, for one thing. For another, the novel form has preconditioned him; mentally prepared for a lengthy sit-down, he doesn't expect rapid story development.

But the same person reading a newspaper is a different man. A single copy of a paper is pathetically cheap, so he isn't reluctant to toss it aside if nothing catches his fancy. His investment in what he reads is so small that it can barely be said to exist at all. He scans the paper idly, impatiently, demanding the instant engagement and quick development that he didn't demand from the novel. In this, his first stage of involvement, he is asking the writer to tease him a little, intrigue him a little, give him some reason for going on with the piece. If the lead doesn't do that he darts away, and a story that may be excellent in all other respects goes unread.

The idea is to get him to make an investment right away. So any lead—and particularly its first paragraph, if it's a longer lead—should not only engage the reader's attention but also force him into what follows. Once he's read a few more lines, that initial investment has been made and he'll be more patient with you. It doesn't matter what the lead is, so long as it's relevant and piques his curiosity. A compelling subject may be enough; if the Martians have invaded New Jersey, that's all the writer need say to be sure of his audience. Or a stage-setting descriptive passage may be written so beautifully that the reader is charmed and wants more.

These attractions aside, many of the leads I like best have one quality in common—mystery. The first paragraph leaves the reader dangling with an unanswered question on his mind, propelling him into the next paragraph and sometimes beyond for an answer. Like this one:

One day last summer during school vacation, a boy named Billy Shannon was at the Don CeSar Beach. He was swimming in the Gulf of Mexico. He was swimming near the deep water markers and he felt something rubbery slide against his leg and he saw a fin.*

This was written by a fourth grader, Karin Fraser of Bay Point Elementary School in South St. Petersburg, Fla. Never mind that the fin belonged to a friendly dolphin; Karin forces us onward to discover that, and so obeys the reader's unspoken command.

A quote lead can have mystery too, as this one illustrates:

LOUISVILLE, Ky.—Charles Davis says, "My job is like getting kissed a lot. My lips get sore, but I love it."

---

*Courtesy of writing coach Roy Peter Clark, associate director of the Poynter Institute in St. Petersburg, Fla., and a part-time instructor and adviser to writers putting out Bay Point's *Cougar Chronicle* ("if a fifth grader needs to know it, we'll print it").

A little corny, but it does the job. We have to find out who this man is and what he does for a living. Reading on, we discover that Davis is a transportation executive for General Electric, that freight forwarders woo him intensely to get his business, and that his company and others now view his kind of work as increasingly important.

Notice also that this lead is stripped of detail; nothing clutters up the central statement. This is a good idea in handling the very top of most stories. Uncommitted at this point, the reader is scanning idly and will be quick to pass over leads larded with extraneous detail. Stripping the lead gives it a simplicity that lets the mystery shine through clearly and, as with Davis, also may heighten that mystery. Contrast the Davis lead with the following on a story about drug marketing:

Isordil is the brand name of a nitrate drug prescribed to heart patients to prevent severe chest pains. Made by the Ives Laboratories division of American Home Products Corp., it was introduced in 1959 and has since grown to claim 46%—the largest share—of a market that now stands at $150 million a year.

This reads like an entry in a drug dictionary. It immediately entangles the reader in a thicket of numbers and names, and it lacks a tantalizing element. An alternative might be:

Isordil is just one of several similar nitrate drugs prescribed to prevent chest pains from heart disease. But it has seized almost half the entire market—not because of what's in it, but because its maker never stops talking about it.

Not great, but better. The lead suggests the importance of marketing, which is what the story is really about, but deliberately leaves obscure the exact nature of Isordil's promotion; we have to go on to find out precisely what is meant. Only the general reason for the drug's success is given, and then simply and baldly. And the clutter is gone. It's not important in this lead to list percentages, numbers, even the name of the manufacturer. These can be worked into the next paragraph or two, when the reader, having made his initial investment, will accept them more willingly.

Sometimes mystery can be added to a lead, as in this one about a fatal flaw in the cargo-door design of the DC-10 jetliner:

Crowded with 346 passengers and crew members, the Turkish Airlines DC-10 rose smoothly from Orly Airport in Paris, bound for London. Terror came at 12,000 feet.

The last sentence is deliberately inserted to lure the reader into what follows, a reconstruction of a crash caused when the rear cargo door blew off and caused explosive decompression that wrecked control systems. All aboard died in the ensuing crash.

More often curiosity is piqued by something the writer omits from the first paragraph rather than by something he supplies. The missing element can be anything: a motive, an identification, an explanation of a general statement. Now and then, in a longer lead, the writer may build suspense by creating a mystery in the first paragraph, solving it only partially in the second, and not lifting the veil all the way until the third. The Mexican migration piece provides one example:

NAPIZARO, Mexico—An astonishingly effective U.S. trade program is operating in this rural hamlet of 1,200 people—but Uncle Sam knows nothing about it. He wouldn't like it if he did.

Two mysteries: What kind of foreign-trade arrangement could function without U.S. knowledge? And why would it arouse displeasure if it was revealed?

Napizaro has street lights, new brick homes with TV antennas sprouting from their rooftops, a modern community center and infirmary, and a new bullring named "North Hollywood California." It is a fitting name. The money for the bullring and all the rest came from North Hollywood in exchange for Napizaro's main export: its male population.

We learn more, but not quite enough. What is the exact nature of the exchange?

For decades this town has systematically sent its men north to work as illegal aliens in small plants and businesses in the California community, and for decades they have sent their pay home, part of it earmarked for civic improvements.

Now we know everything—and have been compelled to make a three-paragraph investment in the process.

It's possible to go too far in trying to include mystery. Leads that have nothing in them *but* mystery, that lack story content and are little more that riddles or advertisements for what follows, are best avoided. The most common one is the billboard or tout lead, which only says, "Hey, have I got an interesting story to tell you." One illustration:

It was a real-life episode with elements worthy of a TV drama.

The story was about the size of a medical bill run up by a woman with a rare blood disorder. After reading it, I was pretty sure *General Hospital* wouldn't buy the script.

Tout leads almost always disappoint. After a breathless introduction a story had better be better than good, it had better be absolutely gripping. That's too much to expect of most pieces, and even those few with riveting drama are better handled by going immediately to the action and letting that drama seize the reader. This kind of product doesn't need advertising.

If anything, it benefits from being deliberately underplayed. Notice how the writer of the following lead, the opening of a story on the ethnic passions aroused by club-league soccer, set up a dramatic incident with a deceptively calm, leisurely approach:

LOS ANGELES—On a nippy, cloudy morn awhile back, one Julio Marchesan, captain of a local Ecuadorean–American soccer team, was watching his boys battle an Armenian team. Things were going badly for the Armenians, and in a spasm of frustration one of their players suddenly assaulted Mr. Marchesan—and bit his nose off.

Next, let's consider the forms good leads can take. When is it better, for example, to use a straightforward, hard-news type lead on a feature story than a soft one? When is it better to use a narrow-focus anecdotal or illustrative lead, one that entices the reader with a quote or slice of life that ties into a broader theme? And when is a more general, summary lead with a feature twist the best form to use?

The selection depends in part on the nature of the story. In writing features, many reporters automatically discard the idea of using a blunt, hard-news type of lead and instead put something cute or tricky at the top; after all, they are working on a feature, are they not? But if the tale develops information with solid news value, the writer must go for the throat, as in this lead:

BEVERLY HILLS—One of the biggest scandals in the history of the insurance industry is beginning to break around Equity Funding Corp. of America, a financial services concern with a go-go growth record in insurance sales.

The story, the first to disclose what was going on in the Equity Funding debacle, then detailed what later proved to be one of the largest and most blatant of all corporate frauds, involving billions of dollars worth of bogus insurance recorded as sold and later peddled to reinsurers; forgery of death claims and policy documents; massive cooking of the corporate books, and more.

The lead is not pretty but it has urgency, immediately telling the reader that something compellingly important is happening. An anecdotal or example lead would have buried that news, and a general lead with a tricky twist might have obscured its importance.

However, most feature stories lack a central development that qualifies as hard news. So the writer's choice usually is between the other two forms. The example or anecdotal type is much overused, probably because it is easier to write and because so many writers see it as a foolproof way to grab the reader's attention with a little color. This is a praiseworthy idea, but it often backfires if the little slice of life a reporter chooses doesn't meet certain standards:

1. Simplicity

The illustration used ought to be clearly and immediately understandable. The reader is not yet inclined to think his way through anything complicated. If the situation you describe requires more than the briefest explanation of how it relates to the theme of the story, the tale bogs down immediately and the reader flees. An ideal example lead can be hooked to what follows in a few words or, at most, a simple line or two.

If this hookup can't be made easily and gracefully, think about using another lead. Save your complex example for the body of the story where the reader, already having made a substantial investment, will be willing to reason it through with you. Replace it with something simpler, like this opening on a story about PIK, the government's plan to reduce future crop surpluses by paying farmers in excess commodities if they agree to idle some of their land:

ROCHESTER, Minn.—Piled up on Joe Thompson's farm is the bulk of two years' corn harvests—270,000 bushels in all, enough to keep the whole country in corn flakes for two weeks. The government wants to give him more.

This illustration is so simple and such a perfect reflection of the whole PIK program that it required no tie-in at all; the mystery is solved by defining PIK, which the writer would have had to do in any case.

2. Theme Relevance

For a story about Little Havana, Miami's Cuban enclave, the writer submitted a lead depicting an old man, known simply as the Man with the Picture, who carried with him everywhere a portrait of Fulgencio Batista, the dictator displaced by Fidel Castro. Hugging the picture to him, the old man is seen holding forth in a cafe about the glories of life in Cuba before the revolution.

This little sketch was well written, evocative, even touching. It would have made a fine lead on a story about how, after all these years, the Cuban exiles in Miami still remain bound to their homeland in spirit, and long to return.

But this story was about how the Cuban community was for the first time beginning to *cut* those emotional ties; Cubans were discarding the possibility of ever returning to the island, settling in as American citizens, and becoming more active politically. The lead was contrary to the thrust of the story.

When this happens, the deception has to be confessed and the reader's expectations shifted 180 degrees. He doesn't like this. No one likes being misled. In this case, the old man would have been better used as a perspective element in the scope section (showing that for some the pull of home is still powerful), or at the very end, which is where he wound up in the edited version.

3. Intrinsic Interest

Slice-of-life leads are only as good as the material used. In fact, dull people doing or saying dull things make worse leads than lackluster general openings. At least the latter get the reader into the story quickly instead of subjecting him to this sort of tedium:

> ESTHERVILLE, Iowa—When John Morrell & Co. announced plans to close beef-processing operations here in November, "everybody was worried," says Dean Hanson, who has slaughtered cattle and cut up beef at the plant for 25 years.

An acute case of the blahs. The quote is unexceptional and predictable, the passage plodding. Hanson's view lacks the quality of intrinsic interest needed in an example lead.

Newspapers use far too many leads like this. If some reporters get seduced by the charm of a contrary example, many more get seduced by the very form of the example lead, believing that the magic of personification can, by itself, turn a frog into a prince. It never does. If you lack vibrant examples, choose a general lead instead.

4. Focus

With certain possible exceptions, the example chosen for the lead should illustrate a key section of the story. Because the reader is conditioned by the lead, he expects the opening example to relate to an important matter treated fully in the body of the tale. If you instead open with an example that relates to a minor section well down in the story, or one that gets no further treatment at all, the reader may justifiably accuse you of false advertising.

By contrast, picking an example from a key section that will be treated heavily and early gives him a sense of promise fulfilled. In the story on farmland, the lead begins with tomato farmer Strano and his loss of land, immediately broadens to Dade County and, before and after the main theme statement, into the national picture. The lead suggests that *scope* will be an important section, and the immediate follow-up bears this out.

But be flexible. If the examples you can draw from key story sections are so-so, and you have a wonderfully engaging anecdote relevant to another part of the story, one that can slide easily into your main theme statement, by all means use it. The focus of a lead is less important than intrinsic interest. A lead that is faithful to every other requirement but is dull as dishwater commits the most mortal offense: It doesn't compel the reader to read on.

Be sure to focus somewhere, however. Don't write a fruit-salad lead, one in which scraps of detail and anecdotal material drawn from different parts of the story are tossed together and served to the reader in one heaping and confusing paragraph. My favorite wafted over the transom many years ago, and the original is lost to history now. But I remember it fairly well except for the names, for which I've made substitutions:

ADDIS ABABA, Ethiopia—From the glass-walled towers of this modern capital with its spanking new jetport, across the arid plains of the Umgatz Plateau, to the jagged hills of the Southwest and the yurts of the Boogie Woogie tribe, where chieftain Abu Blu arises each morning to urinate out his tent flap to see which way the wind is blowing . . .

And on and on.

A diverting passage, certainly, but no lead. Everything but tomatoes and anchovies is in it, but we still haven't a clue about what it means. All we can tell is that we're in Ethiopia, and that isn't enough.

The above laundry list of requirements for a good example or anecdotal lead suggests that more writers ought to think first about using a general or summary one. This type can propel the reader into the heart of the story more quickly, as in this 1977 lead about fraud associated with the rising use of minicomputers (hot stuff then) by businesses:

Here come the minicomputers—and, right behind them, here come the crooks.

In 12 words the writer identifies the main elements in his tale and suggests the connection between them, leaving enough mystery to push us onward. Within a few lines more, we have seen the scope of the minicomputer invasion, and are already learning how the decentralization of data processing these machines make possible is inspiring more embezzlement and other frauds.

The general lead also conserves precious focus-points-and-people material. Often, the writer will have little such material that is worthwhile; if he blows too much on a lead, the body of his story will lack illustration and appear weak and unconvincing.

But general leads can be damnably difficult to write. They are all summaries of story action—but how is the writer to express a summary in an interesting way? Where does the feature twist come from?

As we've suggested, it may simply pop out of the right side of his brain while he's using the left to write the body of the piece. When this *doesn't* happen, a good general lead can be created after he's written the rest of the story by retooling the main theme statement.

In doing this, the writer may adopt a breezier or more dramatic tone than he did in writing the original—and he will leave out of his new version one or more of the important elements he had included before, thus creating a mystery at the top of the story that forces the reader on. In effect, he turns his main theme statement into his lead. Getting no sudden flashes of inspiration while writing the following story, that's what I did after I was finished with the body of it:

FORT McDOWELL, Ariz.—The 360 Yavapai Indians on this small reservation, the shrunken remnant of thousands who once lived on 10 million Arizona acres, have won their first great victory over the white man. He wanted to stuff some $33 million into their pockets. They told him to get lost.

The money would have been paid for a patch of Yavapai desert flooded by the proposed Orme Dam, the keystone of a $1 billion federal water project that practically every element of Arizona's political and economic power structure has lusted after for 13 years. But the huge dam at the confluence of the Salt and Verde rivers would have inundated up to 17,000 of the 25,000 acres the tribe has left, and forced its relocation.

So the Yavapai (pronounced yah-vuh-PIE), who were never even consulted about the dam when it was first authorized in 1968, dug in for a last stand. They lobbied in Congress, marched on a "trail of tears" to the state capitol, and picketed Sen. Barry Goldwater at a public appearance. "This was our last piece of homeland," says tribal chairman Norman Austin. "There was no other place for a people who had been sent wandering over the desert for so many years."

Government Caves In

The government, of course, could have just condemned the property, kicked out the Yavapai, and paid them off anyway. But confronted by their refusal to sell voluntarily at any price, by rising public sympathy for them and by the certainty of a lawsuit by the Indians and their environmentalist allies (the dam would have drowned the South Verde's riparian habitat, bald-eagle nesting sites and archaeological ruins), the dam's proponents are caving in.

Now most of them have reversed course, to support an alternative plan that won't affect the Yavapai. The final decision will be made by Interior Secretary James Watt, who has already informally backed the alternative: official approval won't be announced until environmental-impact statements are completed, but it is generally agreed that the Orme Dam is dead.

"It's pretty amazing," says Lawrence Achenbrenner, an attorney for the Native American Rights Fund, who aided the Yavapai in their struggle. "All sorts of well-intentioned people told the Yavapai they were sticking their heads in the sand, that if they'd just negotiate, they could make a heck of a deal. The $33 million was a tentative bargaining offer, really. What these people have done is an example to other tribes who can now say, 'By God, if we get together and don't give up, we can win too.' "

Meanwhile, on their mountain-ringed piece of Sonoran desert, the Indians celebrate because they don't have to take Uncle Sam's money. When news of Secretary Watt's preliminary opinion was announced a month ago, some elders wept or cried out with joy. "I ran down here hollerin' and my daughter said, 'Are you sick? Are you crazy?' " recalls Bessie Mike, a 73-year-old basket weaver.

A great billowing woman in a print dress, she sits under a tree outside a tiny cinder-block home painted lilac; a rusting Plymouth Fury is sinking into the desert nearby. She has just received $1,100 for basketry it took her four months to make. Couldn't she use $100,000 or so? Why not sell the land? "This is our place," she says simply.

Not all Yavapai opposed the dam. One living off the reservation,

Michele Guerrero of Mesa, has publicly criticized the tribe's decision, saying that the money could have been of immeasurable help in raising the tribe's standard of living and educational level. Many whites also find the decision incomprehensible for the same reason. "I still think they made a mistake," says one state official. "Just think of what they could have done for themselves with all that money."

But some Yavapai cheerfully admit they would probably just blow much of it on a spending binge. One tells of a cousin who got $1,500, part of an overall $5.1 million land-claim settlement distributed among the tribe in the mid-1970s. He splurged on an expensive Western outfit, including red boots, started nipping on a jug, and extended grants and loans to hangers-on. He awoke the next morning sans money and everything else. Even the boots were gone.

So to the Yavapai, the white man's money is ice but the land is diamonds. A profound and mystical connection to that land, something many whites don't comprehend, is at the root of the Yavapai resistance. In a tribal vote five years ago, 144 of them voted to hold the land and 57 voted to sell it, with most of the latter votes apparently coming from tribal members living off the reservation. Today, it is difficult to locate anyone living at Fort McDowell who admits he voted to sell.

Like other tribes, the Yavapai hold their land in common, not as individual plots, and they view it as an integral part of their religion and culture. "Land should not belong to people—people belong to the land," says Virginia Mott, an outspoken opponent of the dam.

Tribal religion and culture have been in decline, slowly eroded by neglect and by white influences. The Yavapai tongue is dying out, the last medicine man is gone, and knowledge of the old faith and customs resides mostly among the elders. But enough of the Yavapai way remains in the tribal consciousness to make even the thought of drowning the land a desecration.

Honored Dead

There are prayer grounds here consecrated by medicine men of old. There is the neatly tended cemetery, all graves aligned to face the sacred mountain called Four Peaks. To the Yavapai, the dead remain a part of the community, and to disturb them would be deeply troubling. (One grave holds the honored bones of Carlos Montezuma, a Yavapai physician and a powerful spokesman for all Indian interests until his death in 1923. He had predicted that the whites one day would try to build a dam that would flood the reservation. "White people's heads are long," he wrote. "They can see many years ahead.")

Finally, there are the Kakakas, the secretive Old Ones who are the guardians and protectors of the Yavapai. In tribal lore, they are tiny people, three or four feet tall, immortal, and live on Four Peaks, Superstition Mountain, and Red Mountain, as well as in ruins at Fort McDowell that the Yavapai avoid. Flood out the Kakakas? Unthinkable.

Beyond their reverence for the land itself, the Yavapai also harbor a historically justified skepticism about white promises. In the 1860s the U.S. cavalry promised them food, clothing and land if they would settle near Army forts; they got starvation and smallpox instead. Lumped in with the far more warlike Apache (they still are called Mohave-Apache, though their language is entirely different), they were mowed down by Army rifles at Skeleton Cave, Bloody Basin, Skull Valley.

Landing on Reservation

Rounded up again on land they were told would be theirs, they were again displaced and sent on a forced march of 180 miles to the Apache reservation of San Carlos. Many died. They finally got their own reservation here in 1903 and have clung to it since, despite repeated threats to move them into the nearby Salt River reservation with their ancestral foes, the Pimas.

Thus, they were wary of white promises about the benefits they would enjoy from the dam. One was exclusive concessions for boating and fishing on the lake it would form. Beyond the fact that Yavapai hate fish and don't like still water, it wasn't made clear until recently that the lake level would fluctuate so drastically that the place would be a mud flat much of the time, which would have left the Indians operating the only landlocked marina in the U.S.

Though they apparently have won the fight against the Orme Dam, the Yavapai and their allies have little confidence that they will be left alone from now on. Carolina Butler, a feisty white housewife from Scottsdale who has aided the Yavapai from the beginning, wants an endangered Indian law to protect small tribes everywhere from destruction by such projects. Tribal member Phil Dorchester, noting that water wells in Phoenix and Scottsdale have been poisoned by chemicals, says fatalistically: "They'll come up here sooner or later to try to get more water from the Verde. They'll have to."

The young will have to be vigilant, says John Williams, 77 and wheelchair-bound. "I am a man of rubber now," he says, indicating his useless legs, "but I would tell the young people this: The God behind blue heaven made this land for his people. Do not sell it. Do not lease it. Pass it down. All this my own father told me too."

The first sentence of the lead shows the reader that the Yavapai are a small, dying tribe driven into a corner by historic white expansionism, and, by citing the size of the tribe, gives the amount of money involved the proper perspective. The last part of the first sentence reveals a surprising turn of events: The Indians, historic losers, have won for a change. The final two sentences are a skeletal, featurized statement of what happened.

Essentially, this is the main theme statement I wrote at the beginning of my work on this story, with a couple of items deliberately omitted. Why offer $33 million? For what? Most mysterious of all, however, is the Indians' motive for rejecting what to them would be an enormous sum, enough to lift the tribe and every reservation resident out of poverty into relative affluence. It's this unexplained element of motive that forces the reader on; he is driven to discover the *why* of things.

In other leads he may be left in the dark about the *how*. He's given a brief summary of everything except the exact operation of the process mentioned in the lead, and this small mystery is enough. It's used in this lead on a simple story about people who make a living telling others how to have fun:

LOS ANGELES—If you can't decide what to do with your free time, you might spend part of it finding out what to do with the rest of it. For a small fee, a leisure consultant will help you out.

We're told everything of importance except what a leisure consultant actually does. The writer is counting on the unusual nature of the business to pique reader interest and is careful not to be too explicit about how that business works, at least in the lead.

A little more mystery could have been inserted if the lead had been written this way:

LOS ANGELES—If you can't decide what to do with your free time, you might spend some of it listening to a new breed of expert tell you what to do with the rest of it. But bring money.

This lead not only obscures the *how* but is a little vague about the *who* as well.

HANDLING NUMBERS

We know that too many numbers are poison, so the writer's first impulse should be to omit unessential ones. But that's as painful as root-canal work to those of us whose days are filled with numbers—numbers vital to the breaking corporate and financial news stories inside *The Wall Street Journal*. In many such stories, numbers define the news or are the news.

It's only natural, then, that some writers come to believe numbers per se possess a magical power of definition. They collect statistics by the bushel and, having gone to such pains, use them at the slightest excuse in every story they do. Then they wonder why editors find their features stupefyingly dull.

A wrenching change in attitude is required when doing features, where story values must be defined in other than just numerical ways. This change is easier to make if the writer remembers that fiction writers, who could bury us under invented figures to lend definition to their tales, never do so. They know better.

I don't imply that we should omit meaningful statistics to avoid boring readers. This would sacrifice substance for form, an error that a novelist may get away with but that we cannot. We need numbers in almost all our stories, and in some a number may be so important or startling that omitting or generalizing it would weaken the whole piece. I only argue that we be choosy in selecting figures and careful in their treatment.

In placing numbers in a story, the good writer tries not to stack too many in one paragraph; this builds a wall of abstraction difficult to breach. It becomes impossible to breach when two or more such paragraphs are butted together, a construction that may lead to more unread prose than any other writing fault. Don't do this. Don't ever do this.

The good writer also recasts as many numbers as he can in a simpler or more pictorial form that removes some of their abstraction. If a precise figure is not important, he rounds it off: $2.6 million is cleaner and easier than $2,611,423. If something increased by 36.7%, he may say it went up more than a third. If it increased 98%, he says it almost doubled. These expressions are pictorial in that they let the reader visualize a slice of a pie, or two pies where there was one before.

Use ratios to simplify large numbers. Instead of saying that 14,654,231 American drivers out of a total of 58,013,261 own foreign cars, a writer may simply say that one in four American drivers owns a foreign auto. Smaller numbers can be grasped, while large ones remain abstract.

If a set of related numbers is involved, the writer must decide exactly what he wants to convey and construct a passage to do that limited job in the simplest way. Say we want to show that a federal agency is getting serious about a certain problem by spending a lot more money on it. Without thought, we might put it this way:

Spending on redundancy research by the Office of Unessential Affairs rose from $847 million in fiscal 1983 to $1.26 billion this year, a 49% increase.

This has four numbers and high density. Our purpose—to show the current magnitude of the effort and how that magnitude has increased—is better served in the following, which also avoids the passive sentence structure:

Over the past fiscal year the Office of Unessential Affairs increased spending on redundancy research by almost half, to $1.26 billion.

If a large, incomprehensible number is important to a story, it'll have a clearer meaning when the writer can supply an equivalent that's easier to visualize. In a story about water waste in Arizona, for example, we must point out that the state's annual groundwater overdraft (the amount sucked out of the acquifers in excess of natural recharge) is about 2.5 million acre feet. But what does that *mean*? I can visualize a foot of water, but I have trouble visualizing an acre, much less 2.5 million of them. The quantity becomes more comprehensible—and more impressive—when I'm told it would submerge New York City 11 feet deep. I know New York is a big place; I now can *see* that the quantity of water is enormous. A number has been turned into a picture, picking up power and interest in the process.

HANDLING PEOPLE AND QUOTES

Too many stories are cluttered by the inclusion of too many people. The few doing or saying something interesting are buried by the many who are just beating their gums, and the reader quickly gets confused trying to keep track of everyone. (This flaw can wreck an investigative story because the writer usually has an intricate plot development problem to begin with. He only compounds it by dragging in platoons of subsidiary sources. His piece may be read with interest by his relatives and law-enforcement sources, but it gives everyone else a migraine by the fifth paragraph.)

I wouldn't pay $30 to watch a play that lacks development of main characters and instead relies on two dozen spear carriers, each speaking a couple of lines. Yet many of us inflict something similar on readers. Our stories are filled with talking heads—forgettable sources who utter a forgettable line or two and are banished or, worse, who are recalled later for another humdrum quote when everyone has clean forgotten who they are.

The writer who does this greatly slows his story pace, impairs its clarity and force, and increases its length. For what?

Many talking heads are there to state the obvious for the writer too timid to do so himself. They are crutches to help him hobble through his tale. No writer, I hope, would bother to quote a leading astronomer on the certainty that the sun will rise to the east tomorrow, but more than a few reflexively use sources to make story conclusions that either don't need to be made, or that they should have made themselves.

Other talking heads are recruited to assure the reader that the writer has done his homework, has talked to a lot of people. See? Here they all are. This writer suffers an anxiety attack if he finishes two paragraphs without quoting someone. He thinks the reader will not believe what he is saying. But the reader doesn't care. He would rather have facts and action anyway.

In both these cases, fear leads the writer to abdicate his job as storyteller and hide behind sources. At other times he may be seduced by them. If he's taken a liking to a genial, cooperative source, he may unconsciously slip that person into his story even if the material supplied is weak or unnecessary. The writer is being a nice guy and saying thank you, but the reader is tapping his foot, impatient for the niceties to end.

A good writer is merciless in deciding who gets into his piece. Each person must have a story purpose or be excluded; scores of sources may have been interviewed, but that's the worst reason for putting most of them into the story.

This doesn't mean, of course, that the omitted interviews were a waste of time. We report exhaustively not to convince the reader but ourselves; seven or eight people may be interviewed without appearing in the story, just so we can make with confidence a single, strong, conclusive statement. This is what the reader pays for, not a procession of talking heads.

It helps to have high standards for the use of all quotations. The source usually ought to offer one or more of the following to warrant being quoted:

Credibility: The source is making a significant statement or interpretation about something in which he is expert by training or experience. His credentials give his words far greater weight than anything you might say, so enlist that credibility.

Every reporter knows this, but some err in paying more attention to the credentials of the source than to what he utters. A luminary who offers muddled, vague, or ambiguous statements, or who is simply spouting the obvious, is a luminary not worth quoting. One wishes the reporter had tacked him to the wall during the interview instead of meekly jotting down whatever pap the Great Man deigned to give him. Credentials are nice, but they mean nothing until married to substance.

Emotional Response: Try to put it in direct quotes. I can't offer an airtight rational argument for this. It just seems best that a person be allowed to express his feelings in his own way. His reasoning and opinions I may summarize, but I don't believe my license extends to editing the inner man.

Trenchancy: The source expresses himself sharply and forcefully, like a small-town real estate man I once met who, at war with the mayor, called him a "plum-assed dingbat." The source may be keenly incisive, or use attractive imagery, regionalisms or slang that give his utterances a distinct and authentic flavor. His words have punch and pungency.

Variety: Now and then a quote is helpful as a final clincher for a point you are trying to make, particularly if that quote provides the last leg on that pleasing construction, the three-legged stool. But if the quote has no substance, emotion or trenchancy, don't use it even as a device.

The writer who sets high standards for quotes finds that good things happen to his work. His stories become clearer because fewer people clutter them up. The action in them becomes predominant, and the pace picks up noticeably. The good quotes he does use stand out because they're not smothered by banal ones. Seeing this, he becomes convinced at last that the sheer number of people in his work is not important in convincing anyone of anything.

I probably interviewed 35 people for the Boomtowns story. Only four are quoted by name, and three other quotes are unattributed, yet I think this is a convincing story. The piece about the loss of prime farmland has only six people in it out of dozens interviewed. I don't think more would have made it any better.

As the number of characters diminishes, those remaining loom larger in the reader's mind. They become more than talking heads and begin to take on identities of their own. The storyteller wants this to happen and works to advance the process.

If one character is more important than others, if he's to appear more than once in the story or is otherwise prominent, the writer may want to use a bit of descriptive detail, just a few words, to build up that character's identity and ensure that he'll be remembered. In the farmlands piece, Rosie Strano is described as "a bull of a man, sweating in air that feels like damp, hot velvet." This snippet is of no importance whatever to story development. It was inserted to build up Strano's identity as an important actor.

The same thing is done to logger Spider Mason. We meet him first as just one of the men on the crew bus. Shortly afterward, when we are about to fix on the tragic history of his family, he is reintroduced: "Spider Mason, tall, dark and talkative ('Spider wore out two pair of lips before he was 18,' says a co-worker) . . ."

While building up some characters, usually only one or two, the writer may want to suppress the importance of others to heighten the contrast between important actors and supporting players. He may do this by giving the latter something to do but nothing to say. They become extras in his movie, animate bits of scenery. In the cowboy story, for one, creating an identity for profile subject Jim Miller out of his own words and actions was the paramount task. Too much gabble by outsiders would have weakened this effort, so only two other people, a cowhand and the ranch owner, were directly quoted in the story.

But it was also necessary to show that Miller was part of a community of cowmen and representative of a certain way of life. So I recruited six extras in silent support of this point. Most appear in two passages of perspective near the end, after Miller says he sees no future in the cattle business:

Perhaps not. But around Yavapai County the cycle of ranch life continues unchanged on the surviving family spreads. In Peeple's Valley, cougars have taken 15 calves this year, and lion hunter George Goswick is tracking them through the Weaver Mountains. In the pastures, mares are heavy with foals; in time, some will find their way into the gentling hands of Twister Heller, the horse breaker. On the Hays ranch, owner John Hays is stabbing a wild-eyed Hereford bull in the rump with a needle full of antibiotics and fretting about the grasshoppers that are all over the property. . . .

Next year, when he's 65, Mr. Miller plans to quit as cowboss at the Rafter Eleven and start collecting Social Security. But he says he will never stop working. Few men around here who have spent their lives on a horse seem able to get off. Jim's friend Tom Rigden still rides roundup and castrates calves on his ranch, though he has been blind for almost eight years . . .

A more common way to suppress identity is to quote anonymously, a device particularly useful in stories that demand a large cast of characters. Making some of them faceless keeps a story from reading like the phone book.

Unlike the cowboy piece, which focuses on one man, the logger story is a collective profile about a group of men divided into subclasses whose experiences are different. Many voices are needed to tell this kind of tale, but the risk of confusing the reader is great. This is why only 12 of the 20 people appearing have names. And with only two exceptions the testimony of each person named is isolated in one place in the story, further preventing confusion.

But anonymous quotes must be used judiciously. They're already a plague, in part because so many reporters are so quick to offer anonymity even before the source opens his mouth. A story riddled with pronouncements from mystery figures makes any reader suspicious, and ultimately irritated; he longs to meet a flesh-and-blood individual who will rip off his mask and say what he thinks. When this doesn't happen, the persuasiveness of the whole story, however accurate it may be, is impaired. It becomes a whispered innuendo instead of a convincing statement.

So at least strive for attribution of every statement where the credibility of the speaker is important in proving a point. Limit anonymous quotes to lesser matters, passing observations or utterances that only clinch or support other evidence like this:

The forest also is unforgiving of error, and a movement's carelessness can wound or kill. About 15,000 men are usually working in the Washington woods; over the past three years they have suffered a total of almost 28,000 injuries and 75 deaths. "It's you against the trees," says a veteran woodsman.

The quote is trenchant, and lends variety to the passage—but it's the figures that convince.

Sometimes the credibility of a source is vital, but what he utters is so dull or rambling that a direct quote would be difficult. Taken as a whole, his meaning is clear but his manner of expression muddies it for the reader. In this event, use the name and credentials of the source but paraphrase what he said. You retain his credibility while providing a clearer, livelier idea of his meaning.

Paraphrasing also can help stories that might otherwise have too many direct quotes, or passages where quotes are being used consecutively. This isn't supposed to happen to begin with, of course, but sometimes you won't be able to get the variety of proofs you seek and will have to rely on multiple testimony. If so, try putting the most trenchant, substantive statement in quotes and paraphrase the other ones. This may give only the illusion of variety, but it's better than stacking direct quotes.

When choosing among quotes, favor the short and sharp over the long and dull, and trim the statement down to its nubbin of meaning. You may find yourself directly quoting only a single phrase or just one word. Never mind. If the word or phrase is an apt or telling one, it'll be all the more forceful when stripped of clutter. But never use several incomplete fragments in a single sentence like this:

Mr. Borland says the prune is "a pretty awful" fruit that is difficult to sell to youthful customers because of its "Ex-Lax" image as something "for senior citizens."

The reader of such a sentence has to strain to be sure of who's addressing him from moment to moment. And he may, as I do, get the impression that the writer didn't fully grasp the central meaning of what the source said and is trying to cover up.

HANDLING ENDINGS

A good ending is an enormous help in meeting the reader's last demand: Help me remember it all. However, one kind of ending that often does that in fiction—the revelation, in which some new and vitally important fact, development or chain of logic is suddenly disclosed, bringing the story to a peaking kind of denouement—isn't useful in newspaper work. We can profitably adopt other tricks of the novelist, but newspaper readers don't have the time or patience to wait for revelatory endings. Instead, we have to drive home our established themes in other ways. Most of the best endings I read fall into the following three broad categories:

Circling Back

This kind of ending reminds the reader of the central message of the story, or of key elements in it. But often it does so indirectly, using material the reporter wouldn't employ as factual proofs—symbols, emotional responses, observations, even snippets of poetry.

At the close of the Disney profile, for example, we are taken to one of the company's "universities," where the writer tells us:

Though these (the "universities") are mainly for the young people who staff the parks, even veteran employees return for refresher courses in Traditions I, II, III and IV—in large part a compendium of Walt's ideas and philosophy. A young Disney instructor shows a visitor a series of placards illustrating the "Disney Ways." The first says: "What do we do? We create happiness."

This simple ending is full of overtones and echoes of the body of the story. We are reminded of the central purpose of the company. We see again, in a different form, the enduring power of the dead founder; his truths are passed through the generations, making him immortal in a way. And we sense subliminally that striving for order and control that is mentioned directly in the story. "We create happiness," says Disney, as if that precious thing really could be summoned forth and commanded, by exercise of the corporate will, to take the shapes of dancing bears and talking Volkswagens.

In the story about the loss of farmlands, the central themes are reflected in Strano's distress and, separately, in a few verses:

In Dade County, Rosie Strano drives out in his pickup to look at his lost land. He does this three or four times a year and gets upset every time. In Washington, Mr. Hidlebaugh, the soil scientist, keeps a poem from a professional journal on his wall. The last two stanzas:

> Beneath the sprawling shopping mall
> That shrouds a hidden secret pall—
> A field that cannot heed the call
> That's made by sun and rain.
>
> Behold the suburbs and their yield;
> Beneath the web of streets is sealed
> The coffin of a fertile field
> The ghost of unborn grain.

Often a simple summary is all that is needed to give the reader the sense of closure he wants. This is done in the last paragraph of the story about the relief pitcher:

For the week, Lew has pitched 9⅓ scoreless innings but doesn't have a win or save to show for it. The season is drawing to a close and his hopes for a reprieve grow dimmer. "I guess it's all been for nothing," he says. There are three more games in Albuquerque, and then it is home to Tucson for El Taco night.

This ending recalls what has already been detailed—the promotion-crazy nature of minor league ball, the sense of impending failure that has been mounting in the reliever, the wearying grind of travel.

Looking Ahead

We've touched on the importance of reporting for future aspects. If that reporting proves fruitful the future probably offers more chances to close stories than any other element, because it tends to fall naturally at or near the end of most tales. There are exceptions, but the future, being always unknown, is seldom a crucial aspect in story plans. In the body of the story we usually emphasize what is happening now, not what might happen.

This is proper. But what might be useless speculation clogging up the middle of a piece can become evocative material at its very end. In the story about Finis Mitchell, the old mountain man, such a close is used to help the reader remember the subject. Mitchell is asked how long he can keep climbing before injury, death or fraility overcome him:

Mr. Mitchell concedes that he is slowing down noticeably now, that the slopes are steeper than they were. But he is convinced that the Creator wouldn't play such a dirty trick on him, not now anyway. "I figure I'm good till about 90," he adds. That would give him 12 years. There are 20 peaks still to go.

If the reader has any imagination, he will see in his mind's eye the old man climbing on, racing time, after the story has ended.

At the end of the Yavapai story we find two Indians looking to the future:

Though they apparently have won the fight against the Orme dam, the Yavapai and their allies have little confidence that they will be left alone from now on. Carolina Butler, a feisty white housewife from Scottsdale who has aided the Yavapai from the beginning, wants an endangered-Indian law to protect small tribes everywhere from destruction by such projects. Tribal member Phil Dorchester, noting that water wells in Phoenix and Scottsdale have been poisoned by chemicals, says fatalistically: "They'll come up here sooner or later to try to get more water from the Verde. They'll have to."

The young will have to be vigilant, says John Williams, 77 and wheelchair-bound. "I am a man of rubber now," he says, indicating his useless legs, "but I would tell the young people this: The God behind blue heaven made this land for his people. Do not sell it. Do not lease it. Pass it down. All this my own father told me too."

Phil Dorchester's future is a factual, dispassionate one based on logic, while John Williams's is poetic and the best quote in the story. They give the piece both a natural closing and a dimension it would have lacked otherwise. This sort of material doesn't just fall over the transom. You have to ask for it.

Spreading Out

To use this kind of ending you must deliberately violate a rule stated earlier, the one about restricting the range of the story so you can tell some of it well instead of all of it poorly.

The rule still holds for the rest of the piece. But by ignoring it at the very end, you suddenly open the lens of the reader's perception by giving him something new to think about. This ending makes the story bigger than it was before, something worth remembering.

The range of the boomtowns story, for example, was severely limited to what was being done about the obvious problems such communities have. It is a practical, nuts-and-bolts piece about the actions of corporations, states and localities, a story about money and things.

But at the end a new and different element is tossed at the reader:

But even with the amenities supplied by corporate and tax money, and even with the jobs for local youths that energy development provides, there is a price for boomtowns to pay. The people of the rural West know it well. "The days when an old person who's lived here all his life could walk down the street and know and greet everyone—that's all gone," says a resident of Forsyth, Mont., affected by mining and power-plant construction. And on the open plains of the North Dakota Power Triangle, where shovels claw at the rangeland and draglines tower over hills of coal like giant black mantises, many ranchers lament the changes now occurring.

One is Werner Benfit, 50 years old, who has been ranching here all his life. Part of his spread is being torn up by the power shovels now. "We fought them for three or four years but we lost," he says. "I wish they'd never come."

The reader now confronts a part of the boomtown syndrome not treated before. The social character of these little communities is being changed by their growth, and the beauty of their surroundings is being degraded. These effects can't be measured and defy practical fixes.

What's more, we are told how people feel about this in a story that otherwise has little or no emotion to it. By introducing emotional response, we are trying to remind the reader that these towns are places where humans live and not just abstract municipal units in a problem-solving exercise.

HANDLING YOURSELF

We know the writer must be in his story. But when should he enter and to what extent dare he impose himself on the reader? Three roles for him:

1. Summarizer/Concluder

Throughout his tale, the writer must pull together bits of related material and give the assembled units meaning. Most often he expresses his summaries and conclusions at the beginning of a passage and then lets the reader see those quotes, numbers and illustrations that led him to make his statement. The process repeats itself: assertion, proofs, new assertion, new proofs.

These summaries and conclusions shouldn't be more forceful or dramatic than the material that supports them. At one point in the Disney story, the author summarizes the opinions of Disney critics by saying that they "view the empire as one huge, multispigoted dispenser of schlock culture." This is strong meat.

But the single quote from Richard Schickel used as illusration is just as forceful:

"Disney's machine was designed to shatter the two most valuable things about childhood—its secrets and its silences—thus forcing everyone to share the same formative dreams. It has placed a Mickey Mouse hat on every little developing personality in America. As capitalism, it is a work of genius; as culture, it is mostly a horror."

Suppose Schickel had said the following instead:

"As capitalism, Disney is a work of genius. As culture, it is too explicit. There is nothing wrong with entertainment, but too many children are getting all their dreams and fantasies from Disney instead of from their own imaginations."

This is still critical, but softer in tone and lacking implications of malevolent design on Disney's part. If this quote was topped by the original summary, it would not justify the strength of that summary and the writer could be accused of overstatement.

At certain times the wise writer backs away from crisp, definitive summaries and conclusions, and walks on tiptoe through his tale or certain passages within it. He does so when he's entering the terrain of the genuine expert, and when he's dealing with particularly controversial or highly charged subjects.

For example, unless he happens to be a plasma physicist a writer has no business concluding that nuclear fusion power is just around the corner because five of seven specialists in the field say so. The writer lacks the expertise to assess their opinions and evidence, and the reader knows that. So any conclusion or summary must be limited and muted. The writer may accurately say that experimental evidence suggests to many scientists that a breakthrough in fusion power has occurred or is imminent. Then he ducks out of the way and lets the experts and the evidence speak, including the contrary evidence. This is no place for sweeping assertions by typewriter jockeys.

Other subject areas are so loaded with emotional charge that the writer hesitates to flex his muscles even when he has uncommon expertise and the weight of evidence seems to dictate a strong conclusion. A medical writer well versed in oncology, for example, might be advised to back off from making conclusions about a possible cure for many common cancers, even though every piece of evidence and opinion he has collected indicates that a new enzyme therapy is working. His conclusions would probably be extremely cautious, only pointing the reader to test results and other hard evidence. There are simply too many lives at stake or otherwise touched by this development, too many expectations that could be raised only to be shattered later. So the writer lets the reader come to judgment by himself.

These exceptions aside, a writer simply has to reject his fear of being wrong, his impulse to fudge and hedge to protect himself, and state plainly and firmly what the evidence adds up to. His conclusions and summaries are the spine of his story and, taken together, impart is central message. Timidity dilutes the power of that message, as here:

The Martian invaders seem to be gaining most ground in northern New Jersey. The only troops in Bergen County have been "wiped out almost to the last man," according to the final radio message from their commander, and civilians fleeing Ridgewood say the aliens have executed all the newspaper editors in town. Aerial photos show no buildings left standing in Hackensack and Paterson, marines attempting a counter-attack from the south have been repulsed with 60% casualties, and all but five combat aircraft have been destroyed by Martian particle-beam weapons. "They have total air superiority and seem to have cut off all our units left in the area," says Gen. James Wiegand, commander of Region III.

A weaseled conclusion. "Seem to be gaining most ground," my Aunt Tillie. The Martians have blown us away while locking up all of North Jersey, and we ought to say so.

2. Referee

A storyteller must seize control of disputants in a story or passage, or he will be left on the sidelines wringing his hands while the antagonists squabble endlessly. Conflict is drama, but when it degenerates into bickering the reader learns nothing and quickly gets bored.

A writer may fall into this trap if he treats a complex dispute as a Ping-Pong match. A has made a specific criticism of B, so in his story our writer dutifully trots over to B, who answers A's criticism and looses a dart of his own at the accuser. The writer scurries back to A and the process continues. The circle of dispute widens and the items of contention grow more trivial, but it's difficult to stop the contest. When it finally does end, the reader is left with an overlong story or passage, spattered with too many quotes and confusingly organized.

The writer avoids this by using critical judgment and a different structure for the dispute. First, he assembles the accusations and criticisms of both sides. Then he throws out most of the gratuitous insults (keeping perhaps one or two to show the depth of feeling of the parties), along with charges that either can't be proved or seem baseless on the evidence. This leaves him with the meat of the dispute.

He then organizes it as an artillery duel, not a Ping-Pong match. One side is allowed to fire its ammunition; its adversaries then do likewise. The arguments of each side become more forceful and easier to follow when kept together this way. The whole passage will be shorter and punchier, too.

3. Observer

In treating the centrally important sections of his story, the writer serves mainly as a guide. He makes conclusions any prudent layman could make, but he must also list at least some of the evidence supporting each of them. Without this, his piece is opinionated and hollow. On the periphery of the tale, however, he becomes more than a guide. Using his license as the reader's agent, he may become another source for the story he is telling.

And why not? He is informed about his subject, or ought to be. He is a trained eyewitness. He has met people, been to places and seen developments the reader has not. All this gives him a measure of credibility, though a limited one.

If he is satisfied that he has the knowledge, he may make flat statements or observations about minor matters, those not at the core of the story and not worth dragging in outside material to develop. The reader, who wants to see convincing evidence behind all major conclusions, will trust the writer in smaller things.

This license should be used to provide a sense of locale and character, elements important to fiction writers. We all have read datelined stories that give us no sense at all of the place or the people in it; the writer could have reported the whole thing by phone and saved the airfare.

Often just a few words physically describing a place or a player are enough to lift them out of the mass of type and given them life. At other times the writer may simply comment on their *natures*. He may call the retirement town of Truth or Consequences, N.M., "a remote provincial capital of the prune-juice belt" or say that San Diego is "so laid-back it sometimes seems comatose."

Now and then the reader will accept the word of his agent on weightier matters, provided there's no one around more credible. We've seen how this license was exercised in the cowboy story when I wanted to show the difference between cowpunching and other work; as an observer of both worlds, I felt qualified to give an assessment myself. Subjective opinion also appears at the end of the logger story, when I tell the reader that the demise of the virgin forest and its replacement by tree farms will rob the work of some of its hazardous glamor.

Writers who shun the observer's role either document minor points they could have handled themselves, or fail to treat them at all. In the first case, this means inclusion of too many marginal sources and too much trivial information: The important sections of the story are smothered by it, overquoting is rampant, the pace slows, the risk of reader confusion increases and the piece becomes overlong. In the second case, the story is flat, drab, impersonal.

But the writer-observer must step in cautiously. His comments should never be based on sheer speculation, sketchy second-hand evidence or his personal leanings. They should come out of his experience in covering the story and the people in it, and he must always hesitate and ask himself: Am I being fair? Do I have enough evidence, from my own senses and from my research, to say what I am about to say? Reckless generalizations hurt people, including those who write them.

Even if the answers are affirmative the writer should hesitate to enter the story too often; his words are digressions too, and slow story action. When there's too much reporter, there's not enough story.

CHAPTER 7

WORDCRAFT

Another heresy: Artful and impeccable use of the language is less important in storytelling than you might think. A well-shaped idea, convincing illustration and interpretation of it, and sound story structure count for more. Lacking these, the writer who follows all the instructions on fine-tuning his prose in all the books extant will produce a well-written failure. The reader may not be able to sense this immediately, but he'll sense it before he's finished. Chinese-dinner stories are tasty going down, but they don't satisfy.

It's equally true, however, that when superior wordcraft is added to a story well wrought in other respects, the results can be arresting. A so-so piece becomes a good one, and a goo one may become a piece of work that lingers in the reader's mind for a long time. This ought to be every writer's ultimate goal.

Wordcraft begins with proper grammar, syntax and usage, subjects I lack the space or qualifications to treat. So we'll assume you have command of them and go on to treat wordcraft as a working writer does. Already versed in the technical fundamentals, he's mainly interested in how to achieve certain effects at certain places in his story.

Some of his considerations:

SPECIFICITY

Some words and phrases are blobs. Others are paintbrushes whose narrow meanings instantly create pictures in the reader's mind. They are specific and concrete, not general and abstract.

A storyteller uses paintbrushes when he can. If nouns like *problem, situation, reaction* or *benefit* tumble thoughtlessly from his typewriter, he immediately stops to ask himself if he can be more specific, more pictorial. What *is* the problem, situation, reaction or benefit he refers to? Can he toss out the blob and replace it with a term carrying needle-sharp meaning?

Sometimes, he can't; blob words were invented for sound reasons. But if he's simply been lazy or careless and can find a better term in his toolbox when he troubles to look, his story will gain a sharper, more definitive edge.

So the storyteller questions every noun he thinks of using, even those that seem respectably specific at first glance. His *passenger ship* may become a *700-foot luxury liner*; a little more specific, more pictorial. His *reaction* becomes *fear, hatred, skepticism, enthusiasm, revulsion* or whatever it actually is. If he's tempted to write *combat*, he asks himself first if *battle* or *skirmish* would be better.

If specific nouns give his tale clarity, specific verbs add vigor and new depths of meaning, as in this fragment from a Barry Newman story on a volcanic politician:

"Don't get the impression I'm a madman!" explodes the mayor.

Wonderful. We see instantly that the mayor is indeed a hothead, and learn at the same time that he's not fully conscious of this quality in himself. (Notice that I've had to use 27 words to explain what one powerful verb conveyed in a picture.)

This whole story, which could have been too talky, was given life by such verbs. Look at what they do for this passage near the end:

Next comes a contractor who is charging $60,000 to repair a city building. The mayor is boiling. "You know you did a lousy job," he hollers. "You farmed it out, and you screwed the city! You're nothing but a pile of bull as far as I'm concerned! I wish I could find myself wrong once; then I'd be patient with you. But not once since I've been here have I been wrong!"

The contractor shuffles out, and a local slumlord steps forward. He wants the building inspectors to leave him alone. The mayor seethes, "How can you let people live like animals? You're probably giving the inspector a quart of liquor."

The slumlord leaps into the air. "I don't give nobody nothing!" he thunders. The mayor jumps to his feet, screaming. "Fix your damned building!" and the two circle each other, snarling . . .

Striving for effects like these, the storyteller constantly refines the verbs he thinks of using. Does Mr. Jones *favor* a certain idea, or does he *embrace* it? There's a difference. Did Mr. Smith just *leave,* or did he *flee, abandon, wander off*? Is the mayor *upset,* or is he *boiling*?

Most writers err in using weak, general terms instead of strong, specific ones, but a good many others need to tone down their prose, not strengthen it. They reflexively hype their copy with words that overstate, giving their work a phony urgency, an overblown quality. To them every passing difficulty is a *crisis,* every set of contradictions a *profound dilemma,* every modification of a White House bill a *resounding defeat* for the President. They cheapen the currency of language. If a genuine crisis occurs, what can they call it to distinguish it from all the ersatz ones they've breathlessly announced? A megacrisis?

The therapy, however, is the same the timid writer must follow—weighing words to balance their precise meaning against the reality they seek to depict.

MEANNESS

The mean writer is always a lean writer. He can't help it.

By meanness I don't refer to a harsh quality in his copy but to his attitude toward himself as he works. You may think it strange to cite an attitude as a consideration in good writing, but often it's the only thing separating the work of two equally talented people. The one turning out fat, flaccid, talky stories is not being tough enough on himself.

The mean storyteller becomes two people, acting alternately as he works. The first is the sensitive artist-creator, the second a savage critic who eradicates every weakness in the creation. He's cruel, derisive and obsessively demanding. He hoots at the writer's affectations and pretty turns of phrase, blisters him for cowardice when he uses soft, passive constructions or hedges on conclusions, challenges every point of logic, demands sound reasons for the presence of every character and fact, and above all flagellates his victim for wordiness. He is a rotten S.O.B., worse than any editor who ever drew breath, and he is the artist's best friend.

Only by shrinking under a barrage of criticism by his alter ego can the artist eventually learn to discipline his art, to get matters right the first time. A gentle critic can't inflict the pain an artist needs to grow to full potential; he's too easy to ignore or argue with. A tactful editor, for example, may persuade a writer to make changes in a specific story, but the odds are good that the same errors will recur in later stories because the writer hasn't been made to suffer for his first sin.

Let's listen to what a self-critic would say about the following passage. The dialogue is invented, but the passage is real, a final draft of an example lead on a piece about increasing cocaine use in the financial community.

At 28, Mike is a successful bond trader with a major firm in the Wall Street area. Like many of his co-workers, he has a comfortable salary (more than $100,000 in a good year), enjoys his work for the most part and has a fairly good home life.

And, like a growing number of his co-workers across the country, Mike uses cocaine. He says he isn't addicted to the expensive white powder but he uses it—sometimes during working hours—for the sense of power and omnipotence he believes it gives him. Mike buys most of his own cocaine but occasionally he gets a gram or two as a gift from brokers who want to keep his friendship—and his business.

ARTIST: Uh, this is what I'll say in this little section . . .

CRITIC: You're kidding. This is full of helium. If it's the top of a newspaper story, it's too long. If it's the beginning of a novel, it's too lousy. The first paragraph reads like a business card and doesn't get us into the topic. I don't give a damn how rich and happy some young jerk in a three-piecer happens to be. What's that got to do with the price of eggs?

ARTIST: But . . .

CRITIC: Shut up and listen. "At 28, Mike is . . ." Weak. You're backing in. Start with the subject and save a word to boot: "Mike is 28." Then you say he's "successful" and right after that tell us he makes a "comfortable salary" of "more than 100K." That's like telling us he's a fat, obese man who weighs 330 pounds. When are you going to learn about redundancy? "A major firm in the Wall Street area," you say. Urban sprawl. Make it "a major Wall Street firm" and clip three of the eight words. That's 37%, dummy. That's a lot. "Like many of his co-workers." Who cares about his co-workers? Are they your friends? Snuff them. "Enjoys his work for the most part." My God, that's wimpy. Does he like his job or doesn't he? Make up your mind. "Has a fairly good home life." Gee, and all along I thought this story was going to be about cocaine, not domestic relations. Snuff the wife and kids too. Remember what you're writing about. And get something related to coke into that first paragraph or everyone will fall asleep; I'm about ready for nighty-night myself.

ARTIST: I was just trying to give a more rounded picture of him . . .

CRITIC: We don't care. This story isn't about him, it's about his problem. He's only one example and we don't have the space to snuggle up to him. Even if we did, your description wouldn't help. Mike sort of likes his job and sort of likes his wife. Gripping. Fascinating. Spare me mush like this.

ARTIST (chastened): But what about the second paragraph? What's wrong with that?

CRITIC: It's better. It's only bad instead of terrible. In the first sentence you drag in the co-workers again. You're straining to widen the story too soon. After this passage we're going to *show* the scope of cocaine use with evidence; why *tell* people when you can *show* them? Keep Mike isolated until you're done with him, then spread out.

Next you've got him snorting the stuff for the "sense of power and omnipotence he believes it gives him." There is a book of words called a dictionary. It tells us that power means power and omnipotence means the quality of being all-powerful. That's too much clout for any man, no? This stinks too: ". . . the sense . . . he *believes* it gives him." You don't *believe* you get a sensation; you either get it or you don't. Enough. Go clean up this mess.

Our artist does, and produces the following:

Mike is 28, a bond trade with a major Wall Street firm, and makes more than $100,000 in a good year. He likes his job. He likes cocaine, too, off the job and sometimes on it.
He claims he's not addicted to the costly white powder; he just enjoys, he says, the sense of omnipotence it gives him. Mike buys most of his own, but occasionally is given a gram or two by brokers who want to keep his friendship—and business.

The artist originally used 120 words. Through painful collaboration with his critic, he got the passage down to 82 words. More than 30% of his solo version was fat. He's gained not only space but pace; shorn of redundancies and irrelevancies, the passage moves more briskly.

Beyond a shared interest in conciseness, important differences divide the self-critic and another alter ego, the self-editor. Entering only at the end of the work, the latter judges the whole. He cares about brevity, but also about rhythm, flow and, above all, persuasiveness. He may even add to the piece to make it more convincing or interesting.

By contrast the self-critic, working hastily along with the writer, can never see the piece whole and is interested only in precision of expression and correct logic within the fragments he inspects. He has no creative ideas of his own. He prunes but never plants.

Why not dismiss him and let the self-editor do everything at the end? A tempting notion, but it usually doesn't work.

Without the relentless pressure his self-critic provides, the artist may gobble up most of his allotted space and still have two-thirds of his tale left to tell. If he plows on as before, he produces a screed so lengthy that the self-editor is overwhelmed;

instead of snipping and polishing, he must fight his way through the jungle with a machete. This isn't what he does best.

If the artist instead tries a mid-course correction, he's likely to begin generalizing and tossing out substance and specifics to bring the piece in at a suitable length. But even if he succeeds, part of it will be windy and the rest weak, again giving the self-editor too much to do. What's more important, the artist has in both cases robbed himself of the chance to gain more mastery over his art. Conciseness is a positive value in writing, and the self-critic is the best teacher of it.

DESCRIPTIVENESS

Nowhere is the writer's ego more troublesome than in his handling of description. Gripped by his muse, he reels off a passage slathered with pretty adjectives and plops it into his tale like a cannonball into a kettle of soup. It's florid, excessive, jarring, but the more he looks at it the more he loves it. It is Art. It is Him. If an editor tries to excise it, the writer will leap at his jugular.

In other places in the story, the same writer has sinned by omission, failing to use his eye and ear and sense of things to paint pictures that would deepen understanding. If his editor calls him on this, he may testily reply that he saw no reason to clutter up the piece with trivia. Taken as a whole, the descriptive quality of his story is out of balance because he was self-indulgent. He wrote to satisfy his literary impulses, and no reader gives a hoot about that. By contrast, the trained storyteller serves readers by using description only with certain purposes in mind. The highest of these is story progression.

Many descriptive passages, no matter how pleasing or brief, are digressions, interruptions in the forward motion of the tale. But when what is described is *central* to the theme, description rolls the story along instead of slowing it up. In a personal profile, to cite one obvious case, every word describing the subject's appearance, attitudes and behavior helps us to know him better—the storyteller's ultimate goal in such a piece. In a story about urban renewal, descriptions of the affected area and its people are necessary if we're to fully appreciate what's happening to them.

Description also aids story progression when it buttresses other evidence that bears on the main thrust of the piece. The whole idea of the Mexican migration story, for example, was to establish the depth and extent of poverty in central Mexico so the reader could understand, with both head and heart, why so many rural Mexicans come to the U.S. Facts, figures and expert testimony are used to inform and convince, but so are descriptions like this:

... As she speaks, a rat creeps boldly toward a small pouch of corn on the Mendozas' dilapidated front porch. Her 69-year-old father-in-law grabs a broomstick and smacks the rodent over the head. "One less mouth to feed," he says.

If the incident described had been put in a different kind of story, one set in Mexico but *not* centering on poverty as a motive for migration, then the description would have been a digression. In the story at hand, it expands the reader's understanding of the central theme, and thus advances the tale.

The storyteller is never reluctant to describe anything that will move the reader along a main thematic channel. Indeed, he knows he must describe in such cases or his story will have no life. But when description is digression, he uses it sparingly.

He will not, for example, even think of describing every secondary character or place, every passing incident. But he may, if needed, use just enough description of one or two of them to serve another purpose—reader involvement.

The reader who stands outside a tale throughout is never touched by it. So, using his previously mentioned license as observer, the writer may take the reader into his tale by letting him walk one or two of its streets, meet one or two of its people, witness one or two incidents. These may be unimportant to story development, but they get the readers involved.

In selecting what he'll describe for this purpose, the writer tries to educate as he involves. He wouldn't bother to describe an executive's office unless there was something strikingly different about it or revelatory of the occupant's character; most people are too familiar with offices to gain from seeing another one. But he will describe strip mining on the Great Plains, "where shovels claw at the rangeland and draglines tower over hills of coal like giant black mantises." Few readers have seen that. He won't describe what goes into a hamburger, but he will give the recipe for son-of-a-bitch stew. He lets agricultural bureaucrats remain faceless (most of us are woefully familiar with bureaucrats), preferring to introduce us to a tomato farmer instead.

A writer may also describe in order to create dramatic contrast. In doing this, he often describes things he wouldn't give space to if his purpose was different. For example, a meek, mild clerkish man, a thoroughly unexceptional type we all know, would ordinarily be a dubious choice for description—but if the man was a mass murderer, the scribbler who failed to set up that fact with the description would have his epaulets torn off by the Writers' Guild. The description of the man makes his crime more startling.

More subtle descriptive contrast helps a lot of passages we encounter more often, like this one from a piece about a mysterious Shell Oil exploration of the Columbia Plateau in Washington state:

> On the surface it is placid country. Orchards and farms nestle among the humpbacked hills and ridges, while the Columbia River waters the land and the white-crowned sentinels of Mount Adams and Mount Rainier watch over it from the west. But just below the orchards is an oilman's nightmare—a layer up to two miles thick of basalt, a dark volcanic rock that scrambles seismic signals and blunts drill bits.

The look of the country has nothing to do with the story theme. But without the picture of a benign, peaceful land, the picture of what lies beneath it loses impact.

So, we always describe for a reason. But how do we describe well?

The question takes us into the realm of art and can't be answered directly. No one can offer recipes that, followed exactly by others, will produce a wonderfully descriptive piece of work every time. Rembrandt couldn't teach a Sunday painter to be

Rembrandt any more than John Updike can reproduce in me his mastery of word play. But it's always possible to improve, and consideration of the following may help:

1. Imagic exactness

The purpose of description is to create pictures of photographic quality in the reader's mind, not blurred images that make him squint and wonder what he is looking at. Descriptive terms must be sharp, at least in most newspaper and magazine work.

When we say a homburg is *black*, the image is precise enough and nothing more is needed. But when we say its wearer is *generous*, focus is lost. In what ways is he generous, and to what extent? We can see his hat clearly but not his generosity. If the writer can't make that quality more pictorially exact, the word *generous* remains mushy. The storyteller usually avoids such terms unless he can illustrate them, then or later. He tries to be as specific with his adjectives and adverbs as he is with his nouns and verbs.

When he succeeds, he can add new layers of meaning to a story in just a few words. Tom Wolfe does so in a story about the Pump House Gang, part of the surfing subculture along the California coast in the 60s. The kids form a tight clan with language, customs and values chosen to set them apart. They are cool. They worship their own youth and beauty, and fear the aging that will inevitably push them out of the clan. Fearing it so, they deride it in others. In the story, a middle-aged, uncool couple is plodding toward them at the stairs to Windandsea Beach in La Jolla. The kids watch them slyly, make a few cracks, wait. The man wants to avoid them and tries to steer his wife away, but she resists:

"Mrs. Roberts," the work-a-hubby says, calling his own wife by her official married name, as if to say she took a vow once and his word is law, even if he is not testing it with the blonde kids here—"farther up, *Mrs. Roberts."*
They start to walk up the sidewalk but one kid won't move his feet and, oh, god, her work-a-hubby breaks into a terrible shaking Jello smile as she steps over them . . .*

*Tom Wolfe, *The Pump House Gang* (New York: Bantam, 1969), p. 17.

Terrible shaking Jello smile. A vivid, complex picture explodes in the mind. We see that this man is mortally afraid of some bizarre, outrageous act that will destroy his dignity, his selfhood, and turn him into a blubbering clown. He is so afraid that he abases himself before these adolescents rather than risk what they *might* do to him. His smile is totally false, a grimace—he hates these punks—and full of dread. The word *terrible* tells us how the writer felt, but we can all share the feeling; the sight of a grown man groveling so makes us want to turn our faces away.

A lesser writer or a lazier one might have skipped a description or used almost as many words as I have to say what the incident meant. Wolfe does everything in one four-word picture. As soon as we see it we see what it means.

2. The people principle

Readers prefer people to places and things, so the storyteller injects humanity into his descriptions whenever he can do so legitimately. In a story about the decay of the Memphis district around Beale Street, Erik Calonius could have stressed broken windows, grime, cracked sidewalks, weedy lots and other signs of physical blight. Instead, he introduces us to the place where the blues were born in this way:

> Morning sunlight washes down Fourth and Vance streets, splashing over the tired facades of the 4-Way bar, the pool hall next door, even the tread-worn stairway leading to the brothel upstairs.
>
> From somewhere above the intersection comes singing, filtering down to the mailman making his rounds and to the men below, some of them passing a bottle beneath a tree, others sitting expressionless in the doorways of a housing project.
>
> Up in the brothel, filling the flung-back French windows and leaning on his elbows on the ornamental railing, is Sweet Charles. He is a big man in a sleeveless undershirt, black wig and a strand of pearls, singing of hard luck and bad love.

Physical deterioration is hinted at in the tired facades, the tread-worn stairway, the nature of the establishments. But people come first, establishing the piece as one about a *neighborhood*, not a jumble of bricks and concrete. This is wise. We often have feeling for our neighbors but are unmoved by the shells in which they live.

3. Animation

While Sweet Charles sings, the mailman bustles about and the men on the street pass a bottle. The human element here is animated.

People like people, but they like them best when they are moving, acting. People like anything better when it moves or acts, so the storyteller describing objects and places that have no human element still seeks ways to make them live, as here:

It is a bare world, done in blues and greys, where the glaciers creak and groan and only the glacier lily, blooming in the melt at the fringes of the vast ice rivers, is a reminder of the flowered fields below.

The creaking and groaning of the glaciers, even the blooming of the lilies, provide animation. Without it, the description is prosaic.

The writer who seeks to animate will automatically avoid most flabby, passive constructions and write more vigorously. In describing the Williston Basin, he will not write that "on the plain are gas-processing plants that look like silver spiders." Instead, he writes that "gas-processing plants squat like silver spiders on the plain." That's shorter, too.

Animation alone can lend descriptive quality to passages that would otherwise lack it. In the loggers story an important paragraph could have been written this way:

Generations of the Mason clan have gone into the forest, and, as with so many other families, they have had to pay for their fascination with it. Spider's uncle, grandfather, father and brother have all been killed there. And at least 10 men from clear across the country, natives of Hayesville, N.C., population about 300, have come to the Northwest woods to die . . .

It was written this way instead;

Generations of the Mason clan have gone into the forest and, as with so may other families, the forest has made them pay for their fascination with it. The forest has killed Spider's uncle, grand-father, father and brother. The forest has reached across the country to exact its price from the little town of Hayesville, N.C., population about 300; at least 10 of its men have come to the Northwest woods to die. . . .

In the first version the forest is just a place. In the second, animation makes it an active, malevolent entity reaching out for its blood price, the center of the whole passage.

4. Poetic license

Glaciers do make noises, and flowers certainly bloom, but when forests reach out to do murder, the writer is exercising poetic license—and, so long as the image accurately reflects the sense of what's going on, the reader only benefits. The descriptive writer who is too literal shackles himself and gives the reader little credit for imagination.

Some writers don't use their poetic licenses because they don't know they have them. They're writing the news, and you don't get fancy with the news; it is sacred and serious, is it not? Others are aware of what is possible but are afraid to spread their wings. To them, poetic license smells like Literature, and newspaper hacks don't write Literature.

Maybe not, but they don't have to, either. In using poetic license to create images, the feature writer doesn't ask himself how pretty they are. He's satisfied if they make what is described clearer to the reader, and if they are entirely accurate reflections.

In one story I say that "it's generally agreed cows will fly before a standard Medicaid measure ever gets through the GOP-dominated Arizona house." Nobody said that precisely, but the image depicts the situation accurately. Cows will never fly and Medicaid will never get through the Arizona legislature as constituted, or so its members believe.

CONVERSATIONAL QUALITY

The story that has this quality makes me feel that the writer is conversing informally with me alone, not giving a speech to a faceless crowd in some coliseum. He has created intimacy between us; he becomes real to me because I sense that I am real to him, an individual and not a cipher.

There are tricks that promote this bonding, but, as with so many other aspects of good writing, the building of reader-writer intimacy begins with the writer's attitude. A good one writes to an individual, never the mass, and this practice is entirely appropriate. Six million people do not sit down together every day for a group reading of *The Wall Street Journal*.

When a writer works with one person in mind, he is less likely to make the mistakes the coliseum orator may make—stuffiness, pedantry, dramatic overstatement, a formality of address that sets him above his audience instead of uniting him with it. The conversational writer avoids most of these errors because he tests whatever he thinks of writing with one question: *Would this be the way I'd tell it over drinks with an interested, intelligent friend?*

I don't suggest that we should always write exactly as we speak, unless we always speak with precision, economy and correctness. I don't. But most of us benefit greatly by coming *closer* to normal conversation as we write.

When we do, we don't lecture—what friend will stand for that?—and we actually find it difficult to be stuffy or overly formal. The tortured jargon of hack newspaperese disappears. Robbers become robbers instead of "perpetrators seen leaving the scene in a late-model Oldsmobile." Instead of a "facility sited at Morrison Industrial Park" we get a factory built there. With our individual reader always in mind, we are naturally inclined toward plainness, to me the most appealing conversational value.

The plain writer may use fewer words to say something than his colleagues, but brevity is a bonus. His purpose is simplicity. So he will be less likely to write this:

Goliath Motors, which incurred $2 billion in development costs on the Belchfire Bobolink, ceased production of the auto last month because of sales levels the company characterized as "far below even minimal expectations."

. . . than this:

Goliath Motors, which spent $2 billion developing the Belchfire Bobolink, stopped making the car last month. Sales were awful, the company said.

When people talk they generally use simpler words than *incurred, ceased,* and *characterized*. They tend to use simpler, more active sentences, too. And they don't quote people as often as they paraphrase them. There's nothing grossly wrong with the structure of the first version or the words chosen, but I like the second for its plainness. It comes closer to what one person might actually say to another.

And what else does a person do when he is having a conversation? Among other things, he may do what I just did—ask a question. Some are rhetorical:

And the trade-off for all this? Membership in a fraternity.

Other questions convey information or reasoning:

BWAB has some 900,000 plateau acres leased for itself and limited partners, but has no plans to drill until it can get a reading on what, if anything, Shell is finding. Everyone else is waiting too; why blow $10 million to $20 million grinding through the basalt when you can sit back, suck your corporate thumb, and let one of the big boys test the water first?

The writer who asks questions keeps his reader alert and enhances the bond between them. A companion who always has the answers to everything and recites them at us with finger-waving certitude is a pendantic bore. We can't feel close to him because we see that he's not interested in us, only in showing off. But a companion who queries us now and then is engaging himself with us. We'll buy another round for *him*.

A good conversationalist also spices his talk with colloquialisms, even slang, when they provide the best illustrations of what he means. A writer shouldn't hesitate to do the same. So the Yavapai Indians tell the white man to "get lost," because that term best fits not only what they did but the spirit in which they did it. Always use what fits best and let the copy editors fret over whether the paper should allow the term. Standards of usage are in their province.

When people talk they sometimes use exclamations, ejaculations, one or two-word sentence fragments and other forms avoided by many writers. Don't be afraid to try these. In a story about oil exploration, a one-word sentence is used to effect:

> Also, under the ethic of the oil patch, a man who receives a favor from another owes him until he can repay. If a debtor stiffs his creditors, he finds himself isolated, excluded from deals, his own phone unanswered. When Mr. Slater recently phoned one source for information and was refused, he drawled, "Ah have reevaluated our friendship and Ah now find that you are an acquaintance." Click.

Without that last word, the passage loses some of the finality it needs.

A little of this goes a long way, however. Avoid overuse of such devices, or your piece will become a parody. Too many question marks, exclamations, fragments divert the reader from the substance of the tale to the performance of its author, and no one buys the paper to watch writers tap-dance through it.

It's enough, really, to maintain the proper attitude. Even if you don't use a single device we've discussed, even if all you do is write to one person and not a mob, you will not be able to help writing more plainly. Just be sure that the person you address is the right one. I'm convinced that much of the stuffiness in newspaper stories creeps in because the writer is unconsciously trying to impress a source or set of sources rather than a general reader; he's overly formal, even stiff, because to be blunt and breezy might indicate he's not taking their subject seriously enough. This may or may not please the little knot of lawyers, bureaucrats, or executives he's writing to, but it certainly leaves millions of other readers unmoved. A spade is still a spade, and readers are happiest when the writer says so.

FLOW

When a story has flow, the reader zips through it so effort-lessly that he's almost surprised to find himself at its end. He's hit no bumps and negotiated no wrenching hairpin turns; the writer has tamped them down, straightened them out.

To do this well, he must pay special attention to three poten-tially troublesome elements:

1. Transitional passages

In moving from one section of a story to another, even from one subsection to another, many writers seem compelled to warn the reader of the shift with a helium-filled transition sentence that says almost nothing but this: "Hey, we're through talking about apples now, and next we're going to talk about oranges." Sometimes even the oranges are missing.

This is one of the worst errors a writer can make. The first sentence of any paragraph or section is particularly important because it gives shape and meaning to what follows. If the sentence is empty, soft, unfocused, if many words are used to shift attention without any development of the new subject, the story flow halts to no purpose and the material that comes next may lose definition.

A good storyteller first tries the shift without using any spe-cial word bridge at all. He just goes on with the action. If he's kept related material together and has been following his road signs, this works an astonishing amount of the time. The urge to *introduce* a shift is so great that many of us drop in words to do so when none are needed. For example, after giving us the views of prune marketers in a story about prunes vs. avocados, a writer might thoughtlessly cross over to the other side with this:

> But champions of the avocado, not surprisingly, don't agree with that at all. "Bullfeathers!" cries Sotworth Weems, executive director of the Avocado Growers Council. "Prunes are just an ugly-looking laxative for old people living on Social Security. Avocados are the upscale fruit."

Instead of crayfishing into the avocado segment, the writer could have—and should have—gone straight to Weems' quote. The transitional sentence is superfluous.

If just rolling along doesn't work, and it's obvious some transition is needed, the writer next tests what he has written for specificity. Poor transitions often center on a blob word or phrase that covers too much ground. Can the writer replace the blob with a paintbrush? If he has written *situation*, can he say what the situation is?

When he can, he will often find himself combining two sentences—his original transition and the sentence after it.

In a story about, say, the impact of a gold strike on Cloaca, Nev., he has reeled off a section on the economic benefits. Trying to cross over to the drawbacks, his first attempt is:

But the discovery of gold has created major housing difficulties in Cloaca. So many miners and construction workers are pouring into town that there is no place left for many of them to live.

The first sentence centers on a blob—*major housing difficulties*. The second sentence explains the blob. So, applying the test of specificity, the writer melds the two:

But the gold strike is bringing so many miners and construction workers to Cloaca that there is no place left for many of them to live.

The Siamese-twin sentences in the first version are a common construction not only in transitional passages but elsewhere. Combine them when you can do so without creating an overly long, complex sentence. One healthy baby is what we want.

Let's see how proper transitioning can help a longer passage from a real story, the piece about increasing cocaine use in the financial community. The passage has been edited except for the transitions.

A broker named Paul is telling us about the effects of cocaine on his life, beginning with the business effects and ending with the personal:

... he has been suffering from unstoppable weight loss and rising blood pressure. There was a painful separation from his wife, and he isn't sure he has permanently controlled his cocaine habit.

Despite cocaine's kick, others besides Paul concede that use during trading hours can create problems. "Cocaine gives you a sense of well-being, and when a position goes against you, you may double your exposure rather than get out of the market," says Frank, a professional trader in Chicago who speculates for his own account. Good money chasing after bad recently cost another trader $8,500 in 15 minutes. "Adding to a losing trade violates the Number 1 rule of trading," this man says, "but I was real coked up."

The destructive power of cocaine on a trader's life can be awesome. The psychological dependence is often extreme, marked by a severe paranoia called cocaine psychosis. The characteristic gregariousness of a trader, for example . . .

The first movement is an expansion; we are broadening out from Paul's individual experience. But the transition says nothing except that others share that experience, which we already know, and the blob word *problems* helps us not at all. Applying the test of specificity, we scrap that sentence and replace it with this:

Under the influence of the drug, brokers and traders may make rash decisions and refuse to alter them because they cannot believe they could be wrong.

That's what the problem *is*.

The second movement is a shift in intensity. We are going from users whose business judgment is clouded to users in danger of mental collapse. But the transition doesn't even say that much. It's so general that it has almost no meaning at all. We've already seen some of the drug's effects on users' lives and judgments, so what's new here? Again, the blob word *awesome* fails to tell us. The fog lifts when we say it this way:

The habitual heavy user eventually may descend into the paranoia called cocaine psychosis.

That's what we wound up saying after the gratuitous transition, so why not say it straight off?

Sometimes being specific isn't enough, and the well-crafted crossover still jars. If this happens to you, it may be that you've missed a road sign in what you have written just before, and are trying to bend the story in a direction it's not ready to take.

Back up and look again. Following the little clues in every story is the best way to avoid transitional difficulties to begin with.

Alas, sometimes nothing works, and the writer is forced against his will to say something that only warns the reader of a major shift in the story. On these occasions he is as simple and terse as possible. Moving from a scope section to a reasons section that is too complex to allow specificity, he may simply say, "Diverse, powerful forces underlie (development)," or something equally brief and plain. Above all he avoids long, contorted sentences that back into the new subject without really saying anything about it. If generalizations have to be written they should be written tightly.

2. Attributions

We may need to identify sources to make their information credible, but the attribution is still a bump in the story road. It may be such an axle-breaker that one wonders if the content is worth it:

"Poetry in America is dying," says Eldridge Bassoon, Rod McKuen Professor of Depraved Pop Literature in the English Department at the McKeesport Campus of the University of the Alleghenies.

This is easy, of course. If we can't throw a pillow over the professor's face and get rid of him, we can always reduce his status. "Professor of English at the University of the Alleghenies" is enough. Similar trains of titular baubles and lace trail behind many middle-level bureaucrats and technologists. Chop them off and tell us what these people do to make a buck.

Collective and institutional attributions, however, require more thought. Many stories are shot through with them: Agencies claim this, banks deny that, doctors assert this, brokers declare that, farmers say one thing, businessmen another.

At first blush it seems hardly worth the writer's time to agonize over these. They are barely noticeable bumps, most of them, and he'll save only a few words by omitting unneeded ones. So why bother?

Certitude, not space, is the issue. Unnecessary attributions sap a story's strength by turning what could be expressed as fact into something akin to opinion, which carries less weight with the reader than fact. And the story flow is impeded whenever a reader must mentally cross-reference a statement with a source; he's not zipping along, but feeling his way.

Deciding which attributions to keep and which to discard depends entirely on the writer's subjective judgment. In exercising it, he asks himself two questions: Am I certain that this is true on the evidence? And even if I'm satisfied it's true, would the information come as something of a surprise to the reader?

If the answer to the second question is yes, then the writer ought to attribute. Whenever we tell people something unexpected they have a natural inclination to check the source. So if you establish something that surprises you, tell the reader where you got it.

If the information wouldn't raise eyebrows, your own certainty is all that matters. There are degrees of certainty, and some choices are easy. If something is universally well-known and observable, it is a truism and no writer will attach an attribution to it. Beyond this point, however, many falter.

They may say that avocado exports in 1978 totaled five million tons, "according to the Commerce Department." Unless someone knowledgeable had challenged that figure, I'd use it without attribution; the Commerce Department is supposed to keep track of outgoing avocados, and I have no reason to doubt that it knows its stuff. Its standing as an unbiased, accepted source of data on such matters allows me to leave its name out of the story.

Often there is no standard, authoritative font of information, and the statements a writer makes are summaries of what several or many sources have told him. He is prudent in handling these; because 11 of 15 specialists in a field agree on something doesn't make it fact. Even if only one disagreed and his arguments were forceful and logical, the prudent writer would hesitate to make a flat declaration. Majority views are not truths any more than mob rule is democracy.

But if there is no serious exception to a statement, if it's widely accepted in the particular community of knowledgeable people the writer is tapping, then the statement is a truism.

Everyone in the wide world may not recognize it as one, but those people closest to the development do. So the writer doesn't have to attribute it. He doesn't have to write that "brokers agree cocaine first gained wide acceptance on Wall Street in the mid-1970s." If he has talked to a good many brokers and all concur, he can just say it.

We miss many opportunities to do this because we are careless, overly cautious or mistakenly convinced that any statement, even a passing factual reference, is somehow more persuasive with attribution hanging from it. And in a few other, more worrisome cases, attribution is used to cloak weak reporting.

The writer may not have bothered to talk to enough people to gain even a rudimentary feel for things, and is too lazy to backtrack and do more reporting when the weakness shows up during writing. He has talked to only two brokers about when cocaine got popular on Wall Street, but he can't very well write, "Two brokers say . . ." Lacks authority. So he writes "Brokers say . . . ," and deceives the reader. That attribution implies incorrectly that many sources have been consulted. The attribution isn't designed to give the statement credibility, but to give the writer a technical defense. He is just covering his rear.

3. Explanation

In every story a writer will have to stop the action now and then to explain some little thing. These explanations are distinct from the material in his reasons section; that part of his story contains the main causative elements underlying his theme, material that is often interesting in itself and always important.

The explanations I refer to are scattered through the story and slow it down rather than advance it. With few exceptions they are mundane, even tedious, dealing with petty matters that crop up in passing: how a machine works, why a secondary character took a certain action, the steps in a procedure, a point of law, and so on.

These are digressions that often lack intrinsic interest, but the writer must fight the impulse to skip them. They may be ugly little interruptions but they are needed, and the writer who omits them only trades a small problem for a bigger one. He is leaving annoying minor mysteries in the body of the story and the reader, who doesn't mind a little titillation at the top, won't stand for it here. If he must stop to puzzle over minor vaguenesses, he may get irritated enough to quit. Always explain anything that might leave the smallest loose end dangling.

But be quick about it. A windy explanation is a serious blockage in the story flow, and you must do all possible to reduce it to essentials. This is dirty work; we're inclined to lavish most of our care on the more important and interesting parts of the story. A natural inclination, perhaps, but a good writer knows it's vital to write the mundane parts of his story tightly and simply so the reader can get to the good stuff.

The writer achieves this by never explaining more than the reader absolutely needs to know at that point. Let's say you are doing a piece about banks battling for depositors against the wiles of the money-market funds. Besides giving away toasters, radios and weekends in a Cleveland motel, the banks are playing up the relative safety their depositors have. This isn't the time to write a long explanatory paragraph about the Federal Deposit Insurance Corp., its history and array of powers. This is the time to say only that bank deposit accounts are federally insured up to $100,000, while money-market accounts are not. This nugget is all that's needed to explain the banks' claim. Even the name of the insuring agency is suppressed to avoid using a few extra words and dragging a new entity into the story. When the reader only needs to know what time it is, don't tell him how to make a watch.

PURPOSEFUL STRUCTURES

These structures are part of the writer's special effects. By engineering the structure and arrangement of his paragraphs and sentences, he can give the reader certain desired impressions:

1. Speed

The writer who wants it may put his reader on board a *freight-train sentence*, in which a central subject (or a subject plus verb) pulls behind it a series of objects or clauses. This kind of sentence conveys maximum information in minimum space, which makes it particularly useful in getting the reader through boggy parts of the tale, such as long explanations that can't be skimped.

In a story about Steve Reynolds, the state engineer and water czar of New Mexico, I had to drag the reader through details of a legal case vital to the story. The passage could have been written this way:

> The engineer proved this with precise, relentless logic. First, he showed that the ground-water supply was connected to the main-stream of the river. Then he was able to prove that pell-mell pumping would diminish the river's flow because the two water sources were linked. This meant, he argued, that New Mexico would be unable to meet its legal obligation to Texas, with which it shares the river. The result: before long, users in the basin would have to be cut off to make up the Texas share, thus turning boom into bust.

Using freight-train construction instead, I got this:

> In his precise, relentlessly logical way, the engineer showed that the ground water was connected to the river's mainstream; that pell-mell pumping would thus diminish the river's flow; that New Mexico would then be unable to meet its legal obligation to Texas, with which it shares the river; and that before long users in the basin would have to be cut off to make up the Texas share, turning boom into bust.

Both versions are tedious, but at least the second releases the suffering reader in 72 words instead of the 93 in the first. This economy, the only mercy I could show him, was made possible by forcing a single subject-verb (*engineer showed*) to haul the informational boxcars. The sentence is very long, but it's no more difficult to understand than the first version because its core structure is simple. The clauses are alike in form, and march along in the same logical sequence as the points made in the actual legal argument.

Still, I wouldn't want to use a sentence like this very often.

The shorter the freight train, the faster it goes and the better the reader likes the ride.

Simple freight-train sentences can lend a crisp certainty as well as speed to conclusions and summaries, such as this one rounding up mountain man Finis Mitchell's thinking about supplies and equipment:

He scorns freeze-dried food ("costs four times as much as it should"), hundred-dollar boots and the other accoutrements of wilderness chic.

This kind of construction also helps the writer give the impression of a flurry of action, a lot going on at once or in rapid succession:

They lobbied in Congress, marched on a "trail of tears" to the state capitol, and picketed Sen. Barry Goldwater at a public appearance.

Amid blood, dust and bawling, the calf is dehorned with a coring tool, branded in an acrid cloud of smoke from burning hair and flesh, earmarked in the ranch's unique pattern (cowboys pay more attention to earmarks in identifying cattle than to brands), and castrated.

Notice the first phrase in the above, "Amid blood, dust and bawling . . .", and the first phrase in the refined water czar passage, "In his precise, relentlessly logical way . . ." They are examples of another speed device I call the *hook-on*.

Digressive material is static and creates flat spots in the story. Everything stops while someone intrudes to deliver a quote, while the sunset over the mountains is described, while the FDIC insurance provision is explained. If there is much of this material, the writer may be forced to choose between some interesting elements and a smooth story flow. But he can have his cake and eat it too if he can turn short digressive sentences into phrases or clauses and then hook them onto sentences with action in them. This often saves a few words, which is nice, but another effect is more important: The reader doesn't notice the flat spot anymore. Stasis has become action, and the whole has become more appealing than the sum of its parts.

So by melding the *atmosphere* of the branding corral (blood, dust, and bawling) into the *action* there (dehorning, branding, earmarking and castrating), I get a passage with more pace and interest than if I had segregated the two elements in separate sentences. And in the refined version of the water czar passage I slip in a characterization of Steve Reynolds in a way that avoids some of the flatness of the original version.

Writers instinctively use hook-ons to avoid choppy, oversimplified sections that read like pages out of Dick and Jane. Their brief compounds may tie *description* to action:

Tourists flock (to the National Elk Refuge) in winter, when the bugling calls of the bulls resound like the notes of silver horns.

As the sun rises over the rolling, dun reaches of the Great Plains, men holed up in motel rooms here reach for their phones and start calling back East.

Get rid of the flat spot that a separate *explanation* might create:

"Hotbedding"—jamming, two, three and even four families into one apartment where they often sleep in shifts—is aggravating health problems and adding to school crowding.

Or do the same thing for a quote:

"Hunger is something we have learned to live with," he says, dispatching a son to scavenge a nearby potato field for anything the harvesters have missed.

One caveat: Don't use a hook-on if it creates a sentence so complex that it obscures meaning or tries the reader's patience.

2. Force

When the writer wants emphasis, he operates differently than when he wants speed. He slows the pace, often using more words than strictly necessary to convey meaning. Instead of combining sentences, he may break a long one into pieces that become hammerstrokes driving home his message. Or, if he does use a longer sentence, he may build it out of independent clauses (those that can stand alone as sentences themselves) instead of dependent ones.

In adding force he relies heavily on *repetition,* a dirty word in journalism because it usually applies to a poorly organized story in which the writer makes the same point over and over in pretty much the same way. This is bad. But some writers go to ridiculous lengths to avoid using even the same *word* twice. (For a while, the humble banana was translated by *Wall Street Journal* writers desperate for variety on second reference into "the elongated yellow fruit.")

Used for effect, there is nothing wrong with word repetition. When people talk, they often repeat words to be more forceful, and the device works. The following is a verbatim quote from a resident of Silver City, Nev., a community threatened by proposed open-pit mining. The company, Houston Oil & Minerals, has been operating just up the road near Virginia City and has wooed that town by donating various civic improvements, but this Silver Citian wants no part of them:

"Our position is we don't want Houston, we don't want their ambulances and their water towers and their smooth talkers from Texas, and we don't want their mine. . . . We've decided to leave 20 times, we've decided to stay 20 times, we've decided to run and we've decided to fight. We can't believe what the company tells us."

This passage could easily be cut, but revised for speed it loses much of the force and feeling that repetition gives it.

So, the writer picks up the conversational cue and adopts the device himself, as in this ending on a story about the migration of city folk to country towns. A community leader in tiny Wittman, Ariz., is talking about why urban migrants are coming there:

Wittman, he points out, can still send volunteer Santas to the home of every school child at Christmas. As a school board member, he can still know personally almost every one of these children. Lacking a bureaucracy to contract such work, townsmen can still pitch in to build cabinets for the school and lay down a basketball court. . . . "People want brotherhood," he says, "and you can't buy that in Phoenix."

The repetition of *can still* gives a measured emphasis to the passage. Remove it and some of that quality disappears.

Force in writing also derives from proper placement of key words within sentences. For maximum effect they should come at the beginning or the end, not in the middle. One of the most stunning openings in literature is the first sentence of Franz Kafka's bizarre tale, *The Metamorphosis:*

As Gregor Samsa awoke one morning from uneasy dreams he found himself transformed in his bed into a gigantic insect.

Gigantic insect carries the shock value. Smother it in the middle of the sentence and force ebbs away:

Gregor Samsa found himself transformed in his bed into a gigantic insect when he awoke one morning from uneasy dreams.

3. Variety and Rhythm

Liking variety in content, the reader likes it in structure too—a lilting, swinging flow in one part of the story, a serpentine subtlety in another, a clipped plainness somewhere else.

Varied sentence length and composition help give him what he wants. They may flow naturally from the writer's other efforts; when he is trying to snuggle up to his reader by being conversational, for example, his one- or two-word sentence fragments, ejaculations and terse questions also provide points of structural contrast. When he is alternating units written for speed with those written for force, as he often will, the same thing may happen:

He scorns freeze-dried food ("costs four times as much as it should"), hundred-dollar boots and the other accoutrements of wilderness chic. His boots are J.C. Penney. He doesn't cook on the trail and relies on the corner grocery for all his food. He isn't fussy about campsites.

As we've seen, the first sentence is a summary, crafted for speed, of Finis Mitchell's attitudes. The next three are hammer strokes, crafted for force, emphasizing his actions.

More variety slips in when a writer uses different sentence forms to treat different types of material. When devising conclusions and summaries I usually find myself writing short declarative sentences or short freight trains; their active voice and simple structure give me the crispness and certainty this kind of material usually requires. But I tend to write longer, compound sentences, sometimes in the passive voice, when dealing with ambiguities, dilemmas, complex reasoning and motivation, or certain involved explanations. This form often expresses subtleties better and in fewer words, at least for me.

Which leaves the ephemeral quality called rhythm. When an editor orders a wage slave to "make it sing," he may refer to several qualities, but rhythm is always among them. He wants a little music, a little poetry, in the writing.

The wretched scribe may fall overboard trying to satisfy, scratching for extended metaphor, alliteration ("what a tale of terror now their turbulency tells!"), even a chance to rhyme internally. Meanwhile, he loses track of the story.

Instead of straining for exotic effects, he can rely again on repetition. We've just seen how one form of it, word repetition, provides power. It can provide a marching cadence at the same time; read again the examples cited under the section on force and you may be able to pick up the beat that word repetition gives them.

Another form of repetition that promotes rhythm is called *balanced parallelism*. A piece of prose is properly parallel when its different elements have some logical connection, and when each element is written in the same grammatical form. In this case structures, not words, are repeated. They are said to be balanced when each is about the same length:

Locusts denuded fields in Utah, torrents washed away rural Iowa, and blazing heat shriveled Arizona's cotton.

Compare the above with this nonparallel version, in which a mid-course shift from active to passive structure destroys the rhythm:

Locusts denuded fields in Utah, rural Iowa was washed away by torrents, and in Arizona the cotton was shriveled by blazing heat.

The following is written in parallel but lacks balance because one of the sentence elements is so much longer and more complex than the others:

Locusts denuded fields in Utah, torrents washed away parts of central Iowa already suffering from a failure of the corn crop, and blazing heat shriveled Arizona's cotton.

Freight-train sentences are properly written in parallel:

The great bulge of Arctic air brought fifty-below readings to the upper Midwest, power blackouts to New England and a killing frost to Florida citrus growers.

A passage composed of several related sentences can form a parallel unit too:

Smith favors ham. Jones likes chicken. Brown loathes both foods.

The music these little sentences make is a childish rat-tat-tat on a toy drum. Combining them into one sentence of independent clauses adds a little smoothness and lilt:

Smith favors ham, Jones likes chicken and Brown loathes both foods.

Even a long, involved paragraph may gain a rhythmic quality from a simple parallel structure imbedded at its core. Look again at the passage from the loggers story cited under *animation* in this chapter. Its cadence as well as some of its power radiate from the combination of word repetition and parallelism in this short central segment:

. . . the forest has made them pay for their fascination with it. The forest has killed Spider's uncle, grandfather, father and brother. The forest has reached across the country . . .

The writer who masters balanced parallelism will find that he can express complex material in very long sentences with both rhythm and perfect clarity. The device is used effectively in this difficult sentence about the simultaneous fight-freeze-flee impulses felt by a man in mortal danger:

Knowing that the tiger would eventually discover his hiding place in the bushes, fearing that if he bolted now the beast would be upon him before he reached the gate, feeling already the crunch of teeth through bone and the bloody rake of claws, Harrison froze in mute terror.

Sentences 49 words long aren't usually recommended. But proper structure lets you get away with them, and helps them sing a little in the bargain.

CHAPTER 8

STRETCHING OUT

Time for a graduate seminar. We've been dealing with stories of roughly 1200 to 2500 words, a bracket that nicely covers most major newspaper features and many that might be done for magazines. The stories studied so far have been in some cases fairly complex, given that length. But the true blockbuster piece, full of intricacies and shadings that require much more space, is geometrically more difficult to execute than features of typical length.

In this chapter we'll see how a gifted reporter handled, in two parts totaling 10,000 words, one of the most riveting human stories I've seen in the daily press. Summarized, it doesn't sound like anything that would make an editor's heart go pitty-pat: A rich Texas widow, aided by a friendly monk and an industrialist, wanted to leave most of her money to a foundation that would help the poor, but there was a nasty fight over the estate and her wishes were thwarted. An industrialist was involved, but no big celebrities. And the whole thing took place 25 years ago.

Who cares about these people? Estate contests aren't worth a line unless media darlings or the hugely rich are in the fray. And even if they had been, isn't this something for the history books instead of the press? A story 25 years old better have more going for it than this one seemed to.

But the reporter, George Getschow, saw something in the

nature of the struggle over the estate, and the makeup of the principal characters, that told him he was on to a potentially fascinating story. He pursued it off and on through most of 1986, on the ranches and in the courthouses of South Texas, in New York, in Chile, and in the monasteries of the Trappist order, where he lived for a time. This is the first of the two stories he got.

> *For I am doing a work in your days*
> *you would not believe if told.*
> *—Habakkuk, Old Testament*

SANTIAGO, Chile—In 1959, a lonely widow from Texas, a devout Roman Catholic, journeyed here with a monk who introduced her to the desperate poor of Latin America. Moved to tears, she resolved to help them—and set in motion a story of chicanery, plunder and unrelenting greed with few parallels anywhere, a sad tale whose end is still unwritten.

Those who would shortly vie for her fortune had many motives, not all of them selfish ones. But the fact remains that out of her good intentions grew a scandal that reaches from the tiny court-houses and the immense, windswept ranches of South Texas to the Vatican. It has sucked hundreds of people and many institutions, including those of the church, into its maw. It has set rancher against rancher, rich against poor, priest against priest. The Texas attorney general, who has been investigating one part of it, calls it "the juiciest scandal" of its kind in Texas history.

The lead is a general one because the events are so many and so complex that they defy summation in anything more than the most general way. So we only tell the reader that this is *a story of chicanery, plunder and unrelenting greed with few parallels anywhere,* and count on his natural curiosity to drive him on. This is close to a tout lead, which I've already warned you about. The justification is that this is the rare story that can deliver on such a promise. It is what the writer says it is.

The second paragraph goads the reader on by giving him an idea of the scope of the story and telling him that its central issue has been an enormously divisive one—but notice that we still leave him hanging as to what exactly that issue is. This is the first mystery.

And we wait still longer to solve it, first introducing in an orderly way the three central figures arrayed on one side of the issue. We only begin to detail the main story thread: the last wishes of a rich woman, and how they were subverted. In a story full of diverse people, motivations and events, trying to cram too much into the top part of the story would be confusing. So we choose orderly development, relying on the powerful statements made at the top to keep the reader reading.

The widow was Sarita Kenedy East, and she had the means to help the poor a great deal. She owned and ran the LaParra and San Pablo ranches, cattle baronies totaling over 400,000 acres. And under her holdings, second in size only to the giant King Ranch, was an ocean of oil—more oil, it developed, than she ever realized.

In January 1960, shortly after returning from South America, the childless woman known to most as "Auntie Sarita" tore up her old 1948 will, which mainly benefited a host of fractious relatives and local church entities, and set up a foundation named in honor of her parents. In a new will, she greatly reduced her previous bequests, instead leaving the bulk of her estate—including oil royalties—to the foundation. In a codicil to that will, she said she wanted the foundation empowered to make grants outside the state, and she frequently told others that her main intent for it was to aid the poor of Latin America. She was the foundation's sole trustee.

To do all these things, she requested and got aid from two major figures in the tale. One was Christopher Gregory, better known as Brother Leo, the Trappist monk and fund-raiser who had taken her to South America.

To do the job his superior charged him with, he was exempted from the rules of silence and the severe, harsh life that make the Trappists the strictest order in the church. But he was a reluctant fund-raiser, wanting only to be back in his monastery.

There was nothing in the new will or the foundation benefiting him or his order; Mrs. East, who had known Brother Leo for many years, had donated separately to the Trappists. The sum included $1 million for new South American monasteries given in exchange for his order's permission to let him help her. In the years to come, he would suffer much at the hands of his church for his stubborn determination to carry out her wishes.

He put Mrs. East in touch with industrialist J. Peter Grace, whose lawyers advised her. Mr. Grace, one of the most prominent of Catholic laymen, a Knight of Malta, had both secular and religious reasons for helping her. He worried that an impoverished Latin America could easily fall under Communist domination as Cuba had, causing the church—and W.R. Grace & Co.'s extensive Latin

American investments—to slide, as he put it, "right down the drain."
He would later bow to pressures that Brother Leo alone would resist
to this day.

Sarita Kenedy East died of cancer in 1961, her foundation in the
hands of these friends. But a quarter-century later, the dream she
had for the poor has not come true.

Thanks largely to a monster oil strike under Mrs. East's San
Pablo Ranch, a find whose extent was unknown when she died, the
foundation's assets are valued today at $300 million to $500 million. Some of the $65 million the foundation has disbursed to date
has gone to religious and secular charities in Texas, but none of it
has gone to the poor of Latin America.

Most of it, in fact, has been used to spruce up church buildings in
South Texas; to finance an opera company, telecommunications
centers and TV programs that include a $100,000 promotional film
boosting the Lone Star State; and to pave parking lots. The first
grant, $7.5 million, built a law library erected "in tribute to the
legal profession"—some of whose members got rich on oil royalties,
taken as contingency fees, for successfully extracting money from
the estate of Sarita Kenedy East.

What happened? Confined mainly to remote county courthouses
and the the privy councils of the church, the struggle for Mrs. East's
fortune has largely escaped public knowledge. Some of the participants are dead. Some, including Peter Grace, will not talk. But
interviews with dozens of others and inspection of tens of thousands
of pages of legal filings, memos and letters disclose this: Almost
everyone fighting for the money felt that charity ought to begin at
home—preferably his own.

John Mullen, an Alice, Texas, attorney who represented one of
the participants in the ensuing battle, says: "There was a pot of gold
there, and greed intervened. In a little while, the question was no
longer, 'What did Sarita want?' It was, 'What can I get out of this?' "

This section, and those following it, foreshadow events to come
without being too detailed about them. We say that Brother Leo
*would suffer much at the hands of his church for his stubborn
determination* and that Peter Grace would *later bow to pressure
that Brother Leo alone would resist to this day.* Suspense is still
being maintained, as is order, while the reader is beginning to
learn something about the nature of the two men and what
drove them. In this story character is a paramount consideration, and we must start developing it early.

Suddenly the story leaps into the present. We get a wry summary of what the money was ultimately used for—everything but what Sarita wanted. Notice the bitter irony at the end of the summation—part of Sarita's estate going for a tribute to lawyers, some of them the very men who got rich countering her wishes.

What happened? echoes what the reader must be feeling at this point and begins the developmental phase of the story. We've told him what Sarita wanted and now he's seen that her wishes did not come true. What we've deliberately left out is how and why this happened. A second mystery, then—and one establishing the story as one that will center on *reasons*. We begin the development with a cutting summary statement backed by a quote, and the rest of the story is devoted to showing the reader why they are true.

Texas vs. New York

The Right Rev. Mariano Garriga, who ran the Diocese of Corpus Christi, Texas, and who lived in a sprawling seaside mansion, presided over an area populated mainly by Anglo Baptists and poor Hispanics. So he took an almost proprietary interest in the few wealthy Catholic ranchers in his domain—figuring, as those who knew him say, that a sizable hunk of their estates would eventually become what he called the "patrimony" of his diocese.

Mrs. East had already put oil royalties worth $300,000 a year into the diocese's coffers, but the bishop had grown increasingly alarmed at her cultivation by the Trappist. He urged her not to see the monk again, but she refused. According to his deposition in a lawsuit, when she told him she was forming a foundation and was thinking about naming Francis Cardinal Spellman of New York (a close friend of Mr. Grace) as a trustee, he counseled her against it and volunteered his own help instead. "Well, we'll see about that," she said, according to the bishop's deposition.

From then on Mrs. East didn't discuss her charitable donations with the bishop. Shortly before her death, she told a geologist analyzing her oil properties that the bishop and his auxiliary had visited her but that she had "told them to go home." Others, including Mrs. East's local lawyer, Jake Floyd, had tried to gain influence over the foundation. Mr. Floyd was the political boss of nearby Jim Wells County, a director and attorney for the Alice National Bank there and counsel to several stockholders, Mrs. East among them. He had a reputation for cunning and was nicknamed *el vibora seca*, "the dry snake."

Mrs. East feared that taxes might drain her estate, and Jake Floyd, knowing this, convinced her that the foundation might lose its tax-exempt status unless she signed papers designating trustees—himself and Lee Lytton, Jr., an ally of the moment. Mr. Lytton was a judge in Kenedy County (which consisted mostly of Mrs. East's giant LaParra ranch) and one of many relatives who lived on the ranch under her benevolence. He also acted as her personal secretary.

To cover his unilateral action, Jake Floyd backdated a letter to the Grace lawyers innocently suggesting that two additional trustees, unnamed, be appointed sometime in the future—when in fact he had already gotten Mrs. East to appoint himself and Lee Lytton. But when Mrs. East was told by the Grace lawyers that she had actually signed over control of the foundation, she demanded and got the grudging resignations of both men.

In a letter to Mrs. East, Judge Lytton said that he could not "help but be apprehensive" that she was listening to outside attorneys instead of Jake Floyd. But he said he did not intend to "butt in"—a position he did not adhere to after Mrs. East died.

As the time of her death approached, the mistress of LaParra sensed the pending assault on her estate. A Washington tax lawyer who advised her said that she had come to regard many around her as "just kind of sitting on the fence like vultures." But she trusted Brother Leo and had put the future of the foundation in his hands.

Since drafting her new will, she had made codicils to it that named foundation trustees to succeed her: Brother Leo, Peter Grace and, later, a missionary priest who shared their views. But the Grace lawyers were unsure that a foundation trusteeship could be willed. So six weeks before Mrs. East's death, the monk, who had been with her ever since she entered a New York hospital, obtained a separate document from her. Duly witnessed, it made him sole trustee upon her death.

Almost immediately after she died on Feb. 11, 1961, Brother Leo appointed Peter Grace as co-trustee and the missionary priest soon joined them. The foundation was under the complete control of what the losing Texans derisively called "the New Yorkers."

At Mrs. East's funeral, Bishop Garriga delivered what seemed to some more a calumny than a eulogy. "I couldn't believe what I was hearing," says rancher Tobin Armstrong. "Obviously, he felt that Aunt Sarita had turned on him by leaving it all where he couldn't get at it."

A few weeks later, the bishop met with Brother Leo and Peter Grace. According to a memo written by Mr. Grace, the bishop castigated the monk "for invading his turf without his approval and taking Sarita Kenedy out from under his nose." He feared that "some hothead would start a lawsuit" unless Brother Leo resigned from the foundation and named the bishop of his auxiliary in his place. Brother Leo refused. The die was cast; it would be Texas vs. New York.

Tale of Two Widows

Mrs. East and her sister-in-law Elena Kenedy, also a widow, lived less than 100 yards apart on the LaParra Ranch, but their relations were not the best. Mrs. Kenedy, born into a society family in Saltillo, Mexico, bridled under the domination of Mrs. East, who ran the ranch as she saw fit. "Sarita was bossy; Elena told her off," recalls Paul Suess, Mrs. Kenedy's brother.

When Mrs. East died, Mrs. Kenedy became the boss—but only a nominal one, since the foundation would now control the ranch. On April 15, 1961, she held a meeting at her house of other South Texans with a lot to lose: Bishop Garriga, Lee Lytton, Jake Floyd and several others.

They had much to worry about. With Mrs. East gone, the New Yorkers wanted to lease LaParra to Robert Kleberg, the overlord of the King Ranch. But an alarmed Mrs. Kenedy wanted the ranch in friendlier hands, those of her favorite nephew, Tom East, who was also present. Tom East was a Kleberg heir. His family had split off its one-fifth interest in the King to form another ranch for which he had great ambitions; someday he wanted to run even more cows, over more land, than "Uncle Bob." He wanted LaParra, badly.

Accounts of the meeting, in depositions, memos and interviews, have Mr. East turning to Bishop Garriga and exclaiming, "Bishop, we just simply can't let this ranch go." The bishop, however, seemed more concerned with his lost patrimony. At one point, he pounded his fist on a table and said of Mrs. East: "You know she was overreached! You know she was overreached!"

Jake Floyd and his principal client, Alice National Bank, were anxious, too. Mrs. East, a director and stockholder of the bank, made it an independent executor of her will and repository for the foundation assets, which were swelling with incoming oil royalties. But these assets were now governed by outsiders who were already skeptical about the bank's management of them—a stewardship that the state attorney general would assault in court 22 years later.

A Grace lawyer wanted the foundation's income, which was held in cash, put into interest-bearing securities. Jake Floyd sent him a snippy refusal that closed the matter for the moment. But the possibility still existed that a pot of money growing into one of the biggest in South Texas might be whisked away at any time.

Mr. Floyd also wanted to control the foundation himself. "Jake was motivated by a desire for power," says Patrick Horkin Jr., who was present at the meeting as Judge Lytton's attorney. A one-time Floyd associate, attorney John Mullen, paints Mr. Floyd as a man with "a nose for money and power" who reveled in the role of kingmaker, paying agents $20 a head to truck in Mexicans who would vote illegally to help him crush a rival machine.

Thus, out of many motives and with Mr. Floyd leading them, the group at Elena Kenedy's decided to sue—to block the leasing of the ranch and to win control of the foundation. Tom East, who wanted to run LaParra, would finance the case. Lee Lytton, Mrs. East's second cousin and personal secretary, agreed to be the nominal plaintiff.

Judge Lytton says the issue of Texas control of Texas money was only one reason for the suit. "They [the New Yorkers] wanted the foundation to be used universally," he says, "but the family thought the funds should be used in Texas. I was just the means to that end." He once testified that he didn't remember reading the complaint he had sworn to.

Notice that a large subhead (TEXAS vs. NEW YORK) takes the place of a transitional passage. We left off the previous section in the present with a quote about greed by John Mullen; suddenly we are back in the past with Bishop Garriga. The same thing is done with the subhead that reads TALE OF TWO WIDOWS.

But the reader is not jarred because we have signaled the sudden shifts with the special subheads. The typographical device tells him that we aren't trying to weave a seamless web here. This device and others like it—star dashes, or simply extra spacing between unrelated passages—is the prose equivalent of the film director's sudden cut to a different scene. Used judiciously it can add an appealing variety to the form of a story, and we already know that variety is attractive to readers.

This section alternates story development with character development. Every time we introduce a player of some consequence, we stop the action briefly to tell the reader just a little about him and what motivates him in the issue at hand. This is important. A man with a nickname like "the dry snake" might be expected to backdate an important letter, as Jake Floyd did. We understand Tom East's actions better when we know how very much he wanted to be a ranch baron like his famous uncle Bob Kleberg. And we are convinced that the lawsuit is a fraud when we find that Lee Lytton didn't read the document he swore to.

But the digressions to establish character and motive are never too long; they are interwoven with action, not lumped together, and the story is always moving ahead.

Four days after the meeting at Mrs. Kenedy's, the suit was filed in state district court at Alice, in Jim Wells County. The defendants included all three foundation trustees, but the main target was Brother Leo. The suit charged that the monk, "a man of extremely strong and persuasive personality," had unduly influenced an ailing Mrs. East "in such a manner as to substitute his will for hers."

In the years to come, virtually every other pleading in this and other cases over the estate would paint Brother Leo as a Svengali who bewitched, through almost hypnotic wiles, an ailing, befuddled old woman too fond of her whiskey and water. At no time would Brother Leo, who vehemently denies such charges, ever get anything resembling a full and fair trial.

The Lytton suit claimed that the monk had used such alleged wiles to get Mrs. East to demand the resignations of Jake Floyd and Lee Lytton as foundation trustees, appointments Mr. Floyd had gotten by playing on Mrs. East's fear of taxes. It wanted the resignations set aside and judgment that the pair were the only valid trustees—in short, total control for the Texas interests.

The Texans also asked for an injunction barring the New Yorkers from leasing LaParra to the King Ranch and from shifting any foundation funds out of the court's jurisdiction. They got it that very day. The New Yorkers had high-priced lawyers, but the Texans owned the battlefield—Jim Wells, Jake Floyd's county.

"An Unholy Alliance"

South Texas has always been a place where a man looks out for kinfolk. So it is not surprising, perhaps, that the first act of the late C. Woodrow Laughlin upon taking the state district court bench in 1953 was the dismissal of a grand jury investigating his brother.

As an elected rather than an appointed jurist, he also had to be politically sensitive to people like Jake Floyd, an early foe who had once tried to unseat him but who now backed him, and the Alice bank he represented. So when the Lytton lawsuit and request for injunction hit his desk—as it had to, since he was the only district judge there—he made the politically correct, if judicially dubious, choice. He granted the injunction without a hearing.

"Laughlin would rule where the power was, and Brother Leo had no power. But the Alice bank did. If Laughlin wanted to get re-elected, he'd need the bank, not Brother Leo," says Wash Storm, who knew the judge well and who himself was on the county-court bench at about the same time.

Patrick Horkin, the lawyer who filed the suit and injunction request, enjoyed warm relations with Judge Laughlin. But he conceded that the granting of an injunction without hearing the other side was still quite unusual. "If it hadn't been for Jake Floyd, I don't think I could have gotten it," he says.

Brother Leo and the Grace layers, believing they could never get a fair trial in Jim Wells County ("There wasn't any way that would happen," agrees Judge Storm), tried to move the case elsewhere but failed. Round one to Texas.

The suit disgusted many who had known Mrs. East. In a letter to the bank, William Sherry, the geologist who had been appraising her oil properties, called it "an unholy alliance to circumvent her will." For his part, Peter Grace dreaded the publicity that a trial might bring and was anxious to convince the church that the charges against Brother Leo and himself were unfounded. So he and the monk sought Rome's help in mediating a quiet settlement. To get one, Bishop Garriga would have to be placated first.

He and the New Yorkers were poles apart. The bishop not only insisted on ousting them but also was now set on getting control of the foundation himself. Jake Floyd (a baptist) was the dominant influence among the Texans, and the bishop feared that a foundation dominated by him would be cool to putting a lot of money into the Diocese of Corpus Christi.

Rome couldn't ignore the appalling prospect of a public brawl over a sick widow's fortune, one that pitted a sitting bishop against a monk and one of the most prominent laymen in the church. Thus, as 1961 melted into 1962 and the long business of taking pre-trial depositions continued, Rome acted. A parallel chain of events began to unfold far from Texas—in Rome, in Philadelphia, in New York, in the silent monasteries of the Trappists—as the church brought its weight to bear.

These efforts, to be detailed in a second article tomorrow, included threats of excommunication against Catholics in the case, the silencing (for a time) of Brother Leo and his virtual imprisonment in a remote monastery, misrepresentation and more. In the matter at hand, they had this result: Under considerable ecclesiastical pressure, Peter Grace left the fight. He cut a deal with the Texans to get the suit dropped.

Reached in July of 1962, the agreement in principle provided that a maximum of $14.4 million from certain oil royalties go to a separate New York foundation established by Mr. Grace, which he named in Sarita East's honor. The original foundation kept all the rest, Mr. Grace and his lawyers resigned from all positions in it, and the Texans got to name as many trustees as they wanted.

Brother Leo resigned rather than give even implied consent to an agreement that would, in effect, deny Mrs. East's intentions. So did the other remaining trustee at the time, Henrietta Armstrong, Mrs. East's best friend.

The new five-member board of trustees was dominated by Jake Floyd, who headed a subgroup of three who voted together and were known as the Alice Bank Group; each of them, including Elena Kenedy, was a bank director. Bishop Garriga was left with half a loaf. He got a trusteeship but would be outvoted by the bank group. (The bishop went to court himself a few months later to try again to get control, but he failed.)

Only days after the agreement was reached, however, a new horde of aspirants to the Kenedy fortune galloped over the horizon and into the probate court at Sarita, Texas. They were the so-called Mexican heirs, and they were quickly joined by others who suffered when Mrs. East scrapped her old will. Their claims threatened the foundation and stalled for almost 20 years the final judgment required to legally settle the Lytton suit.

Mrs. East was the last direct descendant of Capt. Miflin Kenedy, a co-founder of the King Ranch who ultimately split off his piece of it to form LaParra. The Mexican heirs—more than 150 of them— were descendants of a Mexican woman who later became Capt. Kenedy's first wife, and all but a few had been ignored in Mrs. East's new will. Using the same undue-influence charges against Brother Leo that others had, they wanted that will tossed out— and, if possible, the earlier one as well. If that happened, Mrs. East's entire estate would be divided among blood relatives.

The Mexican heirs were joined by some of Mrs. East's relatives, notably the Turcottes, who had gotten bequests of land but wanted mineral rights under it as well. The Oblate Fathers of Texas entered the fray, too. In both wills, Mrs. East had left this Catholic order her ranch mansion for a house of prayer and 10,000 acres around it—but in the 1960 will she cut the order's share of the mineral rights beneath to 10% from 90%, and the Oblates, using the same accusations against Brother Leo, wanted their original share back. (They eventually settled for less land and a 25% slice of the mineral rights beneath the original 10,000 acres. The Turcottes failed to improve on their original bequest.)

All this put the foundation trustees in an interesting legal position. The charges against Brother Leo in the Lytton suit were sworn statements; they were being used by the Mexican heirs and others in contesting the 1960 will—which was the sole source of the foundation's money. So the original sworn pleadings were replaced by amended ones. These new pleadings did not carry the seal indicating they were sworn. "A cute legal point," one lawyer for the bank calls it.

In 1964, while the heirs wrangled on, the agreement in principle to settle the Lytton case was finally converted into a legal judgment. Jake Floyd did not live to see it; his place was filled by his law associate, Kenneth Oden. Brother Leo, at that time under virtual house arrest in a remote Canadian monastery, was forbidden to attend. He almost managed to stall the judgment anyway.

The proceedings required the monk's power of attorney. But Brother Leo, who had revoked his earlier resignation to keep both the Texans and his one-time friend and ally, Peter Grace, from making a deal final, would not grant it despite tremendous pressure from the church.

The church finally supplied it for him. Without his knowledge or consent, his superior in the order sent a telegram to a Grace attorney saying that under an "understanding" he had with the monk, he, the superior, was giving clearance in Brother Leo's name for the settlement to be entered. Accepting this unsigned and unverified message as a valid power of attorney, the accommodating Judge Laughlin allowed its use by the Grace lawyer to remove Brother Leo from the foundation. The judge then transferred it officially into the hands of the Texans.

Hugo Touchy, a Texas state district judge, says: "Under no circumstances would I accept a telegram from a religious superior as a power of attorney to act for someone else. It isn't right and proper."

The new trustees reconstituted the foundation as one that would make donations only in Texas. Sarita East's dream seemed dead.

But the judgment couldn't be made final, and the foundation couldn't disburse grants, until the will contests were settled. As executor of Mrs. East's estate, the bank finally settled the Mexican claims in 1971 for oil royalties with a calculated worth of $10 million; however, with the sudden run-up in oil prices that followed, and continuing major discoveries on the land involved, they became worth many times that. Some of the lawyers who took them as contingency fees became millionaires.

Other contests, however, dragged on into the '80s, paralyzing the foundation. And, as time passed, more of the principals in the affair of Sarita Kenedy East died. Among them were Tom East, who got to run LaParra, and Bishop Garriga, who never saw a cent of his patrimony. The bishop's diocese and his seat on the foundation board were assumed by Bishop Thomas Drury. While on the board, Bishop Drury himself contested the 1960 will that endowed the foundation he was then helping to run; the previous will had been more favorable to the diocese. He finally got a fat settlement—15%

of the mineral rights underlying all but a small portion of Laparra. His successor would do even more.

The writer jumps into this chain of character development/ story action to say that at no time has Brother Leo ever received anything resembling a trial on the charges against him. This not only implies a gross unfairness but gets the reader curious as to why, thus setting up the ensuing material on justice in south Texas.

In dealing with that, we take pains to establish through expert testimony that the handling of the Lytton suit was irregular, to say the least. Readers can't be expected to know exactly how a state judicial system ought to operate, and matters like this have to be put into perspective by believable sources.

Notice the way Peter Grace's change of heart is treated. He did not "reconsider and come to an agreement with his one-time adversaries." He *cut a deal with the Texans to get the suit dropped*. This change from formal diction to a blunt plainness is bracing to the reader, a welcome touch of variety in expression.

Two paragraphs after that we refer to the Alice Bank Group. Throughout the story we've made every effort to introduce and group characters according to their general positions. We have the New Yorkers, the Texans and now a subgroup of Texans, the Alice Bank Group. Right after this we introduce yet another bunch, the Mexican Heirs. In a story full of characters, grouping them in this way helps the reader keep them straight, and the labels attached to the groups remind him of their motivations.

Near the end of the section we make good on an earlier promise. Near the beginning of the story we said that some of Sarita's money went to honor lawyers, including some who had helped keep her money from going where she wanted it to go. The implied promise is that at the proper time the reader will find out more about how they did that. This paragraph delivers the goods.

A Bishop's Business

Bishop Rene Gracida, who was a World War II combat pilot and who carries a scepter made from a pool cue, cleaned house when he was appointed the new bishop in Corpus Christi in mid-1983. He removed most of the chancery staff and diocesan administrators, replacing them with his own handpicked people from Tallahassee, Fla., where he had come from. He wanted the Oblate Fathers to donate the LaParra mansion they had inherited from Mrs. East, along with 1,000 acres around it. They refused.

"He's done a lot of things that don't seem befitting a bishop," says the Rev. David Tonary, who left the diocese. Bishop Gracida, he says, "has got a lot of nerve." He also has got something none of his predecessors could get—control of the foundation, which was in more legal trouble when he arrived to take the "church seat" as a trustee.

The state attorney general's office had sued Alice National Bank in Kenedy County Court at Sarita, Texas, at about the same time the bishop arrived, demanding a full accounting of how Mrs. East's estate was handled. It didn't like what it saw. In early 1984, the attorney general sued again, this time for damages that are unspecified but that could amount to over $40 million. Also leery of the quality of justice in Jim Wells County, where such a suit would ordinarily be brought, the attorney general got special legislation passed to allow its filing in state district court at Austin.

The suit charges that the bank enriched itself at the expense of Mrs. East's foundation. Among other things, it contends that the bank kept almost $1 million of foundation funds in checking accounts on which it paid no interest; that it charged the foundation a $750,000 depository fee "contrary to normal practice"; that it sold Mrs. East's cattle and leased her ranch at below-market prices to Tom East, a client of bank director and foundation trustee Kenneth Oden; and that the cattle appraiser had "personal ties to Oden." It demanded Mr. Oden's ouster.

The action was filed Feb. 8, 1984. Mr. Oden, who later resigned in exchange for immunity from prosecution (the bank itself denies wrongdoing), was due in court Feb. 13, the same day a foundation trustees' meeting was scheduled.

On Feb. 10, Bishop Gracida drove 70 miles to the home of Elena Kenedy, who was 95 and ailing, to obtain her proxy; the reason is unclear, for the trustee meetings were always held at her home anyway. He walked out with the proxy and more—her resignation as trustee and president.

The bishop, who will not consent to an interview, told a local paper at the time that Mrs. Kenedy signed willingly. But her brother, Paul Suess, says she did not realize at the time that she was signing a resignation. The resignation documents shows her signature scribbled diagonally across the page.

Mrs. Kenedy immediately rushed hand-delivered letters to the bishop and other trustees canceling the scheduled meeting and requesting that none be called until Kenneth Oden could be present. The bishop ignored her. With Mr. Oden at the court in Austin and Mr. Lytton there, too, that left only one trustee to attend the meeting—the bishop himself.

Barred from Elena Kenedy's home, he held the "meeting" on the porch. He named himself president, appointed a nun to fill Mrs. Kenedy's place and named two other trustees friendly to him, thus assuming total control. He immediately passed a resolution naming Mrs. Kenedy president emeritus for life. About two weeks later, an investigator for the attorney general called on Mrs. Kenedy to ask her about her "resignation"—only to learn she had died that very day.

• • •

Today, Bishop Gracida is sometimes seen discussing Nicaragua and voter registration on "The Gulf Coast Catholic Hour," one of many local and cable shows turned out by the new Sarita Kenedy East Center, a $1.1 million complex built with one of the foundation grants the bishop has been steadily issuing. He has also joined the attorney general's suit to recover damages from the Alice bank.

Brother Leo is 70. He is currently in New Orleans, where a federal circuit court of appeals will hear yet another argument in yet another case he has brought to see that Mrs. East's money goes where she wanted it to go. It may be his last attempt. He has failed for a quarter of a century, but in the scattered Trappist monasteries he is not seen as a failure; to many of the monks he has become something approaching a legend, and is known throughout the order.

In the slums and rundown villages of Latin America, a whole new generation of the poor has grown up since Mrs. East died. In Aguascalientes, Mexico, she was helping the Rev. Domingo Munoz build a blanket factory so jobless villagers nearby would have work. But Father Munoz, now 75, says the administrators of her estate ignored his pleas for enough money to finish the job.

Near Santiago, where she built a Trappist monastery on 4,000 acres, the monks are planning to auction it off and use the money to house the poor. The Rev. Richard Gans, a former abbot there, says: "It was a gift, and in a way we're only putting it back in the hands of those who inspired her generosity in the first place—the poor, the hungry and the homeless."

With the shift to Bishop Gracida, the reader is now in the near present. The Bishop's personality is implied, not stated. We don't say he is an unconventional type and a go-getter; the business about the pool cue, the housecleaning at the diocese and the quote from the priest who served under him sketches the man in a much more interesting and convincing way than flat declaration would have.

The last four paragraphs, set apart typographically, form a sort of epilogue. It is handled dispassionately, with no intrusion of the writer's feelings, no bells and whistles—and that's why it is effective. The bare recitation of facts in these paragraphs has an emotional wallop that derives from the reader's knowledge of all that has gone before. Embroidering it would ruin it.

The end is a circling-back. We are again with the poor in Santiago, where we were in the beginning. The quote from Fr. Gans reminds us of the good impulse that led to so much evil, the impulse that set in motion the entire tale. And we sense that what the Trappists are doing in Chile may be the only honor ever paid to the wishes of Sarita Kenedy East.

This first story confined itself mainly to the struggle over the estate in Texas, and the clerics in it move in the secular sphere. But there was another conflict occurring at the same time, this one within the councils of the Roman Catholic Church. Author Getschow wisely chose to treat this parallel story separately, and takes us into a world few people know. Also, while Brother Leo is a primary character in the first piece he is still essentially a pawn overshadowed by events; in the story to follow, he emerges in the round as a man of extraordinary principle, tenacity and stubbornness.

This time I won't interrupt the tale with instructional prattle. We'll save that for the end.

Reverend Father, I promise you obedience in all good until death.
—from the Solemn Trappist Vow

SPENCER, Mass.—Within the massive bouldered walls of granite that frame the Abbey of Our Lady of St. Joseph, a ceremony almost half as old as the church itself takes place as the need requires. Completing it, men who have proved worthy enter into a new life bare of luxury, governed by the strictest discipline and full of sacrifice and prayer—the world of the Cistercian Order of the Strict Observance, better known as the Trappists.

This is Brother Leo's order, and this abbey was his home and mother house for many years. Money he raised built it and put up daughter houses elsewhere. But he is a pariah to those who run the abbey now. Separated from his order 20 years ago, existing on the support of those who still honor the memory of Sarita Kenedy East, he lives alone in a cubicle on a mountaintop in Argentina.

All this happened for one reason: Brother Leo took his entire vow of obedience seriously, while the church, anxious to avoid scandal, pressed him unmercifully to follow only part of it. Obedience in all good, yes, said Brother Leo. But what if what is demanded is not good, what if conscience—"the whisper of the Lord within us," as he puts it—speaks against what is bidden?

Brother Leo's choice brought against him powerful figures in the church and in his order, including the apostolic delegate to the U.S., the archbishop of Philadelphia, and the abbot of Spencer, his superior. In trying to bend this one stubborn monk to their will, they tried persuasion, they tried compromise, and they tried threats of excommunication against him and his first lawyer, as well as against other Catholics in the case.

Industrialist Peter Grace bowed to the church's wishes. Brother Leo would not. Failing in all attempts to move him, the powers of the church surrendered to expedience and pragmatism. They sent to a Texas court documents that they knew misrepresented his intentions, documents they also knew would be used to violate the last wishes of Mrs. East. And when Brother Leo then fought the settlement those documents made possible, they cast him out without the ecclesiastical trial the canon law of the church requires.

He is fighting still to see that Sarita East's money ultimately goes where she wanted it to go—to the poor of Latin America. That effort has taken place in a lot of courtrooms, and Brother Leo has not a single small victory to show for it; his case, which entangles the issue of ecclesiastical authority with one of civil responsibility, is one rarely found in the secular courts. It has been suggested to him that he could return to his order if he would only accept a settlement and stop fighting. Why won't he do it?

An Empty Life

In 1938, Christopher Gregory, a handsome, pampered young man of 22 from Auburn, Calif., entered a Trappist monastery in Rhode Island for a retreat. He was an unlikely attendee. The son of a successful author of Western novels, he had been to an exclusive boarding school in France, attended college and lived a high life.

But it was an empty one. "I was adrift," recalls Brother Leo. "I felt humiliated that I could find no meaning in my life. The monastery pushed open a door for me and revealed a life that made a lot of sense. I was smitten with it." Christopher Gregory's retreat never ended. After five years at the monastery, he took the solemn vows of a monk.

The Trappists have moderated their practices since, but at that time their severity was fearsome. Monks could speak only at the request of their abbot or prior, who was second in command. Their sole possessions were a cloak, shoes and one set of underwear woven out of potato sacks. They lived almost entirely on a meatless soup, bread and water. On Fridays, they flagellated themselves with small whips—"the Discipline," it was called—as a reminder of their sinful natures.

Their lives were governed by the Holy Rule of St. Benedict, and a set of some 200 regulations derived from it, prescribing "external reverence and a becoming, modest and edifying demeanor." At the slightest infraction of any of the regulations—glancing sideways at meals, for example—a monk was almost sure to be "proclaimed" at the Chapter of Faults and ordered to prostrate himself before his abbot and beg the forgiveness of his fellows. The Trappists aimed to produce souls strong as iron, and they did.

But they were running out of places to put them. After World War II a great influx of aspirants to the order persuaded Dom Edmund Futterer, Brother Leo's abbot, to do something unheard of—send a monk into the world to raise money for new monasteries in the U.S. and Latin America. He picked a reluctant Brother Leo, who laid down his cobbler's tools and took to the road for months at a time.

He was exempted from the strict rules of the order but still tried to live simply, staying in fleabags and eating canned goods in his room. Louis Shine, a former monk who was the treasurer of the abbey then and would sometimes travel with Brother Leo to inspect monastery sites, says: "I hated to go out with Leo. He'd stay in the most godawful places. Finally I asked Dom Edmund if I could travel alone."

Brother Leo raised about $8 million for the Trappists. An admiring Dom Edmund, who came to love him almost as a son, called him "Leo the Lion," a hunter who never gave up until his prey wrote the check.

Personable and polished, the young monk was readily accepted by the nation's wealthiest Catholic laymen, but the man he grew closest to was Peter Grace. Mr. Grace donated $400,000 toward the construction of a new mother house at Spencer, where Dom Edmund and his monks would move. The monk considered Peter Grace his best friend, and when Sarita Kenedy East decided to set up her foundation, Brother Leo enlisted his help.

Brother Leo first met Mrs. East in 1948 but only began spending a lot of time with her about 10 years later. She was just two years older than his mother, Lotus, who had devoted her life and fortune to helping poor Mexican migrants and whose example had been a profound influence on her son. The two women were later to meet and become friends. In letters, Brother Leo would address Mrs. East, as well as his mother, as *carissima*—dearest one. This would be used against him later.

Mrs. East became a Trappist benefactor and grew increasingly reliant on Brother Leo. "Sarita was a tremendous woman, one of the most remarkable women I've ever met," he says. "She felt she had a responsibility from God to help the poor—the real poor, Catholic or Protestant. She trusted me more than she should have, given how poorly I've handled things."

The widowed Mrs. East had been alone in a 30-room mansion at her vast LaParra ranch in Texas, drinking a little too much, increasingly wary of the droves of aspirants to her estate. "They wanted a piece of the rock," says Maria Langoria, whose husband was Mrs. East's chauffeur. The monk took Mrs. East away from that on trips to monasteries in the U.S. and Latin America, some of which she was helping to build; often traveling with others, they all stayed at the same hotels. These occasions, along with tallies of Mrs. East's liquor bills, would be noted later, too.

Mrs. East asked Dom Edmund Futterer, Brother Leo's abbot, to detach him temporarily to help her set up her foundation. She recognized the request as unusual and promised to underwrite the Trappist expansion in South America in return. Dom Edmund agreed in writing. Brother Leo had the explicit permission of his ecclesiastical superior to join in a civil matter that he came to view as "a sacred contract." When Mrs. East died on Feb. 11, 1961, after a brief illness, his 25-year ordeal in its defense began.

A Very Hot Potato

Archbishop Egidio Vagnozzi, apostolic delegate to the U.S., was the first ranking prelate to juggle what was becoming a very hot potato. Mrs. East had been dead only two months, but the Texas group led by her local lawyer had already filed suit in the name of her relative and private secretary, Lee Lytton Jr., to gain control of her foundation. The apostolic delegate was supposed to make the Lytton suit go away, for it promised great embarrassment to the church.

One of the Texans was the Right Rev. Mariano Garriga, Mrs. East's own bishop, who wanted control of the foundation for himself but had failed to get it. Now, with the others, he was pitted against one of the most prominent Catholic laymen in the U.S., who was a Knight of Malta, and his associate, a Trappist monk. That was bad enough. Worse were the allegations in the suit: that the monk was a Svengali who had charmed a sick old woman into giving him control of most of her estate. And Bishop Garriga, a loose cannon if there ever was one, was compiling a dossier on the monk and the widow. A trial could be ruinous.

Mr. Grace, who didn't want to see his name in the papers either, wanted a church-mediated settlement badly. He had also been told that involving a member of a religious order in a civil proceeding violated canon law. He went to the Vatican—in all, he took 22 trips there to talk to authorities—and the Vatican referred him to Delegate Vagnozzi, back in Washington.

According to a memo written by Mr. Grace, the archbishop listened and immediately wrote out a proposed settlement that gave Bishop Garriga two seats on a five-trustee board, with Mr. Grace, Brother Leo and a priest in accord with their views retaining control. It was approved by the necessary higher authorities.

But according to the same memo, the delegate subsequently changed his mind. Now Bishop Garriga was to have board control, and Brother Leo was to get out of the foundation. At a meeting, the archbishop told Mr. Grace that Brother Leo and Mrs. East "might be guilty of meretricious relations." A stunned Mr. Grace reminded the archbishop that Mrs. East had been 70 years old when she died. The archbishop, he notes, then "went into quite a bit of detail about elderly women, their appetites and desires."

The Grace forces couldn't agree to the archbishop's terms. In his memo, written to his friend Francis Cardinal Spellman of New York, Mr. Grace says the archbishop "threatened me with excommunication, albeit in a friendly way, and then advised me that he would see to it that the Holy See ordered the resignation of Brother Leo."

Archbishop Vagnozzi had apparently seen a copy of a dossier that Bishop Garriga had ordered on the activities of Brother Leo and Mrs. East. The dossier was hand-carried to Rome by the bishop and laid before Pope John XXIII, according to Patrick Horkin, the bishop's lawyer. The document is unavailable, but it is said to have implied that Brother Leo and Mrs. East had engaged in drunken debauchery, listing the occasions when they had stayed in the same hotels (without noting that friends traveling with them had often been staying in the same places) and reporting on Mrs. East's liquor purchases.

No one can be found who, knowing Mrs. East and Brother Leo, gave any credence to what the dossier implied. Friends say that if anything, Brother Leo had a positive and moderating influence on Mrs. East. "Brother Leo got her on her feet and moving," says rancher Tobin Armstrong, "and, if anything, his presence got her off the [heavy] drinking."

Archbishop Vagnozzi brought the undue influence charges the Texans had made against Brother Leo and Mr. Grace before the Sacred Congregation of Religious, overseers of all orders and societies within the church and one of the most powerful bodies of the Roman Curia. There Dom Gabriel Sortais, the abbot general of the entire Trappist order, rose to speak.

Dom Gabriel knew Brother Leo and had visited Mrs. East only a month before her death. He did not find, as the monk's accusers claimed, a woman so addled by pain-killing narcotics that she did not know what she was doing. Mrs. East conversed with him in French, repeated her intentions for the foundation and the monk's role in it, and appeared completely lucid.

Before the Sacred Congregation, Dom Gabriel delivered a blistering denunciation of the charges and the suggested settlement favoring the Texans, which he called "contrary to justice and a modification of the last wishes of Mrs. East." His own conscience forbade him, he said, to take part in it. He warned that removing Brother Leo, whom she had appointed, would signify that the church agreed to the accusations. Any compromise of the issue, he added, would violate "a fundamental moral principle."

Peter Grace was told that the charges would not be pursued. But Dom Gabriel died not long after. The charges lived on.

"Reform of Conscience"

Dom Edmund Futterer, the old abbot at the Spencer mother house, was very ill. Brother Leo says he was closer to Dom Edmund than to his own father. For his part, the abbot knew well the stubbornness and principle of his young monk.

Dom Edmund had a weakness: He loved architecture in the grand European style. Once, Brother Leo recalls, he returned from a fund-raising swing to find a luxurious guest house rising at Spencer. He saw it as a waste of money that could have gone to legitimate charity and told his superior he wouldn't raise more funds for it.

Dom Gabriel, the abbot general, was visiting at the time and sided with Brother Leo. Construction was halted. Furious at what he considered Leo's disobedience, the abbot wouldn't talk to him for months—the worst punishment, monks say, that can occur in a monastery. But when his abbot's health began to fail, Brother Leo relented and told him to build the place if he wanted to.

Dom Edmund finally had to step down as abbot and was succeeded in August 1961 by Dom Thomas Keating. Dom Thomas happened to be the son of a prominent maritime lawyer who had Peter Grace as a client and who sat on the board of a Grace-controlled bank. It was through Dom Thomas that the church would apply its greatest pressure on Brother Leo.

By the fall of 1961, it was apparent that Archbishop Vagnozzi was getting nowhere in obtaining a settlement of the Lytton suit. At a dinner in Paris, Brother Leo says he "told Peter that I didn't see any good coming out of it and that the proper thing for me to do was defend myself in court." While Mr. Grace disagreed—he still wanted a church-mediated settlement—Brother Leo believed that the industrialist understood his point of view and still sympathized with it.

Their parting was amicable, as Brother Leo remembers it. (Mr. Grace wouldn't consent to an interview.) They were still friends; Peter Grace had named a son after Brother Leo; and he and his wife, Margaret, had allowed the monk's mother to live in a retreat house they had at Spencer.

But when Brother Leo came back to Spencer, he found his new superior, Dom Thomas, "trembling, saying to me that I was going to destroy Spencer by my actions."

The abbot had gotten a 78-page memo dictated by Mr. Grace. It said that Patrick Horkin, the lawyer for both Lee Lytton and Bishop Garriga in Texas, was threatening another undue-influence suit—this one to recover all the money that Mrs. East had given the Trappists before she died. (The memo was later filed as an amendment to the original Lytton complaint.) Spencer, which as mother house would be the liable party, had already spent the money on building new monasteries.

This new development, Mr. Grace said in the memo, made it all the more desirable that a settlement be reached. He made it clear that if Brother Leo wouldn't go along voluntarily, his superiors should ensure that he did. At this point, it was beginning not to matter whether the charges against Brother Leo were true; the church and the order were threatened by them, and that proved enough.

Dom Thomas ordered Brother Leo, who was planning legal action himself to block the Texans, to "disengage" from the conflict. The monk, mindful of his promise to Mrs. East and feeling utterly betrayed by his friend, refused. He says today that Mr. Grace "didn't have the guts to say [how he really felt] to a fellow's face. I was terribly hurt by it all."

His abbot, concluding that he suffered from a "badly formed" conscience, then ordered him to halt all contact with anyone outside Spencer and submit to therapy by a monk-psychiatrist. For several months stretching into early 1962, Brother Leo spent hours a day in "reform of conscience" sessions that included repeated references to his solemn vow of obedience. "I renewed my pledge of 'obedience to all good,'" says Brother Leo, "but Dom Thomas and Father Raphael Simon [the monk-psychiatrist] told me I was blinded by pride and in danger of losing my religious vocation."

Dom Thomas grudgingly allowed him to see the Rev. Dominic Hughes, a moral theologian lecturing at Spencer. Father Hughes did not help the abbot's cause. He told Brother Leo that he had not only a right to fight but also a "sacred duty" to do so. The monk emerged unreformed—to face his most powerful challenge yet.

The Archbishop Takes Over

Archbishop John Krol of Philadelphia was a rising star in the American church (he would later get the red hat of a cardinal) and a crack canon lawyer. Alarmed at the delay in reaching settlement of the Lytton suit, Rome put him in charge of negotiating a settlement in February 1962 and armed him with plenary powers of excommunication and full authority over all churchmen in the case.

A few years before, the archbishop had met Bishop Garriga of the Texas group and, according to Patrick Horkin, the bishop's lawyer, the two became friends. Mr. Horkin himself was given the archbishop's unlisted phone number, he says, sometimes stayed in his Philadelphia mansion and called him frequently about the case.

According to a flurry of memos written by Mr. Grace, the archbishop (who has declined numerous requests for an interview) listened only to the Texans while the agreement in principle was being made final, and demanded that foundation control go to them. The Grace forces caved in.

Under the agreement in principle of July 1962, they got a fifth of the foundation's assets to establish a separate New York foundation under Peter Grace. It was a relative pittance; their fifth was in oil royalties that were to be cut off when a maximum of $14.4 million had been paid.

Mrs. East's original foundation, which was to be turned over to the Texans, kept all the rest and had no ceilings on its royalties. Today its assets are between $300 million and $500 million. (Mr. Grace's new foundation, named for Sarita East, has made various donations, some to the Trappists, but little or nothing has gone to the poor of Latin America.)

Disgusted, Brother Leo resigned his trusteeship in the old foundation, though he later revoked the resignation in order to have some leverage in blocking a formal settlement. In 1963, he was sent to a daughter house of Spencer that Mrs. East had given money to build—La Dehesa, near Santiago, Chile. Before long, Archbishop Krol would have need of him.

To take effect, the agreement in principle settling the Lytton case had to be entered as a court judgment. This required Brother Leo's signature on the settlement agreement and his resignation as a trustee. Archbishop Krol wrote him that he could "in good conscience" sign the coming settlement document because "the foundation funds will go to both the needs of the universal Church as well as the Church in Texas."

It arrived in September 1963, hand-delivered by a monk who urged him to sign it without reading it under "orders from Krol." Brother Leo talked the messenger into letting him inspect it—and discovered that the vast bulk of Sarita's largess wouldn't go to any charity outside Texas.

Making the messenger wait, Brother Leo hurriedly sought advice from the Rev. Aldunate Lyon, the head of the Jesuit order in Chile. Father Lyon told Brother Leo he could sign the settlement—but not to return it to Archbishop Krol. Send it to the pope, he urged—with a cover letter explaining that Brother Leo's signature was conditioned upon Pope John XXIII's taking responsibility for altering Mrs. East's wishes. Brother Leo did just that and sent it by a separate courier to the late Bishop Manuel Larrain, a prominent South American prelate who was then in Rome.

The archbishop was beside himself when he learned his emissary had lost control of the document. "Profoundly shocked," he cabled Brother Leo. "Cable identity of person to whom sent and how sent." When Brother Leo replied that he had sent it "to Holy Father," the archbishop raced to Rome just in time to intercept the packet.

A letter by Peter Grace and an oral account by Brother Leo, who spoke with Bishop Larrain afterward, offer slightly different versions of what happened next. But they agree on this: In the presence of Bishop Larrain, the Vatican Secretary of State decided that the cover letter should not stay with the settlement document, and that Archbishop Krol, also present, left with that document. The cover letter never found its way to the Texas court.

However, Archbishop Krol still needed Brother Leo's formal resignation as a foundation trustee, either in person at the court proceedings or by his power of attorney. So the archbishop ordered the monk to Miami and demanded his cooperation. Brother Leo was accompanied by Father Hughes, the moral theologian who had aided him, and the Rev. Luke Anderson, the prior of Spencer. They advised him that he could in good conscience resist the archbishop's demand, and he did.

Dom Thomas Keating ordered Father Anderson never to speak to

Brother Leo again. Dom Thomas sent the recalcitrant monk to a remote Canadian monastery, where he was kept under virtual house arrest, forbidden all contact with outsiders.

Brother Leo says the archbishop also threatened him with excommunication several times over the years. And the monk's first lawyer, William R. Joyce, Jr., says he was told by Father Hughes, who was delivering the message for the archbishop, that the latter would throw Mr. Joyce out of the church if "I filed any papers saying that Brother Leo disagreed with the settlement."

Mr. Joyce, a prominent Washington attorney who represented Brother Leo without fee, is still angry about that and says "He [Archbishop Krol] used his ecclesiastical authority in a civil matter against a man who had been given approval [by his former abbot, Dom Edmund] to do what he did. You don't mess with the civil courts that way, even if you are an archbishop."

In Canada, Brother Leo heard from no one for months. He felt like a prisoner of war and struggled to maintain his sanity by reflecting on the teachings of Gandhi, the apostle of passive resistance. Finally, he got a soothing letter from his abbot, Dom Thomas Keating, telling him that the abbot had intended to ask his aid in getting the settlement through but had decided that "it was too much to ask of you in your present state of mind." He added that there was nothing new to say about the agreement.

That letter was dated Aug. 30, 1964. That same day, Dom Thomas had sent a telegram to a Grace attorney saying that under an "understanding" he had with Leo he was giving clearance in Brother Leo's name for the settlement to take place. With acceptance of this dubious document, the judgment was entered. Dom Thomas waited one month to inform his monk of the action taken in his name.

First of Many Failures

Dom Columban Hawkins had been Christopher's Gregory's novice master. His job was to shape and mature the conscience of his charge, making it a vessel sensitive to the will of God, and the man who became Brother Leo came to love Dom Columban almost as he loved Dom Edmund. Now Dom Columban was the abbot of Our Lady of Guadalupe in Oregon, a daughter house of Spencer, and Dom Thomas Keating had put his former novice, a man torn by conflicting imperatives, back under his old teacher's care.

Dom Columban assured his superior that he would do his best to rehabilitate Brother Leo. But, as had so many others, he too wound up supporting him. Against his own superior's wishes, Dom Columban quietly allowed and encouraged Brother Leo to go back to Texas—to defend the foundation and to unseat the Texans who ran it.

Brother Leo went into the court of C. Woodrow Laughlin, the judge who had allowed the use of his abbot's telegram to seal the Lytton case settlement into judgment. The monk's lawyers filed to set that judgment aside, but Judge Laughlin ruled against them and an appeal failed. It was the first of many failures Leo would suffer.

At that same time, Mrs. East's Mexican relatives—the so-called Mexican heirs—and others were contesting her 1960 will, the only source of foundation money, and Brother Leo testified on behalf of the foundation whose trustees he wanted to remove. On March 7, 1966, he finished his testimony and, stepping down from the stand, was handed a letter by attorney Patrick Horkin. It was his dismissal from the Trappist order. The letter was dated Jan. 12, almost three months before.

When Dom Thomas Keating learned that Brother Leo had gone to Texas to fight the settlement and testify, he had had enough. He sent the letter, which ordered Brother Leo to remove his habit and "live in the world" until he had "removed the cause of this dismissal," to Archbishop Krol. The archbishop sent the letter to Mr. Horkin, who apparently held on to it until Leo had finished testifying.

The monk immediately wrote to the Sacred Congregation of Religious, demanding an ecclesiastical trial as required by canon law and saying that his vocation was "dearer to me than my life." But Rome had had enough, too. It released him from his vows. He refused to be released.

On March 18, the Sacred Congregation, while leaving the door open for reconsideration later, upheld Brother Leo's dismissal. Archbishop Krol was quoted as saying Brother Leo had forgotten "his obligation to observe unquestioned obedience." According to the Rev. Thomas Brockhaus, a canon lawyer who aided Brother Leo, an emissary from the archbishop threatened him with excommunication if he continued to assist the monk.

"Bottom of the Boat"

Grande Canoe, known to locals as "the Bottom of the Boat," is an abandoned hermitage, a tumbledown, spider-infested dump on the island of Martinique. Cast out of his order, forbidden to stay at its monasteries, Brother Leo went there to live as a hermit after his dismissal. He stayed five years, following his monastic regimen, still in his own eyes a monk.

He moved to his present hilltop hermitage in Argentina in 1971 and has lived there since, in a 10-by-20-foot cinder-block box filled with books. For many years he dropped from sight, and his cause seemed hopeless. But Dom Columban and people in Texas who knew what Mrs. East wanted, and saw how her wishes had been subverted, continued to support him.

In 1979, the aging monk took up her cause again, going into Judge Laughlin's court one more time; after 17 years of will contests, the judgment in the Lytton case was at last to be made final, and a preliminary hearing was scheduled. Judge Laughlin converted it into a trial, over the strenuous objections of Brother Leo's lawyers, and ruled after about an hour or two that the settlement was final. Brother Leo lost the appeal in the Texas Supreme Court.

In 1980, he asked the U.S. Supreme Court to review that decision. This time he said he had been deprived of his civil rights in the Texas courts, which had given him "no meaningful opportunity" to defend himself against the undue-influence charges brought against him so many years before, or to prove that his abbot had no authority to assume the power to act in his name. The court denied his petition.

A brief filed on behalf of Peter Grace in that action maintained that Brother Leo had given his "unconditional written consent" to the Lytton judgment. The Rev. Richard Gans, Brother Leo's strong supporter and former abbot in Chile, read it with disbelief. He wrote Mr. Grace, saying, "Can you really believe this? . . . How can it be that you have joined forces with those who heaped lies against you? How can your conscience be at peace?"

Mr. Grace replied, stressing that if Brother Leo had wanted to make his signature on the settlement conditional, he should have noted that on the document itself, not a cover letter. He characterized the position of the church in the matter as "pragmatism in the fullest sense of the word, and that may or may not have been dishonest"—but being no theologian himself, he left such judgments to others.

As for himself, Mr. Grace said: "I have been told insofar as my personal life is concerned that to follow people who are in a superior position to myself, unless it involves obvious immoral conduct, is the way that one should conduct himself."

In 1981, Brother Leo attempted another civil-rights suit, this time filing in a federal district court in Corpus Christi against the foundation trustees at the time, the state attorney general and Alice National Bank, the repository of the foundation funds and the executor of Mrs. East's estate. He claimed they conspired against him to deprive him of his right to trial. This suit was still languishing in the court when Bishop Rene Gracida of Corpus Christi seized control of the foundation in early 1984. He wanted it out of the way.

On April 5 that year, the bishop invited Brother Leo and Father

Gans to his seaside mansion. According to Father Gans, who wrote an account of the meeting, the bishop pointed out that the Alice Bank group that had run the foundation for so long was out and he was in. The way was clear, the bishop believed, for Brother Leo's reinstatement in the Trappists "with full honors"—if he dropped the suit.

Brother Leo and Father Gans were taken aback, for the bishop did not seem to understand what the monk was fighting for. The bishop pressed Leo, saying, "Tell me, brother, what do you want? What do you want?" And ultimately Brother Leo told him he would consider dropping the suit if the foundation gave "substantial amounts" to help Latin America's poor, as Mrs. East had wished.

According to Father Gans's account, the bishop's secretary, who was present at the meeting, told him, "With regard to your poor, you must have faith that God will supply them." The meeting broke up with the parties unable to come close to an agreement.

• • •

Last January, a federal district judge dismissed Brother Leo's complaint without issuing an opinion. Yesterday, appearing before an appeals court in New Orleans, Brother Leo's lawyer was pointedly asked by the panel's chief justice what relief his client was seeking. "We want to have a trial," said Brother Leo's lawyer. "A trial that Brother Leo has never had."

The third paragraph of this story cuts to the central issue: What does "obedience in all good" mean in this context? The different interpretations put on the Trappist vow by Brother Leo and by his superiors, the conflict between them and within the monk himself, torn by another promise he considers sacred, underlies the entire piece and gives it its internal logic. In the few paragraphs that follow, the writer summarizes. Here is the main theme statement, climaxing again in a simple question— why won't this stubborn man bend, and save himself? The rest of the story is its answer.

The same foreshadowing for the sake of suspense that was used in the first story is used in this one too. We are careful to stress that Brother Leo had in writing permission from his direct superior to engage in a civil matter that he views as a *sacred contract.* Then we say, *When Mrs. East died on Feb. 11, 1961 . . . his 25-year ordeal in its defense began.* The word *ordeal* is what drives the reader on here.

In the next paragraph, we again make a sudden, bracing

change from high to low diction when we say that Archbishop Vagnozzi *was supposed to make the Lytton suit go away.* Later, when the head of all the Trappists defends Brother Leo before the Sacred Congregation, we waste words to good effect: *There (before the Sacred Congregation) Dom Gabriel Sortais, the abbot general of the entire Trappist order, rose to speak.* The pause here, the description of Dom Gabriel getting to his feet, signals to the reader that what this man will say has weight and power. We are moving slowly for the sake of force.

Notice that later on the writer steps in and pulls together the meaning of a chain of events in one sharp statement: *At this point it was beginning not to matter whether the charges against Brother Leo were true; the church and the order were threatened by them, and that proved enough.* In long, complex stories the reader must be kept on the track, wants to be kept on the track, and the writer had better move in occasionally to keep him there. Most of the time this involves making a brisk conclusion about what preceding events add up to.

As it was in the first piece, the development of character is of essential importance in this story. The alert student will notice that direct quotations are used sparingly; even Brother Leo has relatively little to say. But his character is detailed in action after action, refusal after refusal. Peter Grace is quoted far more often—he happens to be an incredibly prolific producer of memos—but what he does and doesn't *do* is still more important in bringing him to life. The single passage near the end, where he justifies his actions to Fr. Gans in a letter, contains the longest quote in both stories—and a most revealing one. It stands out not only by virtue of its content, but because it has not been smothered by too much chatter elsewhere in the story. When a writer sets people to talking and talking, pretty soon the reader gets numb and the few important things that are said don't have the needed impact.

At the beginning of this chapter I asked why anyone would be interested in a story about a monk and a widow, people nobody had ever heard of, and what happened to them a quarter-century ago. These stories provide a compelling answer. We are powerfully moved by them because journalism that succeeds in opening a window on the soul of man, that distills both good and evil, weakness and strength, is rare and great journalism. It does not skim over the surface of events but strikes deep and hard at the elemental core of human nature, and so is timeless in its appeal.

The reader doesn't care that he's never seen the names of the characters in *People* magazine, he doesn't care that the events described happened a long time ago, for he is seeing himself and his fellows in what is written. Stories that can be called great all spring from great ideas, and somewhere in most great story ideas there is the promise of the human spirit revealed.

Yes, you say, but you are news people. You want to know what happened to Brother Leo's appeal. It failed.

CHAPTER 9

NOTES ON SELF-EDITING AND STYLE

Your story is written. It's probably a little too long and rough in places, even if you've been tough on yourself, but the desire to get it off your desk is overpowering. You itch to dispose of it immediately.

Don't. Unless the piece is urgently needed by the editors, drop it in a drawer and take a long lunch. Have a beer. Have two. Pat yourself on the back for your achievement; it may be the only praise you get. When you return to the office, leave the story alone and do something else for a day or two, if possible. A piece still warm from the typewriter or VDT is one too close to the writer's heart, and can't be edited with the necessary detachment.

When you do put on your self-editor's hat and attack the story, take your time. I'm continually astonished by writers who spend weeks or even months on a major feature project and only an hour or two on final editing. The writer who doesn't spend at least a half-day editing such a piece is either a supreme craftsman or a masochist begging to see his work truncated and altered by others.

No set procedures govern editing, so again I can only tell you what works for me—a three-step process that in some respects turns the usual order on its head:

1. Editing for Content

Reading quickly through the story, I look first for ways to lengthen it, not shorten it. If I've omitted some bit of reporting that might buttress key sections that now seem a touch weak, some point of explanation that would make something clearer, I include them. At this point I just want to be sure that everything needed to make my story clear and convincing is in it. This doesn't take long.

2. Editing for Conclusiveness and Flow

I pay special attention to my conclusions and summaries, including my main theme statement—do they say exactly what I want them to say, and are they as forceful as the material that backs them up? I also pay close attention to all transitional material, attributions and explanations. If any are verbose or fuzzy, I pare them down and sharpen them up. At the same time, if I'm annoyed by the presence of a secondary character and get the sensation he is only slowing me up, I get rid of him or suppress him.

3. Editing for Pace and Precision

Many writers first try to cut their stories by removing entire sentences, paragraphs or even sections. Only after this do they look for smaller cuts. I do the opposite because I can usually save enough space with word-by-word cuts to preclude major surgery. The latter may create more trouble than it cures because some blood and bone usually comes away with the fat, and an unsightly wound is left that must be stitched together.

Word-by-word editing takes more time than any other step. Even though my self-critic has done much of this work already, he's had to labor in haste and has left enough fat so that I can cut most of my stories 10% to 15% without removing any of their elements.

I look for wasteful little constructions like "due to the fact that" (make it "because"); passive structures that could be made active to save space and add vigor ("he felt it was incumbent on him" means "he felt obligated"); opportunities to use freight-train sentences and hook-ons; lurking redundancies; Siamese-twin sentences that can be combined, and so on. I also strip the lead of any extraneous elements.

Slowly a better, brisker story takes shape. It would be impractical to compare here an entire unedited story with its finished version and explain the reasons for every change and cut, but we can treat one innocuous paragraph:

Boomtowns often suffer severe personnel problems because city workers leave their jobs for better-paying ones with resource companies operating nearby. In Evanston, Wyo., an oil boom that has engulfed the community has given Mayor Dennis Ottley some king-sized headaches. He's lost half the police force to the oil companies, who are employing the men as security guards at 25% more than he can pay, and many teachers who can make much more as roustabouts than they could in the classroom.

This is not terrible, but it is rough. The self-editor first fixes on the blob—"severe personnel problems." What does that mean? It means turnover. Next, "leave their jobs." Let's make it *flee* their jobs." When someone offers you a big raise to walk around a fence for a few hours instead of getting your head broken trying to settle bar fights all night, you don't leave the old job, you flee. "Resource companies." I don't know what a resource company looks like. Can I be more pictorial? How about mines and oil rigs? I can see *them*. "Operating nearby." Pure fat. If the place is a boomtown, the companies will have to be operating somewhere nearby.

Now, this Ottley chap. He is a nice guy, very cooperative, and has seduced us into using him. He is a talking head who isn't even quoted directly. Eliminate him and use his information as fact; as the mayor he ought to know what's happened to his own police force and school system. And the "king-sized headaches" —can we just say what they are? The next sentence does, so let's combine these Siamese twins.

The self-editor arrives at this:

Boomtowns often suffer severe turnover because city workers flee their jobs for better-paying ones at oil rigs or in mines. Engulfed by an oil boom, Evanston, Wyo., has lost half its policemen to oil companies that pay them 25% more as security guards, and many teachers who make much more as roustabouts than they could in the classroom.

The first version uses 82 words to say what the second expresses in 59. Almost 30% of the paragraph has been pared away without loss of substance. Do this throughout a story and the effects will be bracing, to say the least.

If my story is still too long, I then remove elements. The first to go are in the secondary sections of the piece, where the reader won't miss the material as much. Here, I may be able to escape with a simple statement in place of a full set of proofs. If even this doesn't save enough space I'd be forced to take material out of primary story sections, but I've never had to go this far.

Michelangelo claimed that he didn't create images when he sculpted but only released the mighty figures, fully formed, that slept within his blocks of marble. The self-editor's work is a little like that. He refines and releases what the artist in him has already created. The result may be no stunning work of art, but it's better for his effort.

Your own finished piece, containing storytelling qualities and burnished to a gloss by this final step, may also have another quality we haven't addressed directly—style. It may be more than good. It may be you.

I can't teach style. Nobody can. In this context, it's easy enough to say what it is: the character and personality of the writer shining through his work so clearly that the reader senses them. But beyond mere definition is a territory every writer has to explore for himself.

A few years ago I stumbled on an entry in the personal journal kept by my daughter, then a college student majoring in English. The topic was unexceptional, an account of a visit she had made to her grandparents. This is the core of it:

. . . Last night at dinner Granddaddy said the grace; he thanked the Lord for the meal, for the day we all had together, and for having me there to share the weekend with them. Then there was a pause and I looked up at him. His head was still bowed but he was shaking it back and forth and rubbing one hand over the top of the other, as he sometimes does, and his chin was quivering. He stopped, sighed, tried to go on and then just began to cry. Grandmama said, "There, there, Gale, we know exactly how you feel," and then she dished out the dinner and that was it. But I thought I was going to burst.

Another such moment today. I was going for a walk and Grandmama decided to go with me. We went to the park. It was brisk and windy and when we walked down the street with our hands in our pockets we kicked up the autumn leaves. I found an acorn hat under a tree and showed Grandmama how to whistle with it; then we walked around looking for more of them. She was off a little in the distance and I stopped just to look at her—a little woman with a white rain bonnet on and a blue cape, stooping over with her hands on her knees, inspecting the ground with concentration and serious purpose. Then she spied an acorn hat, picked it up, and blew into it. There was a meek little whistle and her eyes got wide; she blew again, harder, and the whistle got louder. Then she stopped and looked at the acorn hat in her hand with a new sense of accomplishment. I laughed to see the child in her and she looked over at me, surprised to be caught, and giggled.

This entry obviously lacks polish, but it's very good. You can't know exactly how good because you don't know the people, so you'll have to take my word for it that a primary characteristic of each is captured here with skill and insight.

The gentleman described was almost inarticulate about his emotions. Indeed, I never heard him even try to verbalize them. But unlike so many of his generation he was never afraid to show physically what he was feeling, and he had an enormous capacity for feeling. His wife, over 80 now, retains a consuming, childlike curiosity; a world grown stale to so many younger people is fresh every day for her, another opportunity to learn something new. These marks of character are defined in action, not declaration, and the writer has a strong presence.

Reading this, I was surprised. I'd never realized my daughter saw so acutely or could write so well. She'd shown me a few of her English themes, and most were awful, stuffed with six-dollar words, Byzantine sentences and tortured or circular logic. When I would point out defects (a nasty business, having a writer for a father), she would say, "Oh, professor so-and-so loves symbolism, so I threw all that stuff in" or "Professor such-and-such is a bug for metaphysics, and I had to say that."

She'd been writing to fit the perceived prejudices of others, and when I saw how she'd written to suit herself I regretted the past suppression of her talent. A shame, I thought. And then I remembered myself as a young writer.

I'm not given to nostalgia, but even if I were my early career was nothing to get nostalgic about. My writing was adequate, even good in flashes, but I got little satisfaction from it. Mostly I remember pain and anxiety—the pain of struggling to wring something decent out of my unfocused, unplanned, completely disorganized reporting efforts, and the fear that what I finally produced would be rejected or dismembered. At 20, my daughter had stifled her individuality because she was afraid her teachers wouldn't accept it—wouldn't accept *her*, really. At 26 and for years afterward, I stifled mine for about the same reasons.

My audience was not an interested, intelligent general reader with whom I could be myself. It was a faceless mob led by a group of editors. To satisfy them, I felt I had to put aside my own natural expression and somehow divine and adopt theirs, even though I'd never met most of them. I had to do things *The Wall Street Journal* Way, whatever that was, or fail.

Many of the hundreds of staffers I've taught are caught in the same trap today. Most have healthy self-esteem as reporters; if it is out there, they say, I'm pretty sure I can get it. But most feel inadequate as writers.

This is why I've put so much stress on the importance of the writer's presence in his story. I crept into my own pieces gradually, timidly—and found that when I did the editors liked them more, not less. Emboldened, I went further. Today, though I'm still gripped by the same anxiety every time I confront a new project, experience tells me that the fear is groundless and will damage my story. So I can dismiss it, and be myself.

My history, my daughter's journal entry, my work with other reporters—all convince me that most of us are better writers than we allow ourselves to be. I hope the nuts-and-bolts instruction in this book helps you approach your potential, but you ought to know this: All it amounts to is a list of terms, arranged systematically, that describe what I consider and do when I'm writing *naturally*. I may have analyzed and defined as devices certain instincts and feelings I had no words for before, but I'm not a better writer because I've tacked names to them. I'm a better writer because I now feel free to use them whenever I please, however I please.

So, the most important parts of this book deal with the writer's attitudes toward himself, the reader, and outsiders that intrude on their conversation. If the writer fails to dismiss these strangers because he's fearful of offending them, if he then models his expression to suit a roomful of people instead of one, writing tricks and devices won't help him. He'll never develop an individual stamp to his work. Style can't grow where fear taints the ground.

APPENDIX 1

READING FOR WRITERS

People frequently ask what they should read to become better writers. The most convenient—and wrongheaded—answer: Read everything. No one has time, and using it to study bad writers is almost as useless as reading no one at all; their clunky phrasing and errors in structure, emphasis, character development and pace seep into the pores of the student and infect him. Hacks only beget more hacks.

Even good writers may be the wrong ones for certain students of nonfiction to read. If a person is most interested in news-papering, for example, I wouldn't recommend he study John McPhee. Though McPhee's work is extraordinary, it rests largely on the skillful layering of detail upon detail upon detail, and he requires a lot of space to tell stories that often are quite narrow in scope. Newspaper writers have little space to tell much broader stories, and if they tried to tell them the way McPhee tells his the whole paper couldn't contain them.

What to do, then? First, the unpopular thing. I recommend that the student put aside his writerly pride, pick up a good basic English text and then do the unthinkable—read it through slowly and thoroughly, no more than a section or chapter at a sitting. Over the years, he should read it again and again.

Whenever I dip into my ancient copy of *Understanding and Using English* (the revised and enlarged edition, written by

Newman and Genevieve Birk and published by The Odyssey Press, New York) I'm mortified to discover how slovenly and excessive I've been with the language since I last read the book. We unconsciously despise the rules that bind us and *want* to forget them, but they can't be broken to good effect unless we first know them in our bones. Rereading a basic text, the serious writer feels the stinging slap of correction and murmurs, "Thanks, I needed that."

The same feeling strikes me when I reread that tiny book no writer can fail to learn from, *The Elements of Style* (William Strunk and E. B. White, Macmillan, New York). If a writer were told he could read only one book about his craft, this would be the best choice. Its instruction in clarity, economy and grace is unequaled. (If the writer were allowed one more book, he could do worse than to see the first put to work in E. B. White's crystalline essays.)

Whole forests have died to fill the marketplace with other writing books. One I've found particularly practical and easy to read is the second edition of *On Writing Well: An Informal Guide to Writing Nonfiction* (by William Zinsser, Harper & Row, New York). The chapters entitled Simplicity, Clutter, Style and Words are particularly good.

Helpful as it is, direct instruction is best taken in small, measured doses; too many writing books and the eyes glaze over, the lids fall. So the student writer should learn mainly by osmosis, spending most of the time reading stories by people who know how to tell them surpassingly well. This is mostly fun, but done for the sake of learning it also involves work. When the reader finds that something on the page creates a vivid image in his mind, arouses an emotion or gives him a stab of insight, he ought to enjoy the moment—and then stop, back up and try to puzzle out how the writer did that to him.

In choosing authors as teachers the student will want to start with those who write in a simple, unobtrusive way and who use conventional structure. He can identify with them—what they do doesn't seem impossible—and their craft is more accessible, as well as more useful to him in what he's likely to write himself.

Isak Dinesen's *Out of Africa* is one of the most beautifully written books I know, but it doesn't arouse hopeless envy in the student's breast. Authors whose expression is complex and vividly original, however, often have that effect, and the despairing beginner can only say, "I'll never be able to write that well." At the top of their form such writers as Norman Mailer, Gabriel Garcia Marquez and John Updike are dazzling—and too intimidating, at least at first.

In my opinion, looking for good writing in the daily press and most magazines is a waste of time. There may be an occasional pearl beneath their oceans of cliched and hopped-up prose, but diving for it isn't worth the trouble. If good journalism is wanted, it's easier to turn to book collections of stories produced by the best authors in the field.

My own favorites are Joan Didion, Gay Talese, Truman Capote (for *In Cold Blood*) and Tom Wolfe. Considering his flamboyant presentation—all the italics, exclamation points, and hammering repetition—Wolfe might seem an odd choice, but beyond all the gee-whiz is work remarkable for its incisiveness, cutting insight and sense of command.

The journalism of Wolfe and the others is enriched by the values that make good fiction, and anyone who wants to write factual material in an arresting way ought to learn at least a little about how fiction works. The second edition of *Technique in Fiction* (by Robie Macauley and George Lanning, St. Martin's Press, New York) is a solid, workmanlike book that covers most of the basics well.

A deeper, more subtle and more meaningful book—if a little harder for the beginner to grasp—is *The Art of Fiction; Notes on Craft for Young Writers* (by John Gardner, Alfred A. Knopf, New York). Gardner is a rarity. A first-rank novelist, he was also a great teacher of writing—not as a literary lion brought to academe to handle a seminar or two for a semester or two, but as a year-round workman.

His book is outstanding on the importance and handling of descriptive detail; on the creation and maintenance of the world into which the writer tries to bring the reader (Gardner calls it "the fictional dream" but nonfiction writers must create dreams

of their own); on the construction of graceful, rhythmic sentences; on matters of taste, and on maintaining suspense. The
chapter titled Common Errors is especially instructive. And the
simple-looking but fiendishly difficult writing exercises Gardner
offers will stretch anyone's talent.

Looking through these books, the student who wants to write
better nonfiction will be struck almost forcibly by the concerns
he shares with the novelist or short-story writer. No Chinese
wall divides writers of fact and writers of fiction. Much more
unites them than separates them, a fact the student will appreciate when he studies—not just reads, but studies—the work of
the best novelists and short-story writers.

The list of nonfiction writers he can learn from is short, the
list of fictionists long. Some are wonderful at one aspect of the
craft, not so good at others. John O'Hara seems hopelessly dated
now and I find his novels, excepting *Appointment in Samarra*,
forgettable even for the time they were written. Many of his
short stories, however, hold up beautifully and his command of
dialogue has taught me much about how to use quotations.
Margaret Craven hasn't written enough to be on anyone's list of
top authors, but her little jewel of a book, *I Heard the Owl Call
My Name*, is a masterpiece of economy.

Again, the student reader must beware of hacks, which means
avoiding most of today's bestselling novelists and a lot of others,
too. (When in doubt, the buyer can always apply this verbiage
standard: All books over 500 pages that weren't written by
Dickens or a dead Russian are better left on the shelf.)

As he did with nonfiction, the beginner will want to concentrate
on acknowledged fiction stylists of long standing whose expression is simple, seemingly effortless. They're the best teachers of
what John Gardner calls the carpentry of writing, and we all
have to see how two boards are properly nailed together before
we can hope to build something beautiful that is uniquely our
own.

There are too many of these writer/teachers to name, and I
don't want to spoil the joy of exploration by offering some kind of
short list. Too many authors who might be helpful to too many
students wouldn't be on it.

But I can't close this without acknowledging a personal debt to one writer who has taught me more about my business than any other, a former newspaperman who long ago went on to better things. I can recommend him without qualification.

He writes with great economy and power about themes worth treating—about obsessive love, about courage where you least expect it, about despair and pity and the finger of God pressing down upon man. Some of his books reveal the cold desert that is the real landscape of espionage, and he's generally credited with fathering the modern spy novel.

He does much with little, and writes plainly about complicated things. In just a few lines, a few words really, he sets me in the square of Mexican village and I can smell the dust, feel the heat, sense a physical and spiritual poverty there. In another book, he gives me just a snatch of dialogue—and I suddenly know what emotion lies hidden behind words that don't express it directly. His characters are full of flaws and redemptive graces both, and he reveals them in action, not declaration. His many books include only a few failures, in my opinion, but I've learned even from these.

Thank you, Graham Greene.

FULL TEXTS OF SAMPLE STORIES

Six stories cited as examples in this book were presented in shortened form, with some of their contents paraphrased rather than quoted directly. This appendix provides the full-text version of each of these shortened stories for the benefit of readers interested in studying them further.

HARD TIMES IN SAN DIEGO (p. 6)

by G. Christian Hill

SAN DIEGO—If awards were given for civic embarrassment or bad luck, a number of candidates would spring to mind. There is Washington, home of Watergate, or Detroit, home of the troubled auto industry. Or that perennial front-runner, Philadelphia, home of Philadelphia.

Then there is this beautiful seaside town of 771,000, the long-suffering victim of a whole string of bumblings, scandals and disasters that make it seem almost a city accursed. The problem has gotten so bad that Doug Porter, ex-editor of an underground paper named The Door, now refers to any noteworthy job of bungling or failure as "typically San Diesque."

Take, for example, the problem of daylight saving time, which became mandatory nationwide last January as an energy-saving measure. In San Diego, however, there may be some baffled residents still walking around two hours behind the rest of the country. That's because the San Diego Union urged them to set their clocks back an hour instead of forward an hour. How could the paper have made such a mistake? "I have no comment, and don't quote me on that," says City Editor Al Jacoby.

The muddle over the time is nothing compared to what has happened to the leading elements of the business and financial community—or what is left of them after a wave of scandals and failures. The crash of collapsing companies and the cries of fraud recently led the San Diego Tribune to comment that the town has seized a leading position as "West Coast distributor of flimflam men and holder of the national record for suede shoes per capita."

Biggest Bank Failure Ever

Some of the noisiest busts have been companies controlled by financier C. Arnholt Smith, honored some years ago as "San Diegan of the century." His U.S. National Bank of San Diego, the town's biggest, was declared insolvent last October after examiners discovered that about half of all its outstanding loans were made to interests related to Mr. Smith, and that much of this total was probably uncollectible. It was the biggest bank failure in U.S. history.

The bank collapse dried up the credit flow to Westgate-California Corp., the city's fourth-largest business, also controlled by Mr. Smith. It swooned into Chapter 10 bankruptcy proceedings in February. Prior to that the Westgate Plaza Hotel, ranked by Esquire magazine as one of the world's three finest hotels, and associated properties owned by Westgate-California separately went into receivership.

Mr. Smith personally set another record for fiscal disaster in 1973, as the Internal Revenue Service slapped him with a $22.8 million tax lien for back taxes and interest allegedly due on his 1969 income. The IRS said it was the largest individual tax lien for one year's income in U.S. history.

San Diego is also the home of the biggest Chapter 11 bankruptcy proceeding ever attempted, according to the federal district court judge overseeing the case. The company is San Diego's largest home-builder, U.S. Financial Inc., which entered Chapter 11 reorganization after the SEC accused its previous management of creating fictitious deals to produce phony profits—a charge denied by the former officer. And San Diego's largest locally based hotel-motel chain, Royal Inns of America, is now laboring in reorganization under the supervision of a creditors committee after suffering a financial flameout early in 1973.

Is It the Sunshine?

There have been other, smaller failures in sufficient quantity to keep the federal bankruptcy court humming. Ironically, this has been of little help to the company that owns the building in which the court is housed; that company recently sought protection under the bankruptcy laws itself.

Surveying the ruins, an investment manager who moved here from the East Coast says: "The business leadership stinks and the place is a lodestone for shady types. I don't know whether it's being close to the Mexican border, the sunshine, or what, but it seems to be a town where nobody gets terribly upset if you pull a fast one. My friends in Boston and Chicago just shake their heads. They can't believe it."

Neither can sports fans in San Diego, where losing has been raised to an art by the city's pro teams. The Chargers of the National Football League (2–11–1 last season) were barely edged out by the Houston Oilers as losingest team in all pro football. They also touched off a drug-use probe of NFL teams by Commissioner Pete Rozelle's office.

The probe was begun after Houston Ridge, a Charger tackle, sued the team, charging he was injured while playing under the influence of a pain-killing drug supplied by the club. He was awarded $260,000 by a state superior court last year.

Meantime, the investigation by Mr. Rozelle's office led to fines totaling $40,000 being levied on players and the club's management for flagrant use of marijuana by the team's members. (Bill Kurtis, a Chicago newscaster, cracked that "the way the Chargers played last year the drug must have been formaldehyde.")

The Padres baseball team of the National League was the cellar dweller in the western division last season, had the second-worst won–lost record in the majors and had the worst attendance of any major league team. The team was recently sold to Ray Kroc, chairman of the McDonald's hamburger chain, by C. Arnholt Smith, the former owner. Mr. Kroc quickly learned what San Diesque means.

Opening the season in Los Angeles, the Padres lost three games straight to the Dodgers. Then they were kicking away (three errors) their home opener against Houston when the hamburger magnate finally lost control. Commandeering the stadium public-address system, he told the fans: "I suffer with you. . . . I've never seen such stupid ball playing in my life." The Padres went down, 9–5.

Two Measures of Success

The most successful pro athletes in town are the San Diego Conquistadors of the American Basketball Association, who edged their way into the league playoffs before losing to the Utah Stars. But few people bother to watch the Qs, as they are called, and the club tells such whoppers about its attendance that the San Diego Union feels constrained to print its own crowd estimate next to the club's figure. In a game last January, writer Jim Hamelin actually counted the crowd and got 471. The club announced attendance of about 1,700 that night.

The malaise that seems to afflict San Diego began to settle on the city in 1972, when it was supplanted by Miami as site for the Republican national convention. The shift was made following disclosure that International Telephone & Telegraph Co. had offered a campaign contribution to support a San Diego convention.

Then came the general fumblings and fiscal disasters of 1973 and into the present. Pete Wilson, the city's mayor, says that the whole thing is just a run of bad luck and that there is nothing about San Diego that particularly attracts disaster. "Maybe we were due just on the law of averages," he says. "It's like catching cold after years of good health."

Dean Dunphy, a building contractor who is president of the Chamber of Commerce, agrees. He calls the town's business busts "Just an unhappy coincidence," adding, "There's no way you can ascribe this to lack of leadership in the community. Nope, no way that argument would fly."

What to Do in San Diego . . .

Whatever the reasons for it, San Diego's misfortunes haven't helped its image much, and it wasn't exactly known as a dynamic power center to begin with. Los Angeles Times sports columnist Jim Murray recently described it as "a body of land surrounded on two sides by water, on two sides by mountains, and on all sides by apathy. There are two things to do in San Diego. You can go to the zoo or you can join the Navy."

Most residents seem to find other compensations, however. Paul Saltman, who left the University of Southern California in Los Angeles to become vice chancellor of the San Diego campus of the University of California, says: "Look, I'm three minutes away from Black's Beach, the surf was four to five feet yesterday, and life is just beautiful, man."

San Diego's string of misfortunes may actually benefit the place, argues Neil Morgan, author, newspaper columnist and informal social historian of the city. He has promulgated "Morgan's Law," which states that the bad luck San Diego has had in the past may discourage a growth that is too rapid and uncontrolled, leaving the city to prosper in a more modest way—unchoked by too many new factories, new skyscrapers, new residents. Mr. Morgan recently expounded on the principle to a group of local public-relations people. Reliable sources say some of them were not amused.

WINO PARK (p. 9)

by Marilyn Chase

SAN FRANCISCO—This town not only tolerates its minorities, it embraces them, wearing ethnic and social diversity proudly, like Joseph's coat of many colors.

Its homosexual community virtually owns two streets and reputedly can deliver an election. There are Chinese, Irish and Italian parades, Japanese and Samoan festivals, a French Hospital and a Russian Hill. San Francisco's ballot is polyglot, and there were city-hall debates over whether to make its gasoline pumps multilingual too.

But ever since the Barbary Coast placed its salty signature on this onetime sand dune, San Francisco has reserved a special place in its heart for drunks. Not the hidden parlor tipplers of Pacific Heights or the virile pub crawlers of Union Street, but what the sociologists call "public inebriates"—winos, of which the city has an estimated 5,000 to 7,000.

San Francisco has long been toasted as one of the world's easiest places to get drunk and stay drunk. It has the requisite amenities; relatively cheap liquor, a temperate climate, and legions of tourists who are easy marks for a practiced panhandler. Now, to these attractions is added another: a park dedicated exclusively to winos.

A Bottle of Thunderbird

Wino Park, officially called Sixth Street Park, is a transformed sandlot tucked amid the transient hotels, pawn shops and liquor stores of the city's tough South-of-Market area. There, a wino can recline with a bottle of Thunderbird or Night Train Express wine, build a bonfire, cook a meal, sleep, loiter or play a game of sodden volleyball without being arrested. A brass plaque commemorates famous people who liked their drink. The winos like to read it aloud, like a roll call of heroes: "Honoring: Winston Churchill, Ernest Hemingway, W. C. Fields, John Barrymore, Betty Ford, Janis Joplin, Dylan Thomas. . . .," they intone.

A $135,000 metamorphosis, incorporating a $20,000 federal grant, has turned the sandlot into a combination campsite and open-air lounge, complete with benches, toilets and trees. It is about the size of a small store. Its sponsor is Glide Memorial Church, a inner-city congregation led by a charismatic and politically powerful black minister, the Rev. Cecil Williams.

Mr. Williams calls his congregation the Moral Minority and says of the park's habitues: "Their place in the sun is on the street." His clout has elicited the official support of the city hall and chief of police.

But if there is a guardian angel of Wino Park, it is Frances Peavey. Mrs. Peavey, a 39-year-old widow, is a rotund blonde who works full time for Glide Memorial as a kind of social engineer. She designed the park's benches extra-wide for sleeping, patiently reseeds its trampled lawns and replaces the scraggly trees that have been ravaged by the volleyball games or torn down for use as improvised weapons against the dangers of night on Sixth Street.

Confidence and Hope

"Before the park, there really was nothing beautiful or fine down there," she says. "It's my belief that if you express a little confidence, put a little hope there, you'll call forth the best in people."

And she believes she has done that. Mrs. Peavey designated a dozen of the park's regulars as "staff" and got them jackets. She holds weekly staff meetings with them to discuss issues surrounding the park, such as a recent infestation of body lice and the proposed installation of showers. She also gave them responsibility for maintaining the park and keeping social order.

"These are civic-minded citizens, who clean the park each morning. At 8 A.M. they're out there raking and sweeping," she says. "We also gave them nonviolent training to try to repel muggings and drug sales. They're a moral force there."

She gets no quarrel from the likes of Hogshead, S.Q., Mickey, Ben, or Peggy, a few of the people who spend their days and nights in Wino Park.

On a mild and sunny afternoon, they are among the three dozen regulars who congregate in the tiny park. To an outsider, the first sensations suggest that this is some kind of crazy, landlocked beach party: blowing sand from the arid planters, the smell of woodsmoke from a midday bonfire, outdoor cooking, the blare of a radio tuned to soul and gospel music, and people drinking from styrofoam cups.

S.Q., 60 and gray-bearded, is the park's elder statesman. He occupies a chair next to the bonfire and despite the balmy spring day wears a fake Persian-lamb hat. It is adorned with a button that reads, "I'm alive," the slogan of Glide Memorial Church. "Winter was rough," he says slowly, "but it's all right now. All right."

Hogshead, glowering and blind drunk, sits alone in a corner. He is the park's wood gatherer.

Ben, about 50, assumed the leadership role from S.Q. He is a robust black man with salt-and-pepper hair, a print polyester shirt and a vest with a nametag reading, "Glide staff. My name is Ben." He surveys the park with a proprietary eye and says the winos are holding their ground in perpetual turf battles with drug traffickers.

"I be here every day, seven days a week, from 6:30 in the morning. If I pick up a broom, everybody here will do the same," he says with an expansive gesture.

Ben's steady lady is Peggy, 34, a plump, freckled, toothless, ponytailed bacchante attired in fuzzy slippers and a shapeless plaid shirt. Her conversation indicates that somewhere, there lurks a proper, middle-class upbringing. She asks a reporter for a stock tip, and when none is forthcoming, explains: "My broker is in Connecticut, and anyway, I don't trust him. But if I were investing, I'd buy Kimberly-Clark, because of the Rely tampon scandal."

When friends guffaw at her investment strategy, she gets indignant. Ben teases, to restore her good humor.

A Designer's Credentials

Joe, 54, a New Orleans native, sidles up and gallantly offers his last cigarette. He talks about plans to redesign the park, and mentions his credentials. "I designed mini-parks when I was with the Department of Corrections," he says.

Drinking is much in evidence, and no one tries to hide it. But the mere mention of drugs draws scowls and denials. "They're going to drink wine," says Ben, "but drugs, no." "Might smoke a little weed," says a handsome young man called Mickey.

Mickey, 36, is a merchant seaman with a wife somewhere that he dotes on. He's trying to go straight for her and has been dry for one day. "I'm afraid of getting the shakes, Fran," he confides to Mrs. Peavey, "But so far, I'm feeling okay. I'm eating and drinking a lot of water." Last winter, when an outsider brought in lice, Mickey obtained a half-case of delousing agent from a nearby clinic and took his friends up to his apartment and bathed them.

Mrs. Peavey points to such acts as vindication of her idealism. "If you had lice, would your friends bathe you?" she asks. "Mine wouldn't." She tries to encourage Mickey's leadership potential.

Asked if it's hard to return to the park sober when all his friends are drinking, Mickey says no. "I've gone 24 hours without taking a drink, and I'm all right," he says determinedly.

This boast irritates Ben, who is feeling thirsty. "Shut up, will you, and bring me one," he says.

Fragile Order

Despite the signs of social order, that order is highly fragile. There are plenty of reminders that the park's residents resist being socialized or tamed. For example, Ben dreamed up a shoeshine business as a moneymaking project for the park, but in the cold of last winter, someone used his stand for kindling the perpetual bonfire.

"They'll burn anything," he says, crestfallen. And an attempted recycling project to turn a few pennies faltered: Their production of empties outstripped the city's ability to pick them up.

There are also reminders that, on some days, anarchy is a hairs-breadth or a drink away. The park's opening-day ceremony last year was a media event gone haywire. The Glide Church staff called a press conference and exhorted the winos to their best behavior. But the press was late, and party manners disintegrated. When a TV crew arrived hours late and tactlessly barged into the park, cameras rolling, the winos rushed the frightened crew and tried to commandeer the equipment.

Although Glide claims that the park's presence is a deterrent to muggings and drug traffic, police statistics over the past year are equivocal. Last fall, crime in the vicinity of the park was down in most categories, but in the first four months of 1981, reported incidents shot up 188%.

Merchants also fault the park for lending legitimacy to derelict behavior. One calls Sixth Street "a corridor to the toilet of the city." Adds his wife: "We have to lock our doors, because the winos fall in."

Even some former habitues of Sixth Street disapprove of the goings-on. "Big Chicago," a big-biceped man with diamond ear studs who now is head cook at Glide Memorial's free-soup kitchen, shakes his head ruefully and says: "The park isn't going well. People are tearing it up."

The winos know well that their park hasn't attained its ideal state. But to keep their goal in sight, they have designed a mural that will depict the park looking as green as the Garden of Eden, and themselves looking like exemplary stewards.

"Then we can always look up," says one wino, "and say: This is the way it's supposed to be."

INSURANCE FRAUD (p. 50)

by Hal Lancaster

LOS ANGELES—The man at the bar is a personnel officer for a large concern. He is well scrubbed, well groomed and as anonymous-looking as a glass of water. All this helps him in his sideline business, which happens to be bilking insurance companies by filing fraudulent claims.

W. T. Stead (a pseudonym he has borrowed, for this story, from an unfortunate passenger on the Titanic) is very good at his avocation. He figures he has netted about $60,000 in settlements over the past few years on 15 staged pratfalls and induced auto accidents. He is not contrite. "I am in every sense a communist," he says. "If you've got a wealthy insurance company out there that will pay out so many dollars, then people should get it."

Is there a grape on the floor of the supermarket? Mr. Stead will slip on it in front of a horde of witnesses and suffer lumbosacral strain; a generous check from the store chain's insurer alleviates it. Is there a distracted mother with a station wagon full of kids on the Santa Monica Freeway? Mr. Stead will abruptly change lanes and swerve in front of her, trying to induce a rear-end collision. A mild collision, of course, but his whiplash injury is just terrible.

Down for the Third Time

Insurance-fraud artists like Mr. Stead have plagued the industry since at least 1730, when a London woman faked her own death three times to collect the insurance money. The toll of such fraud is enormous. While no one knows exactly how much is lost to "scammers," as con artists are called here, various insurance sources estimate that up to 30% of all claims are inflated or fabricated, and that up to 20 cents of every insurance premium dollar subsidizes fraud. This means that the honest policyholders ultimately pay the bill.

The variety of fraudulent practices available is "limited only by the imagination," says Ronald Krauss, assistant to the president of the American Insurance Association. One claimant attempted to collect from his insurer for a knee injury that he claimed prevented him from kneeling at Catholic mass, thus depriving him of full participation and enjoyment of his religious life. All very well, but he turned out to be a Methodist.

Other schemes are nothing less than grisly. One man had been receiving monthly annuity checks in India, where checks are commonly endorsed by thumbprint. But a routine check by Retail Credit

Co., the Atlanta-based credit-rating and business-information firm, which has a sizable claims-investigation arm, showed that he had been dead for two years; his relatives had interred him minus the thumb, preserving the digit in formaldehyde for endorsement purposes.

Large Ante for Maimings

Then there is the macabre case of "Nub City," a small Florida town that insurance investigators decline to identify by its real name because of continuing disputes over claims. Over 50 people in the town have suffered "accidents" involving the loss of various organs and appendages, and claims of up to $300,000 have been paid out by insurers. Their investigators are positive that the maimings are self-inflicted; many witnesses to the "accidents" are prior claimants or relatives of the victims, and one investigator notes that "somehow they always shoot off the parts they seem to need least."

Insurers are moving, albeit slowly, toward stiffer screening of claims, resistance to payment of those that appear dubious, and prosecution of more cases of outright fraud. ("Nub City" residents have trouble getting accident coverage these days.) One principal weapon is the four-year-old Insurance Crime Prevention Institute (ICPI), which has a team of 70 investigators, most of them ex-policemen, ferreting out auto-insurance fraud nationwide.

The ICPI specializes in big-time frauds involving whole teams of scammers, and its ultimate goal is prosecution and conviction—which, it hopes, will discourage potential future frauds. ICPI has already broken many insurance-fraud rings, and its investigations to date have resulted in more than 815 arrests.

70 Indicted in One Case

One of its biggest busts was a ring in Detroit that ICPI says swindled auto insurers out of more than $1 million. Over 70 people have been indicted in the case since it was broken in 1972, including doctors, lawyers, private investigators and policemen acting as "runners"—agents who direct accident victims to particular lawyers and get a kickback in return.

Besides the ambulance-chasing operation, the ring allegedly staged phony accidents, submitted forged doctors' reports and collected for "victims" of bus crashes who, it developed, hadn't been in the buses at all. ICPI director James Ahern says several of the ring members had ties to organized crime, whose role in insurance fraud is reportedly growing rapidly.

The casualty insurance industry, which underwrites ICPI, is now considering expanding its scope to cover property frauds, such as arson and phony burglary rings. This would be welcome, say critics of the insurers' handling of fraud cases, but it won't do enough to solve the industry's chronic and massive losses from fraud. Much of it is perpetrated by lone-wolf operators filing small claims that collectively mount to enormous sums.

"The whole theory behind most insurance fraud is getting the company to make a nuisance settlement," says an official of one insurer.

Investigators are critical of the insurers' propensity to roll over and pay small claims, even when they have strong reason to believe they are fraudulent. Companies should take more of these cases to court for the deterrent effect, says Mr. Ahern, the ICPI director. "They should be willing to invest $5,000 now," he says, "to save $50,000 down the road."

Maybe so, but insurers aren't buying the argument. "It just doesn't pay," says Vestal Lemmon, president of the National Association of Independent Insurers. "It costs so much more to litigate than it does to pay the claim." To combat a lawsuit by an insured whose claim is denied, many companies would have to hire an investigator at $100 to $200 a day (though some have in-house gumshoes, most do not) and a trial lawyer at $50 an hour or more. Companies feel that all this may be worth the trouble if the claim is a large one but not when only a few thousand dollars are involved.

Also, insurers feel the deck is stacked against them when they do go to court. "If you litigate, you often wind up paying the claim and more," says one cynical investigator. "The juries throw in God knows how much for pain and suffering."

Expert scammers like the larcenous W. T. Stead are well aware of this. "You just tell the adjuster that if he doesn't pay, you'll see him in court. He pays. I've never had a case go to trial yet," he says.

One reason is that Mr. Stead is careful to get corroboration for his claim, sometimes from a cooperative doctor. After one staged pratfall, he says, he saw this physician; the latter gave no treatment and never saw the "victim" again, but presented him with a bill for a whopping $800. To Mr. Stead this was not highway robbery. Both he and the insurer knew that if a case came to trial and the insurer lost, the jury would be likely to make a pain-and-suffering award based on a multiple of the doctor's bill. The more their doctor charged, the larger the likely award. The insurer coughed up $8,000 in an out-of-court settlement.

If the insurers have trouble successfully contesting claims, their investigators have even greater trouble trying to get the more blatant insurance crooks prosecuted and convicted. Mr. Ahern of ICPI says prosecutors "would much rather handle a good, simple ax murder" than the complexities of an insurance-fraud case that might take a year to investigate.

"The police aren't really interested, the DAs aren't interested, and if you ever do get a prosecution the guy is apt to get off with a light sentence," complains Joe Healy, a fraud investigator for CNA Insurance Co., a unit of CNA Financial Corp. (He is still smarting over one case he developed against a ring of scammers in Philadelphia; they were convicted, but the judge gave them all suspended sentences.)

Mr. Healy, a loquacious 240-pounder, logs 100,000 air miles a year for CNA, a job not without its hazards. Once, investigating the death of a young man, he was held at gunpoint for 10 minutes by the nearly berserk father of the victim, who demanded to know who had killed his son. Another time, tracking a man who had faked his death, Mr. Healy found himself in a Mexican saloon, surrounded by thugs. Breaking off the ends of beer bottles, he and a companion bluffed their way out.

He has cracked some satisfying cases too—like the one involving the "phantom car" scam. This involved a wandering swindler who would load up on multiple hospital policies, rent a car, drive it into a ditch (while reporting that another car had run him off the road) and spend enough time in the hospital to support claims for back and neck injuries. Then he would move to another state, assume another name and do it all over again. The dogged Mr. Healy kept missing his prey but finally located his ex-wife and, through her, the photographer at their wedding. Mr. Healy obtained a photo enabling the FBI to find and arrest the miscreant, who is now serving a five-to-seven year prison term.

"Preaching the Gospel"

But Mr. Healy concedes that such cases are rare. He estimates that less than 10% of his cases are prosecuted and a still smaller percentage result in convictions. He must often be content with what he calls "preaching the gospel"—letting fraudulent operators know that he is on to their game, even if he doesn't have enough evidence to support a prosecution, and that they had better desist.

A recent case involving a ring of scammers in Los Angeles is a typical one. Knowing he didn't have enough for a prosecution, Mr. Healy assembled the members of the ring. "Hey, you guys—we're not fools," he said. "We're not going to keep paying." (CNA is already out about $10,000.)

The scammers took the news with good grace. "It was a very convivial group," Mr. Healy says. "We all knew what was really going on. One of them even asked me if I knew any good companies who would pay." Mr. Healy says that if the claims dry up, which he thinks they will, he'll close the books on the case. "I know it's not perfect justice," he says, "but it's a solution."

Legal in Itself

One of the most commonly practiced insurance frauds involves something called speculation—the purchase of multiple policies, usually accident insurance and health or disability insurance, followed by a fortuitous accident. The policyholder then collects from all the insurers.

There is nothing illegal about buying multiple policies for the same coverage, and cases of up to 50 policies purchased by the same individual have been documented. Since most of the claims involve alleged back and neck injuries that are all but impossible it disprove to a jury's satisfaction, insurers generally find it easier to pay off than to fight.

One reason this kind of fraud is so prevalent is that insurance firms don't systematically exchange information about "speculators." Nor is there likely to be any such clearinghouse soon. D. J. Chiango, a claims representative for a small Eastern company, has waged a letter-writing campaign in which he has contacted hundreds of insurers, seeking their support for an information-trading program that he feels would do much to stop speculators. He has been unable to win favor for his idea, mainly for two reasons: First, because to be effective the system would have to be a thorough, and therefore massive, undertaking; second, the companies are sensitive about any charges of collusion.

Some insurers have their own way of dealing with suspect policyholders. Claims managers for a few companies say they make threats of prosecution against such claimants, hoping they'll scare them off. One says his company sometimes "forgets" to send premium notices to some prior claimants. "If the guy doesn't notice it and doesn't pay on time, the policy lapses," he says, "and so much the better."

RELIEF PITCHER (p. 56)

by Hal Lancaster

TUCSON—It's a Sunday-night doubleheader, and the veteran relief pitcher is in the bullpen awaiting the call. He sits on a folding chair, arms draped over a low, wire-mesh fence. He fidgets. He picks up a ball, stares at it, rotates it in his hand, tosses it up and down. This is the reliever's time-killing ritual, the battle against boredom that goes on night after night.

There was a time when he was a starting pitcher in Yankee Stadium, Fenway Park, all the big parks of the American League. Now the park is Hi Corbett Field, the league is the tripe-A Pacific Coast League, and he is relegated to the bullpen, such as it is. The pen here is a cramped place, where young curiosity seekers poke the players and giggle or grab their hats and race off with them. "A circus," the pitcher says disgustedly.

He suffers through the first game and two innings of the second before the call finally comes and he begins warming up in the 90-degree heat. The public-address announcer is rattling off an unending stream of promotions: the "royal family," a lucky group chosen by lot who get free tickets, Coke and peanuts; the archery exhibition, the Food Giant attendance-guessing contest (the winner gets $5 in groceries and free Green Stamps) and the "lucky-seat" winners, who get free bowling, free car washes and free child care.

It is all part of promotion-crazy minor-league ball, right down to advertisements on the outfield walls for everything from the Panda Steak House to Kile Jarvis Realty. Atop the left-field fence sit the golden arches of the McDonald's hamburger chain; belt one through them, and you get $500. To the reliever, 30-year-old Lew Krausse Jr. of the Tucson Toros, the whole scene is just another galling reminder that he is now a world away from where he once belonged— the bigs, the major leagues.

Lew pinwheels his right arm, tugs at his sleeve, as he walks to the mound. He has entered the game behind 5 to 2. He gets the third out of the inning on an easy tap back to the box and goes on to blank the opposition over the next three innings, allowing only one hit. By the time he leaves, the Toros have tied the score, and they eventually win. Lew hopes his work has drawn attention in the bigs, among contenders who might need a reliever in the stretch. No word comes.

• • •

The son of a major-league pitcher, Lew graduated from Chester, Pa., high school on June 7, 1961. Two days later, he was in the uniform of the American League Athletics, then of Kansas City, and in possession of a headline-grabbing $125,000 bonus from the A's quixotic owner, Charles O. Finley. Three days after joining the club, he pitched his first game, a shutout—and was engulfed by a tidal wave of publicity.

It was all remarkably similar to the fairytale story of this year's high-school phenom, 18-year-old David Clyde of the Texas Rangers. But Lew Krausse, the can't-miss prospect of his day, couldn't handle the majors. "The second time out," he recalls, "I had a shutout through seven but we wound up getting beat. I started losing my confidence." He finished the season 2–5 and was sent out to wander like a Moses in the deserts of baseball—Binghampton, Portland, Dallas, Vancouver. At Dallas in the PCL, which lost 105 of 145 games when he pitched there, Lew dropped 19, setting a league record that still stands. "My roomie was 4–17," he says. "We drank a whole lot that summer."

Still, the A's brought him back up in 1965. He was good enough to stick in the majors for several years, but his superstar potential never materialized. The Athletics traded him to the Milwaukee Brewers, who cast him off to the Red Sox. They released him this spring. He had won 64 games and lost 88 in the majors.

He called other clubs, seeking a job. There were no return calls. "Nobody wants to take a chance on some 30-year-old road apple," says Lew, "but if I had quit baseball entirely, I would have always wondered if I could have made it back." So he signed with the Toros, a farm club for the A's and his old benefactor, Finley. He makes $15,000 a year, $30,000 less than the Red Sox paid him. Even at that modest salary, he is far better off than many of the young Toros, who labor for $750 to $1,200 a month for the five-month season.

He started three times for the Toros and lost all three. Then he was put in the bullpen, where he has gone 5–1 with 13 saves and an earned-run average among the league's best. Still the phone hasn't rung. "I asked Finley a while ago if anyone was interested," Lew relates. "He said, 'Yeah, the Tokyo Reds and the Nogales Eagles.'" Lew vows not to hang on desperately, like so many veterans who finish their careers in the low minors. Like Denny McLain, who won 31 for the Detroit Tigers in 1968 and now struggles to regain his lost skills with the double-A Shreveport Captains, having failed in Des Moines. If Lew can't make it back to the bigs from Tucson this year, he says he'll quit. The season gets shorter as he speaks.

• • •

The Toros' locker room is small, muggy, strewn with towels. Lew, a slim six-footer, wipes the sweat off his forehead as he assesses a career that is seemingly slipping away from him. He puts most of the blame on himself. "If I'd worked harder, I'd have made more money and I'd still be in the majors," he says. "When Catfish Hunter (a star hurler with the A's) came up in '65, he was only 19 and he was already working on throwing curve balls to spots. I was still just trying to gun the ball past people. I still do. Some guys are like that."

Though he blames himself, he can't escape some bitterness; reminders of the vast differences between the majors and the minors are everywhere. Metal cleats click on the floor as Lew pulls off a stained sweatshirt and pulls on an equally aromatic one. "That's the minors," he says. "Torn shirts, shoes that don't fit. Do you know the trainer on this club is a first-semester college student? And that we get $7.50 a day meal money on the road compared with $19.50 in Oakland? Up there you wear $300 suits and alligator shoes; here it's jeans and sandals."

In the majors, clubs get most Mondays off. Last year the Toros got just four days off all season, this year eight. Road trips are endurance contests; a typical one ended recently with a night game in Tacoma, a 5:45 bus ride to catch a flight to Spokane, there to pick up another team. The plane stops for 1½ hours in Boise, then on to Salt Lake, where the other team gets off. Then on to Phoenix, then Tucson, where they arrive at 3:15 P.M. There is a game at 7:45 P.M., and all Lew has had to eat are "a weak roll and some nasty nuts."

In the PCL, there are two umpires instead of the major-league four, no coaches and a league office whose entire staff consists of two people. The compelling aim of most club owners and operators is to save every nickel they can. "I don't give anything away to anybody," says Toro general manager Merle Miller. It is a philosophy of necessity, for life in the PCL and other minor leagues is a scrape-along existence at best; even the constant stream of promotions doesn't draw the crowds that once came before TV, before expansion, before the upsurge of other sports. The Toros are leading the league and making a little money, but minor-league operators know that a first-place finish and a decent gate attendance one year can easily be followed by a last-place debacle and empty seats the next. That's because the major-league clubs that own them or have working agreements with them are less interested in the farm club winning a pennant than they are in developing young players.

John Claiborne, the A's farm director, says the club signs 45 to 50 new prospects each year, which means that many slots on its four farm clubs must be cleared for the new young players. "You have to move 'em up fast," says Claiborne. "You can stock your farm club with stabilizers (veterans) and win, but that doesn't do the big club any good."

So when the cuts come it is usually the fading veterans who are let go first. Bill McKechnie, Jr., PCL president and a former farm director himself, says: "I've had to cut players like that. Some of them cried. But it's the best thing; all they had ahead of them was to become baseball bums."

Lew Krausse knows all this and also knows that the only possible road back is the one he is on now, risky as it may be. And he wants badly to get back. Sitting by his locker, he says suddenly: "You know, I taught Catfish Hunter how to dress, how to talk to women. Now's he's making a hundred grand and I'm out here in turkey country."

• • •

A week with the Tucson Toros, including tours of Phoenix and Albuquerque on $7.50 a day—

SUNDAY: Lew has just pitched 3½ scoreless innings against the Phoenix Giants and is happy. "Last time I couldn't get the ball over at all," he says. "I got so mad I tore this uniform right off my body and threw it into the beer cooler." His temper is fierce. In Little League, he recalls, a deep fly ball bounced right off the skull of his centerfielder and over the fence, costing young Lew a game. "He took one look at me and jumped the fence," says Lew. "I chased him all the way home." In later years, Lew would lay waste to several clubhouses, rip phones off walls and brawl in bars.

MONDAY: It's Woolco night at Corbett Field, and the message board, a sad-looking structure with hand-posted letters, details the promotions coming up—El Taco night, kids pony night, and so on. A crowd of 4,019 sees a pitcher's duel won by the Toros. Lew doesn't appear.

TUESDAY: The team is on its way to Phoenix by bus. The inevitable card games are under way, and the Latin players are singing and playing guitars. Jose Morales, a catcher (later to be called up by the parent club for the first time in a 10-year career), says the quality of bus travel in the PCL is infinitely better than in the Texas League. "Sixteen hours between Amarillo and Memphis," he says with a moan, "bouncing all the time."

The club stays at the Sands, a large structure with frayed upholstery and holes in the rugs. For dining, there is the Barbeque Pit down the road, where the waitresses wear holsters and sixguns. Some players have come here with their wives, a dangerous practice; the "baseball Annies" of Phoenix, a breed of minor-league groupies, are a fairly comely lot, and a number of players have dallied with them from time to time. "Sure enough," says Lew, "someone will get caught messin' around."

The rematch with the Giants, the third-place club, is played at Phoenix Stadium. A cavernous place the pitchers love, it is 412 feet to straightaway left and right. Before the game, hyperactive Giant promotion director Al Stevens is promising manager Jim Davenport much fan support for the stretch drive. "James, we're gonna go all out with the promotions," says Al. "Hell, if I could get it past Rosy (general manager Rosy Ryan) I'd even have a hooker night."

But only a dismal 1,378 see the Giants take the Toros, 7–4. Lew Krausse pitches to one man in the seventh and gets him on four pitches. Later that evening Toro pitcher Chuck Dobson, Lew's roommate and an Athletics castoff who is due to start tomorrow, is spied at a nearby bar. "I limit myself to nine drinks before a start," he says solemnly. "Doubles."

WEDNESDAY: Lew is up early to play golf, as he does most mornings on the road. When in Tucson, he likes to spend as much time as he can with his wife, Susan, and their two children. Chuck Dobson, a night person, is still asleep and will slumber through most of the day. He should have stayed in bed: Despite a 4-⅔ inning stint in which Phoenix pitcher John D'Acquisto gives up 10 walks, the Giants beat Chuck anyway, 4–2. Lew throws comic blooper pitches in the bullpen to break the monotony. He doesn't appear in the game.

THURSDAY: Glenn Abbott, a lanky young pitcher, rejoins the Toros after a three-day visit with the big club—"a cup of coffee," as the players call it. He is called to the phone, and another player shouts: "Pack your bags again, Abby, the mule died," a reference to Charlie O., the A's mascot. That night the Toros score six times in the seventh and win, 10–4. Lew is limited to playing catch with the rightfielder and warming up briefly. He is testy later. "Everything I do now I do to stay young," he says. "I run to stay young, I throw to stay young. That's all."

FRIDAY: A morning flight to Albuquerque, a town the whole team dreads. "There's nothing to do after you see the skin flicks," groans Chuck. At the airline terminal Lew does his specialty, "the old pro," a relief pitcher coming in for his thousandth appearance. Legs stiffly straight, back bent, upper torso leaning so far forward he seems to defy gravity, he struts past bewildered passengers while players lean against posts, howling.

That night Albuquerque leads the Toros 6–1 when Lew gets the call. He goes 5⅔ innings and gives up only three hits, but a late Toro rally falls short, and his effort is wasted.

SATURDAY: Albuquerque general manager Charlie Blaney is talking about the almost microscopic maladjustments in the pitcher's skill, perhaps the most finely tuned in all of sports, that can turn a good pitcher into a has-been almost overnight. A couple of miles per hour off the fastball, a curve that hangs for a microsecond, and he's through. Sandy Vance is a mystery, says Blaney. A one-time star in the Dodger farm system, which includes Albuquerque, he went up to the big club and came back down. He was released by Albuquerque this year, at age 26 a washout. "He just went downhill," says Blaney. "It's almost impossible to say why, but he just stopped getting people out."

Blaney's present pitching doesn't get anybody out that night. The Toros crucify his staff, winning 20 to 1. In the clubhouse later, Toro pitcher Randy Scarbery, a reported $50,000 bonus baby in his first season, is talking about how he'll invest the money. Lew listens. Though far from destitute, he has blown almost all his own bonus on cars, clothes and booze, besides paying about $40,000 in taxes on it.

What will he do if he quits? "I don't know," he says. "I've got some money in a used-car dealership, and I've got a real estate salesman's license. I could try that. But I'd really like to be a pitching coach."

For the week, Lew has pitched 9⅓ scoreless innings but doesn't have a win or a save to show for it. The season is drawing to a close, and his hopes for a reprieve from the minors grow dimmer. "I guess it's all been for nothing," Lew says. There are three more games in Albuquerque, and then it is home to Tucson for El Taco night.

WALT DISNEY PRODUCTIONS (p. 59)

by Earl C. Gottschalk Jr.

BURBANK, Calif.—In a buff-colored building at the corner of Dopey Drive and Mickey Mouse Boulevard, there are two rooms in which time has been suspended, by executive order, for more than five years. This is where Walt Disney dreamed his dreams.

Nothing has been changed in these offices since the co-founder of Walt Disney Productions, Inc. died of lung cancer in 1966. His last notes lie on the low black desk, and the scripts he was reading are pigeonholed in the rack behind his desk, where he left them. In his outer office is the piano on which musicians would play tunes for his approval. On it stands a tiny wind-up toy—two birds in a gilded cage—on which he based his idea for audioanimatronics. This is the process by which models of everything from pirates to presidents are made to move and speak in an eerie imitation of life.

Once asked to state his greatest accomplishment, Mr. Disney replied: "The fact that I was able to build an organization and hold it." The shrine made of his office symbolizes the strong grip he still has on his company. His photo smiles down from the walls of every office in the Disney Productions complex here. Mickey Mouse clocks tick away incessantly, Mickey Mouse watches adorn many an executive wrist, and the supreme accolade for a good piece of work is "Walt would have liked it."

Following Walt's Dreams

His corporate heirs remain harnessed to his ideas. "We took advantage of Walt's concepts, but we haven't gone in any new directions," says E. Cardon Walker, president. He and other executives make it clear that they don't intend to make any radical departures; instead, their goal is to skillfully manage those of Mr. Disney's dream that are already reality and to develop those that aren't—including a planned city in Florida crammed with new technology that Walt Disney hoped would be a test for a better urban life.

All this makes Disney Productions a striking anomaly in American big business. Usually corporate chieftains, even founders, depart without leaving a lasting imprint on corporate policy, let alone on the individual values and attitudes of those who work for them. The new bosses pay lip service to the old, wait a decent interval, and then try to make their own marks with different products, management techniques and goals.

But no new brooms are sweeping away the old ideas at Disney Productions. Everyone makes it clear that Walt would *not* have liked that. And neither would his brother, Roy, who died last December after serving as chairman and chief executive officer since Walt's death. Considered by far the shrewder of the two as a businessman (he was primarily responsible for raising $262 million in public offerings to build Disney World in Florida), Roy, too, devoted himself to developing Walt's ideas.

Is It Time for a Change?

To some critics, however, a change in the Disney way would be welcome. They view the empire as one huge, multi-spigoted dispenser of schlock culture—from amusements, architecture and art, to movies and music. They feel that the Disney influence has been too pervasive already. In his book, "The Disney Version," critic Richard Schickel says:

"Disney's machine was designed to shatter the two most valuable things about childhood—its secrets and its silences—thus forcing everyone to share the same formative dreams. It has placed a Mickey Mouse hat on every little developing personality in America. As capitalism, it is a work of genius; as culture, it is mostly a horror."

The men at Disney take strong exception to that. What is wrong, they ask, with exposing countless millions of children to American history, to the ways of nature, to "good, clean" entertainment?

"We've furnished a wholesome service with a good deal of inspiration and education to it," says Donn Tatum, the new chairman. "We have a platform of public acceptance. We sell something of quality. And we never take for granted the legacy of the Disney brothers."

Pleasing the Public

Even if the critics are right and the Disney complex is inundating the country with treacle and escapism, then treacle and escapism seem to be what people want. In movie production, which President Walker calls "the rock on which the company is built," this is apparent.

Disney films—a great number of which seem to feature Dean Jones talking to horses, computers and Volkswagens—roll on monotonously making money while some other studios producing critically acclaimed pictures have trouble keeping their noses above the red ink. In the past five years Disney Productions has released 25 new films; all but five were profitable.

But what of the critical complaints that these movies are bland, corny, cutesy-pie and overloaded with gimmicks? "True, all true," amiably concedes Ron Miller, vice president and member of the executive committee, head of the movie division and Walt's son-in-law. "But lots of people are looking for relief, fantasy, an escape from their problems for a couple of hours. If The New York Times or Time magazine says it likes one of our movies, I know that movie is going to be in trouble."

It is the same way at Disneyland in Anaheim and at the company's huge new 27,000 acre preserve in central Florida, site of Walt Disney World. Critic Schickel, attributing to Walt a "lifelong rage to order, control and keep clean any environment he inhabited," says of Disneyland that there is "no sex or violence, no release of inhibitions, no relief of real stresses and tensions through their symbolic statement, and therefore no therapeutic effect." In short, no reflection of real life at all. That much is true enough of both parks.

At Disneyland, a cigarette crushed carelessly on the pavement is an abomination to be quickly scuttled out of sight by a clean-cut, white-jacketed attendant. Disney World in Florida is similarly immaculate, similarly artificial—from the surf machine in Bay Lake that makes fake waves to the plastic trees in the lobby of the new Contemporary Hotel that are cleaned every night with a dust mop on a long pole. Sex is banished from the magazine shop, where there are no racy paperbacks on sale; you can get the Reader's Digest or The Wall Street Journal, but you have to smuggle in your own copy of Playboy.

And the people seem to love it. Traffic jams 15 miles long occurred over the Christmas holidays as fun seekers struggled to get into Disney World. The two hotels are booked so solidly that Disney says it will build others immediately; more than 500 conventions have been scheduled over the next three years to fill up the times when tourism normally slacks off. "Fort Wilderness," a camping area in the park with 260 spaces, has been full every night—at $11 a space. By next summer there will be 1,000 spaces.

Mr. Walker now says that attendance is running at a rate that will put it "substantially above" the 10 million originally estimated for the first full year of operation. He also expects Disneyland in Anaheim to show gains from 1971's admissions of 9.3 million. And he also sees higher profits in the company's ancillary businesses, including music publishing, educational materials and the merchandising of all sorts of Disney-connected clothing and paraphernalia.

Mickey Mouse Defeats the Bears

As the Disney machine rolls on, talking to securities analysts who follow the company and the industry becomes more and more like talking to Disney cheerleaders. The company has become one of Wall Street's darlings; its stock has risen to $163 a share from $15 in 1957—and split twice along the way.

Profits have continued to soar since Walt's death. In 1966 Disney Productions earned $12.4 million on revenue of $116.6 million; last year the company earned $26.7 million on revenue of $176 million. Analysts predict 1972 per-share net of $2.40 to $3, up from last year's $2.07. Joe Fuchs, an analyst with Kidder, Peabody & Co., calls Disney World "one of the most exciting private-enterprise projects of this decade" and expects it to contribute heavily to earnings immediately.

Those who watch the company concede that no one of Walt's inventiveness is around now. But they praise the company's management and see another ace in the hole. Says Michael Del Balso, an analyst with White, Weld & Co.: "There is a tremendous repository of creativity in WED Enterprises. This group is unknown to the public."

WED Enterprises (short for Walter Elias Disney) is the company's subsidiary for design and engineering—or, in Disney's corporate jargon, "imagineering." Established by Walt in the early 1950s to build the audioanimatronic figures at Disneyland, its 200-odd artists, architects, engineers and other employees are now responsible for designing and planning every Disney project. WED designed all the rides at Disneyland, planned the park layout and designed the entire Florida project.

An Ever Changing City

It is gearing up to tackle another of Walt's dreams—an Experimental Prototype Community of Tomorrow, or EPCOT, which would be built on the Disney holdings in Florida. Shortly before he died, Walt became interested in urban planning. He conceived of EPCOT as a city that would never stop changing, incorporating all the new wrinkles and new materials that he had found in corporate and other research facilities, where they had never been fully developed because of cost and other restrictions.

He envisioned a downtown covered with a climatic dome. Through traffic would pass completely under the city, residents and shoppers would park their cars on a level just below the surface, and the surface would be ruled entirely by pedestrians. Disney says it will begin planning EPCOT in earnest in five years and hopes to begin construction in 10.

The second-in-command of WED is John Hench, a vice president. Like many others the Disney organization, he is happy to be a fabricator of neat, clean dreams, not an interpreter or elaborator of an often-untidy reality. And, like many of the others, he is hugely pleased with what Disney hath wrought. "Look at that Main Street," he says, referring to the quaint, pasteled rows of shops on Disneyland's principal thoroughfare. "No main street like that ever existed—but that's what a Main Street *should* be."

He tells of following a family from Akron around Disney World and of how "their mouths fell open" when their monorail zipped right through the massive dining room of the Contemporary Hotel. "I can imagine them returning to Akron," rhapsodizes Mr. Hench, "a little like the people who'd come back to a small town from a trip to Europe decades ago. They would never be the same. They had seen a new country."

That new country, if that's what it is, took the Disney organization almost 50 years to arrive at. In 1923 Walt, born in Chicago and reared on a Missouri farm, arrived in Hollywood with drawing materials, $40 in the pocket of a well-worn suit and a few ideas. He joined brother Roy, already in California, and they set up shop in a garage. Mickey Mouse made his screen debut in 1928 in "Steamboat Willie," the first sound cartoon. Walt became famous, but it wasn't until much later that he was able to turn his company into anything but a small, struggling business; in most of the early years Disney Productions grossed $3 million to $6 million and was often in the red.

In 1948 the company had to bend the arm of a Pasadena theater owner to get him to exhibit the first of its widely acclaimed nature films, "Seal Island." It won an Oscar and was followed by many other such films, shot by cameramen whose patience and endurance have become legendary. Cameraman Al Milotte and his wife once camped for six straight weeks next to an alligator egg, waiting for it to hatch. (The nature films, most of which are now made for TV, are under the supervision of Vice President Roy E. Disney, son of the late Roy O. Disney. Roy E. Disney was made a member of the executive committee recently.)

They'd Rather Join Than Fight

In 1952 Walt came up with the idea for Disneyland. Brother Roy called it "another one of Walt's screwy ideas" and gave him only $10,00 of the studio's money to work with. Walt borrowed on his life insurance to commission plans and drawings. Two years later Disney Productions and two other partners committed themselves to big investments and began building. By 1960 Disney had bought out the others and was sole owner of the most successful amusement park in the U.S. From then on the company grew rapidly.

Analysts and competitors credit Disney with some shrewd management moves along the way. While other movie studios were fighting TV, Disney Productions joined it, producing Disneyland and Mickey Mouse Club shows that were marginally profitable but that provided priceless free advertising for the company. And when other movie studios sold out to TV, marketing their film libraries for showing on the tube, Disney hung on to its own productions and began rerunning them in theaters.

This has proved to be like mining an infinitely thick gold vein. Disney's movie executives figure that their primary audience turns over every seven years; as each crop of kids gets old enough to shave, a new one is ripe for the same movies.

Hanging onto the films is in keeping with a Disney management credo that has developed over the years: Always seek absolute control of whatever you're involved in. That way you can do everything your way, guard the precious Disney image most effectively, and maximize profit.

Nowhere is this more apparent than at the Florida preserve, which is Disney County in all but name. The company has obtained all governmental power in its area except police. It has its own building and zoning codes that permit it to test all sorts of new products, building materials or other developments—a vital necessity for EPCOT.

The company controls and operates its own phone company, a central energy plant powered in part by two giant jet engines, its own avant-garde transit system of monorails, trains and boats, and its own sewage and trash-collection system, which includes pneumatic tubes that whisk away offensive garbage to a central disposal plant. There are a Disney laundry, an insurance agency and a construction company. There is even a Disney Wilderness—7,500 acres set aside for conservationists only.

Here and there, however, the realities of a changing world outside intrude upon the Disney scheme of things. Disney finds it harder and harder to discover books and stories upon which to base its movies; Mr. Miller, the movie-division chief, notes that "people aren't writing that kind of thing anymore." Its animators, the men whose artistic skills are essential to so many Disney film productions, are growing old and harder to replace; many young artists don't want to work in the Disney style.

Animation That Doesn't Move

Animators who have left Disney say it is behind the times now. "I admire their craftsmanship, but their thinking hasn't advanced one bit in 35 years. Their work becomes more sterile all the time," says one Disney alumnus, now working for a competitor.

There is some minor grumbling among the clean-cut cadre that staff Disneyland—despite a rigorous screening of job applicants that weeds out the sloppy, the withdrawn and the ugly, leaving only good-looking youngsters who have "personality" and who "fit the Disney image."

That image bars moustaches, beards and sideburns longer than the bottom of the ear and specifies that hair be neatly tapered in the back. This would mean that Roy E. Disney, who is bearded, couldn't work here. (A few years ago the park tried to impose hair standards on visitors also but found itself hopelessly at odds with the times and gave up.)

"Even the Army and Navy have altered their hair regulations; Disney is now stricter than the military," complains Rocky Miller, who used to work as Brer Bear at Disneyland and took part in a performers' strike there last year. He now is an organizer for the American Guild of Variety Artists, one of the unions representing Disney employees.

But these are minor ripples on an otherwise placid surface. Disney Productions is loaded with people who have worked nowhere else, and most seem totally attuned to the "Disney Way." This concept is being preserved in part by a Disney archivist, and is continually reflected in training courses at Disneyland and Disney World "Universities." Though these are mainly for the young people who staff the parks, even veteran employees return for refresher courses in Traditions I, II, III and IV—in large part a compendium of Walt's ideas and philosophy. A young Disney instructor shows a visitor a series of placards illustrating the "Disney Ways." The first says: "What do we do? We create happiness."

THE AGRICULTURE DEPARTMENT (p. 87)

by Karen Elliot House

WASHINGTON—Dalton Wilson has a nice salary, a long title and a clean desk.

Mr. Wilson, 52, is an assistant to an assistant administrator for management in the Foreign Agricultural Service of the Agriculture Department. The other day, when a reporter dropped in to chat, Mr. Wilson's desktop held a candy bar, a pack of cigarettes and Mr. Wilson's feet. He was tilted back in his chair reading real-estate ads in the Washington Post.

Exactly what, the reporter asked, does a man with that title do?

"You mean, what am I supposed to do?" said Mr. Wilson with a chuckle. "Let me tell you what I did last year."

It turns out that Mr. Wilson, whose annual pay is more than $28,000, spent the entire year trying to assess the adequacy and timeliness of the department's fats and oils publications. He says 1977 is shaping up as another slow year; he is planning another study, this one designed to justify the use of satellites to forecast crop production.

One Bureaucrat for 34 Farmers

Mr. Wilson's pace is typical of life at the Agriculture Department. With 80,000 full-time employees, the department has one bureaucrat for every 34 U.S. farmers. Now that President Carter is setting out to reorganize the government to make it more efficient, a close look at the Agriculture Department provides a vivid picture of the problems he faces.

As the number of farmers has declined in recent years, the Agriculture Department has turned increasingly to self-promotion and has adroitly managed to continue doing old jobs while thinking up new jobs to do. The result is a huge bureaucracy engaged in scores of dubious tasks and seemingly beyond direction.

"No Secretary of Agriculture runs the department," says Washington Democrat Thomas Foley, chairman of the House Agriculture Committee. "It's too big."

The department's full-time employees, plus 45,000 part-time helpers, occupy five buildings in Washington and spill out across the country into 16,000 others. Its employees direct self-awareness programs for women, write standards for watermelons and measure planted acreage for a dozen crops—even though government limitations on planting no longer exist.

The department is the government's biggest moneylender (it will lend $9 billion in 1977). It has also built more dams—two million so far—than any other government agency. And it is one of the government's top three publishers, with a $16 million annual printing bill. Part of that goes to print 28,000 types of forms used internally to keep track of department activities.

Agriculture Secretary Bob Bergland says he soon will ask every employee to furnish a written justification for his job. Mr. Bergland, who worked at the department in the 1960s, says it is distinguished by inefficiency and a lack of clear goals. "I intend to find out what's really necessary and eliminate the rest," he says.

Time on Their Hands

But employees don't seem worried. "He'll never do it," says a young statistician, heaving his feet onto his desk. "He wouldn't have time to read them," a second man adds. A third man says, "Don't worry, guys—those with the least work to do will have the most time to justify their jobs."

Even a casual stroll through the department suggests something is awry. Throughout the main office building, old clocks are stopped at various hours as if time, too, had stopped. At all hours, hundreds of people mill about the corridors or linger in the large, sunny cafeteria.

Loafing became such a problem last year that the secretary's office sent a memo to supervisors requesting a crackdown on "significant problems of attendance in the Washington, D.C., complex." A second memo went to all employees warning that "tardiness, eating breakfast immediately after reporting for work, extended coffee breaks, excessive lunch periods and early departures" convey a "poor image to the public."

Today, laziness is still apparent and is a standard source of humor. Says a young man resting on a bench outside the cafeteria, "My only concern about work is breakfast, lunch, two coffee breaks, and being the first one out the door each evening." Sometimes the humor is unintentional. "I'd like to be sick tomorrow," a woman tells her elevator companion, "but I can't. The woman I work with plans to be."

This lackadaisical attitude irks J. P. Bolduc, the department's top management official. "There's too much deadwood around here," he says. "The answer is for every administrator to get rid of that in his agency, even if it causes a stink."

Rewarding Dead Weight

But instead of getting rid of the dead weight, the department rewards it. An internal memo shows that of the 49,000 employees eligible last year for merit pay increases, 44,956 received them. "We don't have that many super performers," concedes Mr. Bolduc, when asked about the memo.

Motivation is difficult for many employees because their tasks seem pointless. Paul Beattle in the department's Agriculture Marketing Service spent much of last year drafting a standard for watermelons, including sketches illustrating a good one. He concedes that the standard, which defines a bad melon in terms of its deformities and disfiguring spots, is rarely used by growers or retailers. Anyway, he says, most consumers know a good watermelon when they see one.

Ava Rodgers, the department's deputy assistant administrator for home economics, says she spends half her time traveling the country to coordinate activities of 4,000 home economists. Asked to describe a typical day in her office, Miss Rodgers says, "I've answered the phone a couple of times this morning. That's about it. It's a normal day." She is paid $33,700 a year.

Elsewhere in the department, 2,000 people are busily planning new dam projects even though there is a 10-year backlog of such projects already planned and awaiting construction. Secretary Bergland says he issued an order several weeks ago halting further dam-construction planning, but Joe Haas, assistant administrator for water resources, says he hasn't heard of such an order. So the planning continues. "You need new planning to have a continuous workload," Mr. Haas explains.

One reason the department remains so big is that it continues to perform outdated tasks. A notable example is the Rural Electrification Administration, begun in 1935 to provide electricity to rural America. Today, 99% of the rural homes have electricity, but the REA is still around and is getting bigger.

No longer does it simply lend money to build electricity lines. This year the agency will guarantee $3.5 billion in government loans for generating electricity, up from $1.2 billion last year. "We make a $40 million loan before lunch and never think a thing about it," says David Askegaard, deputy REA administrator.

An amazing ability of officials to dream up new tasks also contributes to the department's size. During the Depression, President Roosevelt created the Resettlement Administration, currently known as the Farmers Home Administration, to make loans to help farm families remain on their land. To qualify, a farmer could have no more than one hired hand, two mules and two cows. Today, he doesn't even have to be a farmer.

The department and Congress have expanded the program to permit loans to any poor person in a community of fewer than 50,000 residents. And loans may be used to finance sewer and water systems, recreational centers, and business and industrial construction. These low-interest Farmers Home Administration loans this year are expected to total $6.7 billion.

"Now the rural areas have everything towns have got but grime and crime," says Mississippi Democrat James Whitten, chairman of the House Agriculture Appropriations Subcommittee since 1949.

Preserving Conservation Payments

Having powerful congressional friends like Mr. Whitten is a big reason some of these outdated programs survive and grow. Every president since Harry Truman has tried to curtail conservation payments to farmers, who often use the money to enhance production rather than preserve their land. But Mr. Whitten always blocks such cutbacks. This year, farmers will receive $190 million in conservation payments. These payments help keep the 13,800 Soil Conservation Service employees busy.

Congress also strongly influences where the department spends its research fund—$592 million this year. Largely because Southern lawmakers are prominent on the agricultural committees, the department spends twice as much money—about $22 million a year—on cotton research as it does on corn, wheat or soybean research, even though the latter crops are more important to U.S. farm income.

There are other contradictions. The department will spend $4 million this year on peanut research, including efforts to increase yields, at the same time it doles out $188 million in payments for surplus peanuts.

Another questionable activity is the department's market research. A typical project is aimed at producing oranges of uniform size to make packing easier. Recently the department spent $45,000 on a study to determine for the food industry how long Americans commonly take to cook breakfast. Similar research projects are planned for cooking lunch and dinner.

The department also spends considerable time and money on self-promotion. With a $16 million annual public-relations budget, the department's 600 publicists crank out 2,500 press releases a year and about 70 television films. Another $16 million a year is spent printing an estimated $54 million books, brochures and pamphlets to distribute to the public.

The "Bank" Account

A large portion of these publications are distributed on behalf of congressmen—a practice publicity-conscious lawmakers remember when voting on the department's appropriations. Each member of Congress is entitled to 10,000 agriculture publications a year for his constituents.

The department maintains six full-time employees to mail the requested brochures for each congressman and to keep track of how many remain in his "bank." Those who run the "bank" say that some senators save their annual allotment to blitz constituents in an election year and that other urban congressmen trade the brochures to rural colleagues for football tickets. By law, the records of all these transactions must be kept secret.

Overall, the department hasn't any resemblance to the nine-employee agency created 105 years ago. That department's goals were limited and clear: "to procure, propogate and distribute among the people new and valuable seeds and plants."

Secretary Bergland wants to streamline the department and focus its resources on rural development. He says he won't fight if President Carter moves the 45,000-employee Forest Service, which grows and cuts timber in national forests, to the Interior Department. And he would accept a decision to move $7 billion in feeding programs to the Health, Education and Welfare Department. These two moves would eliminate half of Mr. Bergland's full-time employees and about half of the department's $15 billion annual budget.

Those familiar with the department are highly skeptical, however, that Messrs. Carter and Bergland will be able to do much about the scores of programs that have outlived their usefulness. "Survival is the strongest urge in Washington," says former Agriculture Secretary Earl Butz, currently a professor at Purdue University. "Carter and Bergland are going to find it difficult to reorganize because Congress won't go along with much. You can move the boxes around, but then all you have is the new program plus the old one."